THE CHRISTIAN VIEW OF SCIENCE
AND SCRIPTURE

The Christian View

of

Science and Scripture

By

BERNARD RAMM, B.D., M.A., Ph.D.

WILLIAM B. EERDMANS PUBLISHING COMPANY
GRAND RAPIDS, MICHIGAN

ISBN 0-8028-1429-8

PHOTOLITHOPRINTED BY EERDMANS PRINTING COMPANY
GRAND RAPIDS, MICHIGAN, UNITED STATES OF AMERICA

PREFACE

I HESITATE to put before the Christian public another treatise on Scripture and science. The task has been done many times before and by more capable men than this writer. The hesitation comes not only from a sense of incompetence but from a sense of futility. It is difficult to determine the actual gain of such a treatise. Such works have not been marked with an influence *where it counts*. But knowing that something *must* be said, we have added one more book to the now large collection on the Bible and science.

If someone writes on Christianity and science he should indicate some of his qualifications. Concerning a knowledge of the Bible, we have studied it for twenty years—at home, in devotions, at school, in the study for lectures. We have tried to keep close to the original text by the use of Hebrew and Greek, commentaries, translations, and good reference works. We have tried to keep good reading habits in theology by reading the old and the new, the home and the foreign, the liberal, neo-orthodox, and conservative. We have also tried to maintain a wide selection of periodicals in our monthly reading.

My scientific interest stems from days of early youth. One of my playmates was the son of a Russian engineer who had to flee Russia at the time of the revolution. The father followed along with his son's studies. Evenings, Saturdays, and Sundays were frequently spent in working through the homework with the boy. I sat in on many of these sessions, and although much went over my head, I did imbibe a deep interest in physical science, and the name of Einstein had a halo around it standing for the holiest in science. At the level our minds could understand we discussed relativity theory, atomic theory, and much chemistry. Because of these conversations I purposed to spend my life in science and so I proceeded to prepare myself in school and university, taking as much science and mathematics as my time-table would permit. However, in the summer between school and university I was converted to Jesus Christ, and this made a radical difference in every dimension of my life.

After graduating from the University of Washington I attended Eastern Baptist Theological Seminary. In my last year at "Eastern" I attended graduate courses in philosophy at the University of

Pennsylvania. From 1945–1950 I studied philosophy at the University of Southern California. Here my early appetite for science asserted itself, and I found myself much interested in the philosophy of science. Lectures on the cosmology of Descartes played a special role in this reawakening process. I had two courses in philosophy of science with Dr. Bures (a student of Feigl, of the Vienna Circle) who later went to the faculty of the California Institute of Technology. In my philosophy work I wrote several papers on philosophy of science or philosophers of science. My M.A. thesis was: "The idealism of Jeans and Eddington in modern physical theory" (1947), and my doctoral dissertation: "An investigation of some recent efforts to justify metaphysical statements from science with special reference to physics" (1950).

I have spent untold hours with the philosophical journals, especially *Philosophy of Science,* and the *Journal of the Proceedings of the Aristotelian Society.* I have had to delve into the many labyrinths of atomic theory, relativity theory, the mathematical revolution of the nineteenth century (which, though little known, was a great epoch in the development of mathematics, science, and philosophy), logical positivism, and naturalism. I have read materialists, naturalists, positivists (by the dozen) and idealists. In that psychology was my subsidiary, I probed much into the philosophy of science as it pertains to psychology. For the past ten years I have been teaching and among the courses taught have been Bible and science, Christianity and science, and philosophy of science.

Poring over such material does not mean competency in itself. It at least means conscious and willing exposure to the relevant material. I am simply trying to be honest and not to claim more than the "facts in the case." With reference to technical details of the sciences I must depend on what other men say, and I am thereby at their mercy. The only reservation is that there is no monopoly on logic, and granted the facts, conclusions may be wrongly drawn by an expert, and may be rightly made by the informed amateur.

In research for this book I discovered that there are two traditions in Bible and science both stemming from the developments of the nineteenth century. There is the ignoble tradition which has taken a most unwholesome attitude toward science, and has used arguments and procedures not in the better traditions of established scholarship. There has been and is a noble tradition in Bible and science, and this is the tradition of the great and learned evangelical Christians who have been patient, genuine, and kind and who have taken great care to learn the facts of science and Scripture. No better example can be found than that of J. W. Dawson but we would also include such men as John Pye Smith, Pratt, Dana, Hugh

Miller, James Orr, Asa Gray, Bettex, Ambrose Fleming, Rendle Short and Malcolm Dixon.

Unfortunately the noble tradition which was in ascendancy in the closing years of the nineteenth century has not been the major tradition in evangelicalism in the twentieth century. A narrow bibliolatry, the product not of faith but of fear, buried the noble tradition. The sad result has been that in spite of stout affirmations that true science and the Bible agree and do not conflict, science has repudiated the ignoble tradition. It is our wish to call evangelicalism back to the noble tradition of the closing years of the nineteenth century.

We have purposefully omitted discussions about history and psychology because we have limited ourselves to natural science. History is best dealt with by the archaeologist; and psychology is too involved in theology and philosophy to be treated here. We have also foregone a chapter on medicine because of our lack of competency in that field.

Sometimes we have used other than the Authorized Version of the Bible and we have indicated which version we use in parentheses. Special thanks go to Dr. J. Laurence Kulp, of the department of geology of Columbia University, who read the manuscript for technical accuracy; to Dr. E. J. Carnell of Fuller Theological Seminary for reading parts of the manuscript which pertain to theology and philosophy; to Dr. Wilbur M. Smith of Fuller Theological Seminary for turning over to me his large collection of books on Bible-and-science for my use; and to Dr. Elving Anderson, Professor of zoology at Bethel College, for corrections with reference to biology.

Evangelicalism as used in this book means the historic Christian faith as reflected in the great creeds of the ancient Church, and in the spirit and writings of the Reformers.

Bernard Ramm

Chevy Chase, Glendale,
California.

CONTENTS

ABBREVIATIONS
USED IN THE TEXT AND FOOTNOTES

ARV—*The American Revised Version of 1901*

BASA—*Bulletin of the American Scientific Affiliation*

BS—*The Bibliotheca Sacra*

CB—*The Cambridge Bible*

ELLICOTT—C. J. Ellicott, editor, *The Bible Commentary for English Readers*

ERE—Hastings, editor, *Encyclopaedia of Religion and Ethics*

HBC—C. Cooke, editor, *The Holy Bible Commentary*

ICC—*The International Critical Commentary*

ISBE—*The International Standard Bible Encyclopedia*

JASA—*The Journal of the American Scientific Affiliation*

JFB—Jamieson, Fausset and Brown, *A Commentary on the Old and New Testaments*

JTVI—*Journal of the Transactions of the Victoria Institute*

KD—Keil and Delitzsch, *Commentaries on the Old Testament*

KJ—*King James Version (Authorized Version)*

LANGE—J. P. Lange, *A Commentary on the Holy Scriptures*

MS—M'Clintock and Strong, *Biblical, Theological, and Ecclesiastical Cyclopedia*

RSV—*Revised Standard Version*

WC—*Westminster Commentaries*

WD—*Westminster Bible Dictionary*

WHITE (followed by volume and page)—Andrew Dickson White, *A History of the Warfare of Science with Theology in Christendom* (1896), 2 vols.

CHAPTER I

THE IMPERATIVE NECESSITY OF A HARMONY OF CHRISTIANITY AND SCIENCE

I. THE PRESENT STATUS OF CHRISTIANITY AND SCIENCE

IF we were to examine the faculty of a large medieval university we could be sure that practically to a man the faculty would be composed of those who accepted without any reservations the full inspiration of the Bible, and its reliability in all matters pertaining to Nature.[1] If we were to visit the faculty meeting of some American or European university of a hundred years ago the situation would be changed somewhat. We would find materialist and atheist, but we would also find some of the greatest men of arts, letters, and sciences, to be sincere and devout believers who trusted all the Bible said on matters of Nature. If we were to go from one department to another in our modern American universities we would discover that considerably more than ninety per cent of the faculty are either completely naturalistic or materialistic in creed, or very nominally religious. In many schools not a single firm believer in the trustworthiness of Scripture can be found; in others there may be two or five at the most. From medieval universities with faculties composed completely of Bible believers we have now reached the point where very few modern American universities have Bible believers on the staff.

The battle to keep the Bible as a respected book among the learned scholars and the academic world was fought and lost in the nineteenth century. The astronomy of Copernicus did not begin to have the influence on human thought as did the events of the nineteenth century. During that period there was a mushrooming of anti-Biblical, anti-Christian movements. There was the growth in radical Biblical criticism, and the emergence of religious modernism. In philosophy able representatives defended positivism, naturalism, materialism, and agnosticism. Orthodoxy was barraged from every side.

The battle was a battle of strategy. The victors were on the side of modernism and unbelief; not of evangelical faith and the Bible. *Why did the battle go as it did?* Why did the populace, the universities, and even much of the clergy yield to the critical and

[1] For notes see page 32.

scientific attacks on the Bible? Why was Huxley or Tyndall or
Colenso or Lyell so eagerly heard, and why did Gladstone or
Mivart or Pratt have such a limited success?

1. At the most fundamental level was the continuing revolt of
man from the religion and authoritarianism of the Roman Catholic
Church in its medieval expression. These roots go back through
the *Aufklärung* to the rise of modern philosophy in Descartes and
Spinoza and to humanism and the Renaissance. It was at first a
revolt against Catholicism, but it also became hostile to Protestant
orthodoxy. This deep-moving secularism—life without God,
philosophy without the Bible, community without the Church—was
all in favour of the radical and the critic, and against the Christian
and the apologist. It was an irresistible tide which set men's mind,
the popular and the scholarly, in favour of Huxley or Spencer.

2. The development of modern philosophy from Descartes, and
of modern science from Galileo, have shown the value of sharp,
critical, non-conventional mentality. Descartes impressed modern
philosophy from its very source with his principle of radical doubt,
and Galileo and his trial prophesied that science would only progress
when freed from clericalism. Locke set before men the results
of a refined analysis of concepts, and Hume showed how little was
left of the world of common sense when dipped in acidic scepticism.
Kant ponderously but deftly showed the impossibility of metaphysics as traditionally conceived. The progress of modern
thought is then such as to put a premium on criticism and scepticism, and to put anything religious, theological, or synthetical at a
great disadvantage even before the debate commences. In less than
one hundred years Paley is moved out of place in British thought and
Huxley or Spencer takes over. In this atmosphere Bible-and-
science fought its battle with modern mentality and came out the
loser as far as which was to dominate the thinking in academic and
learned society. The entire psychological and social advantage was
with the radical or the critic as over against the orthodox. It was
far easier for the radical to draw blood than for the Christian to do so.

3. In the nineteenth century battleground of the Bible and science
another advantage accrued to the critic. Science was developing
with an amazing rapidity. All the practical and theoretical success
of science added weight to the arguments of Christianity's critics.
The rapid strides of science in the nineteenth century were enormous. We have become so accustomed to the scientific marvels of
the twentieth century that we have forgotten the days of the scientific
giants of the nineteenth century. It was the century of the founding of sciences, of the development of the sciences, of the birth of
many fundamental theories of science, of the creation of remarkable experiments. The scientists could point to such concrete

things and to such remarkable successes.   Then, too, the theoretical aspects of science found practical expressions which reached into every civilized hamlet.   Steam engines, electricity, and chemistry were powerful and practical apologists for the scientific point of view.   Inoculations, surgery under an anaesthetic, and brilliant new progress in surgery were medical marvels which preached irresistibly the gospel of science.

What could theologians offer as a parallel to this?   A theologian's product is a book, but so few of our population read the books of the theologians.   Further, the reasoned argument of a book cannot compete popularly with the practical gadgets of science. Here again, Huxley could vex and tease the theologians, and carry with his vexing and teasing the enormous prestige of the practical and theoretical strides of the progress of science.   The theologian's use of logic, history, or reason seemed like confused sputterings to common people unaccustomed to such argumentations, and very much accustomed to the scientist's claims demonstrated very concretely and at times so dramatically.

4. Another one of the reasons why the radical and the critic made such headway and the orthodox and evangelical so little was that divisions plagued the Church.   There were the major cleavages of Eastern Orthodoxy, Roman Catholicism, and Protestantism.   In Protestantism there was denominationalism with seemingly unlimited powers of spawning new denominations or cults or sects. There was deep and serious division as to the interpretation of the revelation, and right in the midst of it all developed religious modernism which created another great cleavage in Protestantism. Science, to the sharp contrast, was developing a measure of unanimity.   Newton formulated the law of universal gravitation, and fellow physicists could check it and agree with him.   Pasteur discovered the principle of immunization and all bacteriologists eventually concurred.

Once again, the psychological thrust here is great.   There is less unanimity among scientists than the layman is aware of, but that is usually considered one of the growing pains of science. Scientists for the most part seem to be able to agree on certain things when these things are adequately demonstrated, but theologians never seem to be able to agree.   The anti-Christian philosophies (materialism, naturalism, positivism, agnosticism) lost no time in pre-empting science to themselves, and presumed that orthodoxy and science were divorced.   This was taken as proven fact.   The divergences among theologians enervated their case, and the measure of unanimity which prevailed among scientists enhanced the position of the anti-Christian philosopher who taught his philosophy in the name of science.

5. The very strategy of the hyper-orthodox and even the orthodox was such as to defeat itself. We must be charitable at this point in the realization that the orthodox had little time to develop a strategy to combat the critic. He had to pitch in and fight the best he could. But this was not good enough. Sometimes he was woefully ignorant of the simplest facts of science. It must be kept in mind that university training up to the early part of the twentieth century was principally literary and classical. Science courses and scientific laboratories on the grand scale now found in the modern university are strictly phenomena of the twentieth century. Most of the clergy were trained in the classics, and were strangers to the sciences. Therefore, they did not even have the facts to create a telling strategy.

The other deficiency was that of improper spirit. Too frequently orthodoxy fought the critic with sarcasm or vilification or denunciation. This too often involved a similar treatment of the *facts* of science. Such a strategy was futile. The sure advance of empirical data, and the analytic mentality modern science developed in her devotees, could not be coerced or routed by ridicule or wholesale depreciation of science.

6. Another cause for the success of the critic and the defeat of the evangelical was that science was developed by non-Christians in increasing numbers. Men like Newton and Pasteur and Clerk-Maxwell were devout men, but they were replaced by men of atheistic or at least anti-Christian bent of mind. The God-fearing scientist became rare, and the conservative or orthodox scientist (with reference to religious belief) became an oddity. This had many ramifications. The prestige of science went to the scientists and to their philosophical and religious views. Science was developed on non-Christian premises. The thousands of students passing through science courses were influenced for naturalism and against religion by the anti-Christian or naturalistic convictions of their professors of science.

7. Orthodoxy did not have a well-developed philosophy of science or philosophy of biology. The *big* problems of science and biology must be argued in terms of a broad philosophy of science. The evangelical always fought the battle on too narrow a strip. He argued over the authenticity of this or that bone; this or that phenomenon in a plant or animal; this or that detail in geology. The empirical data is just there, and the scientists can run the evangelical to death in constantly turning up new material. The evangelicals by fighting on such a narrow strip simply could not compete with the scientists who were spending their lifetime routing out matters of fact.

It must be admitted that the discipline of philosophy of science is a development of recent years.   True, all great philosophers have had a philosophy of science implicit in their works, and even a philosophy of biology, *e.g.* Aristotle, Aquinas, and Descartes.   But these matters have not been sharpened up till recently, and they could hardly have been till more empirical data were on hand.   In view of this the evangelicals cannot be blamed for not having either a philosophy of science or biology on hand to meet modern science.   But the case is the same.   It was impossible to settle the complex problems of Bible-and-science, theological and empirical fact, without a well-developed Christian theism and philosophy of science.

For example, the idea of creation is rather complex.   Evangelicals were not always aware of the great deal of thought put into this matter by Augustine and Aquinas.   As a result evangelicals posed the problems of modern science as resolving down to: (i) fiat, instantaneous creationism; or (ii) atheistic developmentalism.   This is certainly a gross over-simplification, not a genuine probing, of the entire concept of creation.   By putting the question this way, every bit of developmentalism in science made the evangelical position that much more difficult of defence.   Evangelicals, by putting such a premium on *discontinuity*, had no recourse but to fight any *continuity* in any of the sciences as if it were the devil himself.   With no real philosophy of creation, evangelicals defended a position that violently countermanded the findings of science.   Evangelicals of today who fail to see these problems in their larger dimensions are but perpetuating the losing strategy of their brethren who lost the battle in the previous century.

The result of losing the battle of the Bible and science in the nineteenth century is simply and tragically this: Physics, astronomy, chemistry, zoology, botany, geology, psychology, medicine and the rest of the sciences are taught in disregard of Biblical statements and Christian perspectives, and with no interest in the Biblical data on the sciences, and no confidence in what the Bible might even say about the same.   Evangelical Christianity is obtaining a measure of success in education, in evangelism, in missions, in journalism and publications, in church expansion, but in the field of science evangelicalism is apparently the lost cause.[2]   For all practical purposes science is developed and controlled by men who do not believe in the scientific credibility of Holy Writ.   Evangelicals in science are considered by scientists as anachronisms or unnecessary perpetuations of the medieval mentality into the modern period.

The detrimental influence of this on Christianity is beyond any possible calculation.   To enumerate the resultant influence on the Christian church is heartbreaking.   First to be mentioned is the revolt within the church itself in the nineteenth century in which thousands of ministers forsook an evangelical theology under the pressure of radical criticism and scientific allegations against the Bible. The principle of the uniformity of Nature became the first axiom in all theology and Biblical criticism. All miracles and all supernatural activity of God had to go under this royal principle. Evolutionary biology and uniformitarian geology made serious inroads on theology. Next to be mentioned are the numerous intelligent and gifted young men who could have served the church with distinction but who live and work outside the church in the belief that Holy Scripture is scientifically untrustworthy. Thousands of splendid, trained, capable men now lost to secularism could have provided the church with an imposing array of scholars in every department of learning and provided for a stronger ministry and a more intelligent laity. Today these talented people in education, business, and professions, using their talents and energies for these tasks, leave a crippled and weakened church in their wake. Finally, the influence on the masses is a great imponderable quantity. The spirit of the times is such as to make evangelical headway difficult. It is the popular belief that the Bible and science are at odds, that intelligence is on the side of unbelief, and that only childish or sentimental or uneducated people still trust the contents of the Bible. No longer do people respond to Scripture because it is the voice of God, but armed with the belief that science has broken the credibility of Scripture they cynically ask how we know the Bible is God's voice. Apart from those circles in which the church exerts its influence early in life it is very difficult for Christianity to get a sympathetic hearing.

The immediate prospects are that unless something very revolutionary develops in science to reinstate the Bible before the scientists of the world the situation will continue in its aggravated state. The world of scholarship will continue to ignore Biblical teaching; the liberals and neo-orthodox will still hold to the scientific fallibility of Scripture; and the masses at large will believe that the development of science has exploded the scientific reliability of the Bible.

Before we leave this subject of the embarrassment of Christianity by science, we must indicate that it is not evangelical Christianity alone that is embarrassed. Religion in general has been embarrassed. The strict naturalist or positivist or materialist is opposed to neo-orthodoxy and modernism as well as to orthodoxy. It is not only difficult to get a hearing for evangelical Christianity on our large state campuses; it is hard to get any sort of religious hearing. Metaphysics is also embarrassed by science.[3] Naturalism and materialism are philosophies which have renounced any special philosophic methodology and have espoused the scientific method for philosophy. Even more extreme are the logical positivists or scientific empiricists who rule out all metaphysics whatsoever. These scientisms are the dominant philosophies of our times and they all affirm the universal applicability of the scientific method, and sternly oppose any type of idealistic reconstruction. Science has thus made a cleavage all the way through modern mentality and culture, and not merely in evangelical theology alone.

In fact, the so-called *modern mind* is the scientific mind. Although somewhat of an over-simplification it could be said that there has been the classical mind, the medieval mind, and the modern mind. The modern mind is distinguished from the classical and medieval by the impact of scientific theory and attitude in formulating it. The making of the modern mind is actually the formulating of a mental attitude guided by science. Idealism, metaphysics, and religion are all under suspicion by modern scientific mentality. Parenthetically, we must insist that one of the greatest mistakes of modern scholars is to equate the Christian mind with the medieval mind, and then to accuse the Christian mind of all the mistakes and fallibilities of the medieval mind.

II. THE APPROACH THAT CREATES DISHARMONY

In view of the present antagonism of science to evangelical Christianity, the situation will continue and perhaps grow worse if no reconciliation takes place. The movement of reconciliation may come from the scientist or from the evangelical. Although the movement from the scientist is less likely to occur, it must not be completely ignored. Recent studies in astrophysics suggest a moment of creation; and the sobering considerations over atomic power have reawakened some scientists to the important role of religion in civilization. Perhaps in another hundred years of experimentation, geneticists will admit that the evolutionary theory must be abandoned, and if they do they will be amenable to some sort of creationism.

However, for any positive and successful reconciliation of science and evangelicalism the obligation is upon the evangelical. It is up to him to set forth the terms of *rapprochement*. Evangelicalism has been exceedingly slow in learning certain fundamental lessons in this controversy. In this regard the Roman Catholic scholars have far outstripped us. They have worked out a set of principles setting the boundaries of science, the boundaries of theology, and the canons of interpretation. These matters are set forth in the encyclical *Providentissimus Deus* (1893) of Leo XIII, and in the decrees of the Pontifical Commission for Biblical Studies (1902 and following years).[4]

One wing of evangelicalism whose orthodoxy and zeal are commendable but whose judgment is to be seriously questioned is that group which took a very negative and castigatory attitude toward science, and in many other ways was very inept in its efforts.   Men of this group are not limited to any country nor to the past, but are with us to this day.   Although there was some good in such journals as *The Bible Champion* or *Christian Faith and Life,* most of the articles reflect not orthodoxy, but hyper-orthodoxy.   So many articles lacked the measured control of cultured men, and a judgment seasoned through much use of logic and experimentation.

Taking as its watchword the "oppositions of science falsely so called,"[5] hyper-orthodoxy assumed that since unregenerate man is in open rebellion against God, he will use science as well as anything else to oppose Christianity.   The Bible, it asserted, was in accord with true science, but obviously in conflict with most of the world's practising scientists.   These scientists, unregenerate and anti-Christian, must be written off the record in science as well as in religion.

Sad has been the history of the evil that good Christian men have done in regard to science.   Bettex laments that far too often the Christian attitude toward science is an attitude unworthy of itself and "where not positively hostile, treats it with petty distrust, and an admixture of scorn, or at least with some aversion and distaste."[6] Dawson complains of "slipshod Christianity" which rests smugly in dogmatic theology, and has the most contemptible estimation of geology.[7]   John Pye Smith complained:

> [Evangelical castigators of science] are unwittingly serving the designs of [Christianity's] enemies [and are] secret traitors to the cause of Christianity.[8]

The judgment of White is proved a thousand times that the cheap weapons of religious opposition to science are like "Chinese gongs and dragon lanterns against rifled cannon."[9]

Does not the most hyper-orthodox among us realize that most of the views he now holds about the Bible, medicine, science, and progress which he thinks are so orthodox, safe, sane, and Biblical, would, a few centuries ago, have cost him his life?

If evangelicalism continues to have a strong, outspoken group within it with such a negative approach to science, the prospects of making clear the scientific respectability of Scripture are not good. If this "pedantic hyper-orthodoxy"[10] continues to be the representative voice in evangelical apologetics, the great cleavage between science and evangelicalism which occurred in the nineteenth century will not only be perpetuated through the twentieth, but it will be widened.

But pedantic hyper-orthodoxy must not be allowed to speak for all evangelical Christians, as the position it holds is impossible of credible defence.   We present the following reasons why such a position is indefensible.

1. It is, as already asserted, *hyper-orthodoxy*.   We can sin to the right as well as to the left.   Patriotism can degenerate into jingoism and enthusiasm into fanaticism and virtue into prudishness.   It is possible not only to have slack theological views, but to have views far more rigid and dogmatic than Scripture itself.   Hyper-orthodoxy in trying to be loyal to the Bible has developed an exaggerated sense of what loyalty to the Bible means.

2. Hyper-orthodoxy does not believe its platform "to the hilt." It is willing to retain faith in the Bible no matter what the scientists say.   But would they really believe the Bible if at *every* point the Bible and science conflicted?   If the differences between the sciences and the Bible were to grow to a very large number and were of the most serious nature, it would be questionable if they would retain faith in Scripture.   True, we may believe *some* of the Bible "in spite of" science, but certainly the situation would change if we believed *all* of the Bible in spite of science.   That is to say, the hyper-orthodox have made a virtue of disagreeing with science, and have not set any sort of limits as to how serious the divergences with science may go before they must rethink their position.   Their guiding principle cannot be extended without making their entire position indefensible or simply absurd.   We question that the hyper-orthodox would follow their principle through to its extremity, and therefore can only judge that it is an inadequate principle.

3. Hyper-orthodoxy is inconsistent in actual practice, for it will certainly use the *practical* achievements of modern science, *e.g.* radio, television, 'phones, cars, medicines, furnaces, glasses, artificial teeth, and so on.   It is not intellectually respectable to condemn science as satanic while having teeth repaired by scientific technicians, wearing glasses prescribed and ground by other scientists, being covered with clothing produced by chemists and engineers, with a body saved from premature death by an appendicectomy performed by a scientist, and with a mind trained in a school system working with methods provided by educational scientists.

4. Such a position makes the words of God and the work of God clash.   Certainly, the pragmatic truthfulness of science as witnessed by a modern industrialized society, modern rapid transportation and communications, modern medicine, and modern warfare, cannot be denied.   This is incontrovertible data that in many regards science is on the right track.   To this extent science has opened up the secrets and meanings of Nature, the creation of God.   To set theology against science is simply to oppose Creation to Revelation,

and Nature to Redemption.   Yet, it is the uniform testimony of Scripture that the God and Christ of redemption are the God and Christ of creation.

Further, without a rather extended tour of the sciences the hyper-orthodox have no idea of the relationship of Scripture to science. Scientific knowledge is invaluable for a knowledge of the Bible— at least to know it fully and completely.   We do not see how it is possible to gainsay what Shields has written in this connexion: "Without astronomical knowledge he cannot tell whether the astro-nomical scriptures are in accord with the discovery of suns and planets.   Without geological knowledge he cannot tell whether the order of the creative days agrees with the order of the earth's strata. Without ethnological knowledge he cannot tell whether the Mosaic genealogies include or exclude pre-Adamite and co-Adamite races of mankind.   Without archaeological knowledge he cannot tell whether the Mosaic cosmogony was of Hebrew or Chaldean origin, or derived from primeval tradition still more ancient; nor whether the Elohist and Jehovist sections were original or compiled docu-ments; nor whether Moses wrote the whole or parts of the books which have always borne his name.   Without historical science he cannot tell whether the Mosaic codes formed a logical or chrono-logical series; nor whether they date before or after the Babylonian exile.   And without some knowledge of psychology, sociology, and comparative religion he cannot even approach the higher problems of the soul, the Church, and the future of Christianity."[11]

5. Even though the non-Christian scientist is unsaved and even though he is spiritually ruled by the Evil One, yet that is no basis for writing scientists and science off the record.   That this cannot be done can be proved on the sole ground that in the vast majority of cases of matter of fact the scientist who is Christian and the scientist who is not Christian concur.   Chemical formulas, laws of physics, occurrences of fossils, physiological processes are not deter-mined by being Christian or non-Christian.   Granted, when we deal with wider problems such as the *why* there are any laws at all, and as to the *origin* of matter and its properties, the metaphysical issue intrudes and there is a definite Christian answer.   But if a Christian should write an introductory text-book on physics or chemistry it would be practically identical to the one written by a non-Christian save for a note in the preface which might say (i) matter is created by God; (ii) the laws of Nature are as they are because God so made them; and (iii) the rationality of both man and the universe derive from the same God.   That iron has a certain specific gravity, that the chemical families of Mendelyeev's tables have certain common traits, that tadpoles go through stages x, y, z to become frogs, is common property to Christian and non-Christian.

We conclude that it is impossible for us to follow the pattern set by the hyper-orthodox in their proposed relationship of Christianity to science.   Their efforts in the past have increased the gap between Christianity and the scientists, have embittered the scientists, and have done little to provide a working theory of any creative dimensions for the *rapprochement* of science and evangelicalism.

III.   The Approach that Creates Harmony

If we believe that the God of creation is the God of redemption, and that the God of redemption is the God of creation, then we are committed to some very positive theory of harmonization between science and evangelicalism.   God cannot contradict His speech in Nature by His speech in Scripture.   If the Author of Nature and Scripture are the same God, then the two books of God must eventually recite the same story.   Therefore, in place of resentment or suspicion or vilification toward science and scientists, we must have a spirit of respect and gratitude.   In place of a narrow hyper-dogmatic attitude toward science we are to be careful, reserved, open-minded.

We are to pay due respect to *both* science and Scripture.   Neither adoration of one nor bigoted condemnation of the other is correct. We must be ready to hear the voice of science and the voice of Scripture on common matters.   The spirit of mutual respect for *both* science and Scripture preserves us from any charge of being anti-scientific or blindly dogmatic or religiously bigoted; and from being gullible, or credulous or superstitious in our religious beliefs as they pertain to Nature.

There are two attitudes toward the Scriptures which this view is opposed to.   Obviously, it is opposed to hyper-orthodoxy, for hyper-orthodoxy will have no serious interactions with modern science. It is also opposed to neo-orthodoxy and religious liberalism, both of which believe that the message of the Bible is entirely religious or theological, and therefore the science of the Bible may be ignored or "demythologized."   Neo-orthodoxy does take a more serious view of much of the Bible which liberalism simply casts off as incredible, but it takes such passages mythologically or metaphorically but not literally, and so concurs with liberalism as to their unscientific nature.   In contrast to neo-orthodoxy, religious modernism, and hyper-orthodoxy (the first two refusing to take the science of the Bible seriously and the latter refusing to take science seriously) we defend a position which asserts *that a positive relationship must exist between science and Christianity*.   It is as foolish for the hyper-orthodox to write off science as it is for the religious liberals and neo-orthodox to write off the Bible.   The truth must be a conjunction of the two. The reasons for this position are as follows:

1. *The doctrine of creation is fundamental to Christian and Biblical theology.*   As Dawson observes, "The first article in the creed of inspiration relates to physical nature (Gen. 1: 1)."[12]   It is not possible to separate the theological and ethical teachings of the Bible from the references to Nature.   Divine creation is asserted continuously from the Pentateuch through the book of Revelation.   The unity of husband and wife is based upon creation, and is so taught in both the Old (Mal. 2: 10–16) and New Testaments (Matt. 19: 1–5). The defection of the original man and the curse pronounced upon him is part of the theological framework of the New Testament. The Jehovah of the Law asserts that He was the Elohim of creation (Ex. 20: 9–11).   The Christ of the New Covenant is the Logos of Creation (John 1: 1–14).   The Creator of heaven and earth (Rev. 4) also holds in his hands the book of eternal judgment which He gives to Christ the Lion and Lamb of God (Rev. 5).   The prohibition against idolatry is argued in terms of God as Creator of the visible universe, and it is the power of God and omniscience of God as exhibited in His control of Nature and history which differentiates the true God from the idols and gods of the pagans.

The theological, the ethical, and the practical are so conjoined in the Bible with the statements about Nature or creation that it is impossible to separate them, and to impugn one is to impugn the other.   It is therefore suicidal for the hyper-orthodox to pass by the findings of science which cannot but have a most important bearing on the Biblical references to Nature and matters of fact; and it is inconsistent for the neo-orthodox to try to separate neatly the theological elements of the Bible from the statements about Nature and fact.

2. *Science needs the light of revelation.*   Modern science has explored with remarkable success the world of the infinitely small (atomic physics) and the world of the infinitely large (molar physics).   In complex mathematical formulas we express the nature of atoms and the stellar universe.   Scientists use infinitesimal units of measurement to deal with electromagnetic vibrations, and employ enormous measurements to deal with astronomical phenomena.   We also have reliable knowledge of millions of years of geological history.   Exhaustive researches have been made in physics, chemistry, biology, and psychology.

After looking over an immense factory with miles of complex machinery, huge presses, impressive batteries of automatic devices, thousands of workers, researchers, and executives, we would be shocked, if we were to ask "what do you manufacture here," to be told "nothing."   In the domain of human experience such a situation would be sheer irrationality.   It would be judged as a case of perverted and fantastic mentality if one were to put into operation an automotive plant so fixed that as the finished products were driven off the assembly line they would drop into the maws of the huge smelter from which they were originally derived.   Yet this is precisely the type of analogy much of modern science persists in following.   *Teleology and final causes are sternly and systematically driven out of modern scientific mentality.*

If it is the intent of science to amass all the facts about the universe in its countless facets *it is the function of theology to give these data their purpose and teleological ordering.*   Through revelation we know that this great system we call the universe (in all its levels from the physical to the psychical and the atomic to the astronomical) is from God.   From the same Book of revelation we know its divinely appointed function and purpose.   Without theology science sets forth the vast universal scheme as blind, meaningless, purposeless, never knowing an hour of creation, never knowing of an hour of consummation, and in the perspective of an infinity of years and an immensity of space our human hopes, joys, tragedies, aspirations, civilizations, intellectual and artistic achievements, are meaningless, insignificant and trivial.   The humanist who tries to put a little colour and thrill back into human existence—while still believing in a universe that is inhuman and meaningless and impersonal—cannot but sound either cheap or ironical.

But with the help of theology the vast system which science creates for us takes on meaning and we see it from a credible perspective. It has a personal, meaningful, worthwhile core.   Human life with its hopes, joys, tragedies, aspirations, civilizations, intellectual and artistic achievements *is now the very centre of the universe.*

Furthermore, the contributions of science to morality are problematic.   In teaching the priority of science to metaphysics and religion, the relativity of all knowledge, and the ateleological character of the universe, science has weakened the hold of moral principles upon mankind.   Morality tacked upon materialism, positivism, naturalism, and pragmatism, always appears as an *ad hoc* affair,[13] or a wise concession to public sentiment much like Descartes' safe treatment of the Catholic Church.   However, with immense powers of destruction in man's hands through science, science now realizes it has need of moral safeguards which it is not able to produce of itself.   At this point theology can give to science the necessary moral safeguards.   Truth established through the reliability of the scientific method is now guided in its use by truth through the reliability of revelation.

3. *Revelation needs the perspectives of science.*[14]   Certainly one of the

sharpest criticisms of so many religions of the world is their provincialism. Too many gods are local gods or tribal gods. It is the insistence of the Biblical revelation that God is the God of all humanity, of all the world, and of all the visible universe. As our conceptions of humanity, the world, and the universe enlarge so does our idea of God. A knowledge of geography and anthropology certainly enlarged the Christian understanding of the scope of the gospel. Being world-minded and missionary-minded is considered a necessary feature of a healthy Christian mentality. But far more important for pure theological considerations is our expanded knowledge of the universe. The discoveries of modern astronomy underline dramatically our conception of the immensity, infinity, and eternity of God. As Shields writes:

> Take the Bible without astronomy, and there would remain the infinite and absolute Jehovah enthroned in the skies of our little planet as the only scene of his abode. But bring the two together, and at once the author of Scripture becomes the author of nature with all his revealed attributes in full manifestation; with his immensity extending through the boundless regions of celestial space; with his eternity unfolding through the endless periods of celestial time; with his omnipotence expending its potential energy in the tremendous forces and velocities of the celestial orbs; with his immutability expressed in the mechanical and physical laws which govern these ceaseless movements; and with his omniscience displayed in a universe of order and beauty and grandeur which all our science has but begun to apprehend. Astronomy thus yields overwhelming evidence in favour of revealed religion.[15]

4. *Both science and theology are fundamental human pursuits.* Both science and theology deal with the same universe. The goal of science is to understand what is included in the concept of Nature, and the goal of theology is to understand what is included under the concept of God. The emphasis in science is on the visible universe, and in theology the emphasis is on the invisible universe, *but it is one universe.* If it is one universe then the visible and the invisible interpenetrate epistemologically and metaphysically. Through theology we discover the origin, purpose and end of the created universe. Through science we find clues, analogies, and confirmations of the existence and nature of the invisible universe. We cannot be true to the Biblical revelation and be Kierkegaardians who affirm that God is secretly present in Nature and therefore Nature ceases to be of importance to theology and theism. Nor can we be religious liberals who too neatly separate science and religion. Nor can we be hyper-orthodox and ignore the enormous accumulations of valid information by modern science. *Only a serious, intelligent, discerning*

Biblicism can hope to hold in happy relationship Christian theology and modern science.

IV. THE IMPORTANCE OF BIBLE AND SCIENCE

It might be asked: why the concern as to whether the Bible and science agree or disagree? Is not religion independent of such matters? Is it not of the spirit, of the eternal?

These questions have been partially answered in our discussion up to this point, but they are worthy of further consideration. There are three fundamental reasons why evangelical Christianity is concerned with science.

First of all, science is used by men to create anti-Christian systems. If it be said by some that science has nothing to do with the domain of the spiritual, it is said by others that *in the name of science* no such domain exists. This is either a theistic universe or a non-theistic universe. If it is declared a non-theistic universe in the name of science, then the evangelical must show reason for dissent. Therefore, if we are convinced of the truthfulness of the evangelical faith we cannot help but lock horns with those men and those philosophies which deny our faith. If this denial is done in the name of science, the evangelical must interact with science to see if the charges are true, and if not, why not.

The second fundamental reason is that religion is not pure spirit, pure eternal fact. The evangelical faith has doctrines which directly pertain to the world of fact. The verse which opens the canon of Sacred Scripture refers to Nature, namely, its creation by Almighty God. The Incarnation and Resurrection are in the stream of history. *Bible-and-science is therefore part of the Christian apologetic.* It fits into the Christian apologetic as follows.

The most general term to describe our faith is *the Christian religion.* In more detail we are Protestant, not Catholic; conservative, not liberal. In more extended form our faith is *Protestant, Biblical, Conservative,* and *Trinitarian.* The teachings of our faith are summarized as *Christian theology,* and the verification of Christian theology is termed *Christian apologetics.* Christian apologetics may be divided into *Christian theism* and *Christian evidences.* In Christian theism we work with (i) the unique revelatory material of the Bible, and (ii) methodology of philosophy, and so construct a Christian theism which we defend as the truest explanation of the totality of facts, or experience. In Christian evidences we endeavour to show the correlation of Christianity to fact. First, Christianity is in accord with material fact; secondly, with supernatural fact; thirdly with experiential fact. In showing the correlation of Christianity with *material fact* we must deal with all the major sciences which have any relation to the Biblical record.   From this analysis it will be seen that the study of Bible and science is part of Christian apologetics, and a sub-division of Christian evidences.

The third important reason for the evangelical concern with Bible-and-science is that certain miracles of the Bible have been attacked as non-scientific.   Positively, the miracles of the Bible enter the domain of Nature which is the special province of science.   If the biologist denies the virgin birth and the astronomer the long day of Joshua and the geologist the creation record, the evangelical must explain why he chooses to go counter to modern science at these points.   One cannot be true to the Biblical record and not be con-cerned with the miraculous.

Both modernism and neo-orthodoxy are retreats from fact.   Both have affirmed that (i) the science of the Bible is simply the outmoded science of antiquity, and (ii) the science of the Bible has nothing to do with the theology of the Bible.   As much as modernism and neo-orthodoxy differ, they concur on these two judgments.   But the evangelical feels that this is a retreat from fact, a distortion of the true nature of the Biblical religion.   The relation of the Biblical religion to fact must be maintained.   One generation of evangelical-ism might survive if we seriously divorce the religion of the Bible from its necessary relevance to fact, but we feel that the second generation would drift away from anything similar to Biblical reli-gion.   The issues at stake, therefore, in Bible-and-science are enormous.

The major scope of this work will be to show the relationship of Biblical data to scientific knowledge.   It will not be an elaborate Christian philosophy of science nor a discussion of the relationship of Christianity to scientific knowledge on an extended basis.   Both of these problems would require development beyond the purposes of this book and are more properly theological problems than Biblical.

Recent works such as John Baillie, *Natural Science and the Spiritual Life* (1951); W. A. Whitehouse, *Christian Faith and the Scientific Attitude* (1952); D. R. G. Owen, *Scientism, Man, and Religion* (1952); E. L. Long, *Religious Beliefs of American Scientists* (1952), and *Science and the Christian Faith* (1950); and D. L. Morris, *Possibilities Unlimited: A Scientist's Approach to Religion* (1952), are efforts at describing the relationship of modern science to theological know-edge.

Having taught Bible-and-science over a period of years the author is aware of a very difficult psychological problem in discussing the matters of this book with his conservative brethren.   The psychol-ogical problem is that so many Christians *fail to differentiate interpreta-tion from inspiration*.   For example, if from childhood a student has heard only of a universal flood, he will consider a local flood as a heretical innovation.   Or, if a Christian has known only the gap theory of Gen. 1, having read it in *The Scofield Reference Bible* or in the popular writings of Harry Rimmer, such a person will feel that other interpretations are trifling with Sacred Scripture.   In both cases it is clearly a mistake in failing to distinguish between inspiration and interpretation.

First, one must realize that *revelation is not interpretation,* and conversely, *interpretation is not revelation.*   Revelation is the communication of divine truth; interpretation is the effort to understand it.   One cannot say: "I believe just exactly what Gen. 1 says and I don't need any theory of reconciliation with science."   Such an assertion identifies revelation with interpretation.   The problem still remains: *what does Gen. 1 say or mean or involve us in?*   Our mutual problem is not this: is Genesis inspired?   On that we agree.   Our problem is: what does Gen. 1 mean—how do we interpret it?   To profess belief in its divine origin does not necessarily help us in understanding how it relates to science.

Nor can we identify our interpretation with the infallibility of revelation.   We can dogmatize if we wish and equate our interpretation with orthodoxy.   John Pye Smith must have had a difficult time with some of his contemporary hyper-orthodox brethren for he wrote:

> It is not the Word of God, but the expositions and deductions of men, from which I dissent.

Later he mentions:

> [The dogmatic orthodox] represents his own interpretations of Scripture as unquestionable; and so confident is he in the infallibility of his own deductions as to identify them with the Divine Veracity, and to think himself entitled to take it for an analogy to his own reasoning.[16]

All the interpretations we ourselves shall defend in subsequent pages are tentative, exploratory and not given in a dogmatic spirit.

Second, we must recognize latitude of interpretation in these matters and not confuse differences of interpretation with belief in inspiration.   The fact that men believe in a local flood does not mean they believe less in divine inspiration.   Nor because Christian men seek harmonization of Scripture and science are they to be accused of trifling with Scripture.   These are extremely serious matters and there is no legitimate place for small minds, petty souls, and studied ignorance.

The author of this book believes in the divine origin of the Bible and therefore in its divine inspiration; and he emphatically rejects any partial theory of inspiration or liberal or neo-orthodox views of the Bible.   If what follows disagrees with cherished beliefs of the reader, be assured it is not a difference over inspiration but over interpretation.

NOTES

1. Because the word *nature* has so many meanings we have capitalized it in this work at all places where it stands for such notions as "the universe," or "creation," or the material dimension of reality.

2. Cf. "If Protestantism is to win America it must win science." C. C. Morrison, "Protestantism and Science," *Christian Century*, April 1946, p. 524.   Evangelicalism is certainly not winning science, which makes winning America that much more difficult.

3. Cf. E. W. Hall, "Metaphysics," *Twentieth Century Philosophy* (1943), pp. 145–194.

4. Exposition of these principles and their importance for the Catholic dealing with Christianity and science will be found in Canon Dorlodot, *Darwinism and Catholic Thought* (1923), Vol. I.

5. 1 Tim. 6: 20.   The Greek word here is *gnōsis,* "knowledge," not science in its technical meaning.

6. F. Bettex, *Christianity and Science* (1903), p. 123.

7. J. W. Dawson, *The Origin of the World According to Revelation and Science* (1877), p. 323.

8. John Pye Smith, *On the Relation Between the Holy Scriptures and some parts of Geological Science* (1840), pp. 148 and 150.   In many stalwart treatises which we have read on Bible and science, the learned authors have complained that they were more bitterly attacked by the hyper-orthodox than by unbelieving scientists.

9. White, I, 225.

10. An expression used by such a loyal believer of the Bible as J. W. Dawson (*op. cit.*, p. 135).   Although most evangelicals would not appreciate a reference to Maynard Shipley's *The War on Modern Science* (1927) they cannot deny the very words of the hyper-orthodox which Shipley quotes.   There they are in all their extremisms, and even fanaticisms.   Just as heartbreaking and deplorable is the story told by Norman F. Furniss in *The Fundamentalist Controversy, 1918–1931"* (New Haven, Yale University Press, 1954) whose elaborate documentation cannot be denied even though at some points he fails to see the controversy in its fuller dimensions.

11. C. W. Shields, *The Scientific Evidences of Revealed Religion* (1900), pp. 35–36.

12. J. W. Dawson, *Nature and the Bible* (1875), p. 48.

13. Hans Reichenbach, *The Rise of Scientific Philosophy* (1951), labours hard to make a good case for philosophy being constructed in the same spirit and precision as science. In his chapter on ethics he rejects normative ethics, but then admits that it is best to live *as if* ethical rules of a given society were valid. But the ghost of normative ethics stalks his treatment as he speaks of a "distorted morality," rebels against the charge of anarchism, and argues for the "democratic principle."

14. Shields, *op. cit.*, p. 56.

15. Shields, *op. cit.*, p. 56. Cf. also the judgment of Guyot as to the relationship of Bible and science: "Let us not, therefore, hope, much less ask, from science the knowledge which it can never give; nor seek from the Bible the science which it does not intend to teach. Let us receive from the Bible, on trust, the fundamental truths to which the human sciences cannot attain, and let the results of scientific inquiry serve as a running commentary to help us rightly to understand the comprehensive statements of the Biblical account which refer to God's work during the grand week of creation." A Guyot, *Creation* (1884), p. 6.

16. John Pye Smith, *On the Relation Between the Holy Scriptures and some parts of Geological Science* (1840), pp. 70 and 157.

CHAPTER II

AN ANALYSIS OF THE CONFLICT BETWEEN THEOLOGY AND SCIENCE[1]

I. INTRODUCTION

THAT evangelicalism has not been in the good graces of science has been indicated in the previous chapter. The causes of such a condition are therefore an important consideration. Our task in this chapter, is (i) to describe the tasks of theology and science, and (ii) to seek to understand how in the pursuit of these tasks theologians and scientists have come into conflict.

II. THE SPECIFIC TASKS OF SCIENCE AND THEOLOGY

To define the task of science is difficult because to define science itself is difficult. School textbooks define science with an ease that we envy, but the task is not so simple in philosophy of science. The vexing problem of defining science is best seen when one tries to classify the sciences. The usual result is to identify science with all knowledge. By science we mean that approximate knowledge we possess of Nature and its phenomena, and this would include the pure sciences and the mixed sciences such as geology and astronomy (or if one prefers, the composite sciences). By extending our notion of science to include anything capable of a measure of systematic treatment and verification we would then include psychology, sociology, history and anthropology. If we were to identify the terms science and knowledge, then theology would be included. The scientist working in pure science thinks that all other types of knowledge are too loose to be classified as sciences, but the psychologist and sociologist do not readily acquiesce in this. However psychologists and sociologists usually draw the line to exclude theology, and this does not please the theologians. Any definition of science will be part arbitrary and conventional. We, therefore, in speaking of science mean to emphasize that body of knowledge dealing with the *structure* and *causal* or *functional relationships* of the *physical* and *space-time* aspects of the universe. Hence, our emphasis is on that which is *external* in contrast to the internal;

[1] For notes see page 43.

on that which is *causal* or *determined* in contrast to that which is free or novel or spontaneous; on that which is *formal* in contrast to that which is personal; on that which is capable of *description by law* in contrast to that which is unique; and on that which is based on the *continuous* or *uniform* or *regular* in contrast to that which is novel, vertical, and occasional.

The definition of theology is almost as difficult as that of science, for there are those who wish either to annul religious knowledge or those who wish to make religious experience more fundamental than theology. Orthodox theologians insist that theological knowledge is valid knowledge, whereas liberals define theology as the science of religion. We define theology as the task of setting forth the claims of our knowledge of God, the verification of these claims, and the systematic and organic connexions of our theological knowledge. Theological study has, however, two foci, one in experience and one in Scripture, and for this reason the study of theology has moral and spiritual considerations which the study of science does not have. Hence, there is an important subjective element in the study of theology as well as an objective element. Theology is a study by the regenerated heart and mind of (primarily but not exclusively) the Holy Bible to determine the system of truth it presents. Although in theology we believe we have objective and real knowledge, we believe that in large part it appears credible only to those who have had an inward experience of the grace of the Holy Spirit. The requirements for a scientist are such things as honesty, integrity, intelligence, patience and fairness. There is no crucial experience which makes one a scientist. The requirements of a theologian include all those of a scientist and the additional spiritual ones. (The hyper-orthodox frequently make the mistake of thinking that because they have the spiritual requirements they can treat with great disregard the scientific aspects of theological scholarship.) In defining theology as our knowledge of God and of His relationships to creation we must add: *as carried on by a Christian man*.

It is, to speak as a theologian, the task of the scientist to explore the works or creation of God, and that of the theologian the speech of God in the Bible, Nature, and history. From the Christian perspective the true scientist should work in humility and reverence, believing that he is delving into the workshop of God. Whatever theology brings forth from the scientific investigation of Nature comes at the end of the task and consists of the generalizations indicating how our knowledge of Nature dovetails with our theological knowledge. In the main, the task of science is the understanding of Nature; and the task of theology is the understanding of God. It is the thesis of this author that the two tasks and the two bodies of conclusions should exist in a state of harmony.   The speech of God in Nature and in Scripture must accord.

III.   Why Theologians and Scientists have Conflicts

Ideally in their mutual pursuits the scientist and the theologian should supplement each other.   Their efforts should merge into each other to form one harmonious continuum of reliable knowledge.   But, much to the contrary, the relationship in many cases has been bitter and antagonistic.   Blame is on both sides.   The dogmatizing theologian has a blood-brother in the dogmatic materialist, and premature judgments in theology are akin to immature judgments in science.   Out of the mistakes of both theologian and scientist has come the unfortunate history of their unfriendly relationship.

Mistakes peculiar to the theologian.   The first mistake peculiar to the theologian is that of attitude.   He has been unsympathetic with science, or suspicious of it, or he fails to understand science.   In this the theologian is to blame.   If he is censorious of the scientist who makes amateurish remarks about theology, and wishes that the scientist would learn a little theology before he spoke, the scientist can also ask the theologian to learn a little science before he speaks.   To view science as the work of scheming atheists, iconoclasts, or plotting infidels is not true to the facts nor felicitous of the spirit of the Christian theologian.   Slurring the name of science, branding it all as devil-inspired, chiding it unsympathetically, further aggravate the situation that is already bordering on the incurable.

The second mistake peculiar to the theologian is either (i) to identify a given world view, with its science, with the Bible or (ii) to derive too much empirical or specific data from the general assertions of Gen. 1.   For example, the identification of the Aristotelian science with Christianity as occurred during the Middle Ages has done harm beyond any possible calculation.   Much of the conflict between scientists and theologians was really between Aristotelianism and science, not Christianity and science.   Theologians must be exceedingly careful to not identify Christianity with any perishable scientific world view.

Just as mistaken as identifying Christianity with Aristotelianism is the mistake of making the Bible speak too specifically on scientific matters.   We have in Gen. 1 a broad, general sketch of creation.   To try to prove minute points of geology, biology, botany or anthropology from it is therefore impossible and should not be attempted.   When we try to do it, we force the record to speak in detail beyond its real purpose, and we are in danger of running into contradiction with the empirical facts established by the sciences. Few reliable conservative scholars today would state that we can positively identify the Hebrew word *kind* (Hebrew, *min*; LXX, *genos;* Vulgate, *genus* and *species*) with the modern scientific notion of *species*. None would certainly identify *min* with varieties. To attempt to identify *min* with species or varieties is making the record speak with a scientific particularity it does not possess. We judge it improper for the theologian to try to settle specific details about scientific matters by forcing the Bible to speak with a degree of particularity its language does not indicate.

Mistakes common to both theologians and scientists. First, theologians and scientists may pronounce some scientific theory as final, and this can cause conflict. The theologian may presume a hypothesis to be a fact, and then have later developments in science demonstrate its falsity; the scientist may prematurely accept a hypothesis as true and find himself in conflict with the theologian. There have been no less than ten theories as to the origin of the solar system as listed in W. M. Smart's *The Origin of the Earth* (1951). Which is the true one? Which is the Biblical one? Premature judgment by either scientist or theologian may cause unnecessary friction. There are several schools of contemporary psychology, as there are of basic theory of acculturation in anthropology. "Denominationalism" afflicts science as well as the church, and for this reason both scientist and theologian must be careful of too easy an identification of any current school of scientific theory with the final truth.

Secondly, theologians and scientists must be keenly aware of the imperfections of human knowledge in both science and theology. Scientific theory is somewhat fluid under our feet. The history of atomic theory from 1885 to 1950 is so rapid it is almost breath-taking. Each removal of a past imperfection is a prophecy of a future imperfection. The same is the case with exegesis. Archaeology, philology, and history are constantly enriching our knowledge of the Old and New Testaments. With this enriched knowledge attends a more careful and accurate exegesis. Thus exegesis, to a certain extent, is in a state of flux.[2]

We can at this point take the advice of Pratt:

> The Book of Nature and the Word of God emanate from the same infallible Author, and therefore cannot be at variance. But man is a fallible interpreter, and by mistaking one or both of these Divine Records, he forces them too often into unnatural conflict.[3]

The third cause for conflict is misinterpretation of the Bible by scientist or theologian. If the scientist affirms that the Bible teaches creation at 4004 B.C. he needlessly makes science and Scripture conflict through misinterpretation. If the first step toward truth is the removal of error, the Ussher chronology should at this point be abandoned. If the scientist insists that the Bible teaches that the earth is flat, or the heavens solid, or that there are pillars supporting the sky, or that the entire solar system came to rest at Joshua's command, then through his own misinterpretation he brings the Bible into conflict with science.

If the theologian teaches that the earth is the centre of the solar system, or that man first appeared on the earth at 4004 B.C., or that all the world was submerged under water at 4004 B.C. and had been for unknown millennia, he is misinterpreting Scripture and bringing Scripture into needless conflict with science. Both scientist and theologian must exercise unusual care in the interpretation of the Bible and it is just as mistaken to follow after improper interpretations of the Bible as it is to follow after unproved hypotheses in science.

Mistakes peculiar to scientists. Just as there are certain mistakes that a theologian is susceptible to there are ones that the scientist is just as susceptible to in the relationship of theology to science. The first of these mistakes is to have an anti-religious attitude. No system of knowledge can be learned without some sympathy or kindly feeling toward the system—something pointed out long ago by Augustine but never fully appreciated by educators or epistemologists. Dogmatists study science as well as theology.

The evangelical indicates that man is a spiritual rebel and his spirit of rebellion is reflected in all his activities. Unregenerate man opposes the doctrines of creation, sin, redemption, and eschatology. A man may be religious and yet anti-Christian. Opposition to Christianity at the level of science is in many instances simply localized or vocalized opposition to Christianity in general. Therefore anti-Christian man takes pleasure in making the gap between science and Christianity as wide as he can make it, and will heartlessly ridicule any efforts at reconciliation. In this instance, the gap between science and Christianity is in reality the gap between faith and unbelief.

However, conservatives need to be careful that this is not exaggerated in their dealings with scientists. All science and all scientists cannot be dropped overboard on the sole grounds that they are not Christian. All of geology cannot be declared specious because geology has been developed principally by unregenerate men. Truth is truth and facts are facts no matter who develops them. Man as a spiritual and intellectual rebel is part of the reason why there is tension between science and Christianity, but *it is not the entire reason.*

Putting the same truth positively we assert that a scientist's lack of faith incapacitates him from truly harmonizing science and Scripture. The evidence of Heb. 11: 3 cannot be controverted at this point ("Through faith we understand that the world came into being by the command of God, so that what is seen does not owe its existence to that which is visible"—Weymouth). Nature as the creation of God can be appreciated properly and interpreted correctly only by the man of God, and the Bible as the Word of God is so recognized only by the man of God. Only the man of faith has the correct perspective and motivation to harmonize Scripture and science. Men without faith cannot but clash the gears.

However, the most drastic difference between science and evangelicalism arises from the usage of the scientific method and knowledge by the scientists. We must now examine why it is that scientists persist in creating a so-called scientific world view which clashes with the Biblical world view.

Science, narrowly conceived, is not partial to any philosophical system but forms a body of material which any philosophy must reckon with. Philosophers may claim that science is on their side or that their philosophy is constructed by the use of the scientific method and so lend the prestige of science to their philosophy. In either case science is made to serve metaphysics or philosophy. The materialist claims that science presents the same world view from empirical and experimental considerations that materialism presents from philosophical considerations. Similar use is made of science by pragmatism, naturalism, and positivism, all of which may be termed *scientisms*. All have in common the exaltation of the scientific method and scientific knowledge with reference to philosophical construction.

Obviously, if science and the scientific method be used to exclude the spiritual the Christian feels that the scientific method and scientific knowledge are abused. It is the Christian's obligation to show wherein is the type of reasoning employed which leads to scientisms.

1. The Christian philosopher indicates that all scientisms *oversimplify both the scientific method and the scope of reliable knowledge.* In reference to the over-simplification of the scientific method we mean that only certain aspects of the scientific method are emphasized and made important. The scientific method as usually listed in college text-books in connexion with the sciences is epistemologically disrespectful. What is presented is correct, but what is left unmentioned is as vital to the scientific method as what is mentioned. Included in the scientific methodology are: (i) requisite ethical norms on the part of the experimenter, *e.g.* honesty in reading his various meters, reporting variations, not faking the evidence; (ii) the necessary integrity of the personal powers of the

scientist, *e.g.* his memory, his sensory equipment, his judgment; (iii) the validity of the laws of logic as he manipulates his data; (iv) the necessity and validity of communication to other selves, for science is a community project and a social activity.[4]   When the scientific method is usually discussed such notions as testability or intersubjectivity or experimentation are to the fore.   This is a clear case of evasion, and it is only by such methods that a plausible case can be made for scientisms.   If we seek a grounding for (i) ethical norms, (ii) logical procedures, (iii) the integrity of personal powers, and (iv) the existence of other selves and our communication with them, in the same sense in which scientisms seek a grounding for experimentation, uniformity of nature, and sensory experience, we will discover that none of the scientisms can carry the burden.   In the history of philosophy it will be discovered that philosophers can find a locus for ethics, logical realism, selves, knowledge of other selves, only in some sort of theistic system, and rightly so.   Scientisms must admit that ethical norms, etc., are (i) operational procedures, or (ii) necessary assumptions but devoid of any metaphysical standing, or (iii) conventions judged solely by their utility.   The Christian philosopher insists that scientisms evade this point, and it is the crucial point.   With no possible justification one segment of the scientific method is given royal status (experimental, sensory, etc.) and the other segment (ethical norms, etc.) *just as important as the first* is written off as having no metaphysical importance.   In a very clearly written essay Brightman has exposed this entire procedure, and shown that a *knowing, ethical, dependable, integrated, rational self is a necessary part of the scientific method.*[5]

If the scientific method is construed in terms far simpler than it actually is, obviously knowledge is also cut too short.   Reliable knowledge must be enlarged as to include knowledge about ethics, logic, human personality and social communication.   Such an enlarged notion of knowledge would permit theology its rightful place in the domain of reliable human knowledge.

2. The Christian indicts scientisms for their *reductionistic spirit.* Reductionism is the effort to explain the complex by the simple, and the higher by the lower.   A typical reduction chain is as follows: what we call the mind is in reality a very complex set of nerve networks called the brain.   These fibres are made up of complex organic compounds.   These organic compounds can be resolved into their original chemical elements.   *Ergo,* the brain is nothing but a highly complicated arrangement of several of the basic chemical elements.   What is called mind turns out to be a complex grouping of matter.   A typical reductionist statement, valuable for its simplicity and frankness, is that of Russell:

The evidence, though not conclusive, tends to show that everything distinctive of living matter can be reduced to chemistry, and therefore ultimately to physics. The fundamental laws governing living matter are, in all likelihood, the very same that govern the behaviour of the hydrogen atom, namely, the laws of quantum mechanics.[6]

Then speaking directly of mental life he affirms:

In the chain of events from sense organ to muscle, everything is determined by the laws of macroscopic physics.[7]

Another form of reductionism is to say that religion is a disguised sex-response. Religion is thus reduced to physiology. Or, with reference to conscience, to call it the accumulated result of the countless "no's" we heard as children from parents and teachers, conscience is reduced to psychological conditioning. We have said "spirit of reductionism," for scientisms vary in their application of the reductionist principle. The materialists and positivists are the extreme reductionists. Naturalists have tried to avoid the reductionist's fallacy, but that they have is to be doubted.

The reductionist mentality is complex as it springs partly from the scientific ideal of simplicity, and partly from an anti-metaphysical or anti-religious mood. It amounts to depriving something of its own right and status. The Christian objects at this point. Mind, as we know it, functions in organisms, but if mind is equated with the brain the facts are butchered. Conscience may have numerous correlations with heredity, environment and physical elements of one's own body, but these modifications do not destroy its being and autonomy. In some instances religious feelings and sex feelings may merge or be confused, but that does not give us the right to discount all religion as disguised sex response.

The Christian philosopher urges at this point that *adequacy* is as much a guide as *simplicity* is, and that the reductionist in seeking simplicity murders facts. Only when reductionism kills off a large measure of the fact-population can scientism make good its claims. But if we are fair to all experience, adequacy must be also reckoned with, and any procedure which sacrifices adequacy to simplicity is an abortive procedure.

3. The Christian philosopher indicts scientisms for their *irrational prejudice against teleological thinking.* By teleological thinking we mean that thinking which recognizes the validity of purpose, meaning, intelligence, wisdom and guidance as possible categories of the Real. Teleological thinking has always been associated with religious, spiritual, and idealistic thought. Scientisms have steadily ruled in favour of ateleological thought. They have unfairly

tagged teleological thought as "sentimental" or "emotional" or "soft-headed," and have prided ateleological thought as "factual" or "hard-headed" or "scientific."

We brand this prejudice against teleological thought as unjustifiable on the grounds that it is completely impossible of practice, and if completely impossible of practice it cannot be a true philosophical position. It is obvious psychological fact that people without will or purpose or motivation are already psychopathic or shortly will be. It is common knowledge among anthropologists that uprooted primitive peoples suffer from melancholia and eventually die off. All normal psychological life is held together with purpose. The most ardent materialist or positivist is guided and motivated by purpose. The very fibre and glue of the philosophical activity itself is the purposive. Yet, in mental life, scientisms must brand purpose as deceptive and of no metaphysical import. This is why we consider the ateleological mood of scientisms as unjustifiable. How is it possible that, if all is materially or causally determined, such a misbehaving, deceptive item like purpose should be the very cement of healthy personality?

4. The Christian indicts scientisms for their *prejudice against the supernatural*. The problem of the supernatural is actually the problem of the conceivable or the inconceivable. Bett, in his work *The Reality of the Religious Life* (1949), ably argues that the entire concept of conceivability is a slippery one. A vast array of modern attainments were all at one time declared inconceivable. When the history of things considered inconceivable is reviewed one shudders at ever uttering a statement, "it is inconceivable." That is to say, we are hardly in a position to dogmatize on inconceivability. Admittedly, *conceivability* does not prove actuality. But the deep-seated spirit of anti-supernaturalism among scientisms is built upon a theory of inconceivability which is not justifiable.

The categorical, dogmatic, officious and contemptuous excluding of the very conceivability of the supernatural we consider a most improper procedure, and entirely untrue to what an examination of the concept of conceivability would warrant.

A *scientism* can be constructed only by its being partial and limited in its conduct of the philosophical quest. Combining abuses of the interpretation of the scientific method, and deep-seated prejudices in the interpretation of reality, scientisms created anti-Christian philosophies. The Christian philosopher affirms that a fair treatment of the scientific method, and a thorough appreciation of all the facts, lead not only to a fair and adequate appreciation of science and scientific methodology, but also to an appreciation of the Christian system of philosophy, and an appreciation of the Christian faith.

The main burden of this chapter then is simply this: *if the theologian and the scientist had been careful to stick to their respective duties, and to learn carefully the other side when they spoke of it there would have been no disharmony between them save that of the non-Christian heart in rebellion against God.* There would have been no stupid exegetical mistakes of theologians, nor misunderstandings of the Bible by scientists. The theologian would not have needlessly stung the scientists, and the scientist would not have needlessly provoked the theologian. The issue between Christian and non-Christian would not have been a morass of blunder, mistake, and bigotry, but clearly that of belief or unbelief, faith or disobedience. *It is our purpose to show that there is nothing between the soul of a scientist and Jesus Christ save the disposition of the scientist himself.* We hope to show that whatever else is put between is put there improperly and that if the total facts are known its impropriety will become apparent. It is therefore not our purpose to coerce faith, but to remove the needless timber that men are wont to throw between themselves and the Saviour.

NOTES

1. Studied historically by: A. D. White, *A History of the Warfare of Science with Theology* (1896), 2 vols.; D. O. Zöckler, *Geschichte der Beziehungen zwischen Theologie and Naturwissenschaft mit besonderer Rücksicht auf Schöpfungsgeschichte* (1879), 2 vols., and a corrective to White's history; J. Y. Simpson, *Landmarks in the Struggle Between Science and Religion* (1925); J. W. Draper, *The Conflict between Religion and Science* (1875); C. W. Shields, *The Final Philosophy* (1877).

2. Clay tablets from the ancient Biblical lands have been the source of much new information—religious, political, and grammatical or linguistic. Even with reference to the famous virgin passage of Isa. 7: 14 there is information to be learned from the clay tablets. Cf. Cyrus H. Gordon, "Almah in Isa. 7: 14," *The Journal of Bible and Religion*, 21: 106, April, 1953.

3. J. H. Pratt, *Scripture and Science not at Variance* (1872), p. 8.

4. J. H. Woodger, *Biological Principles* (1929), p. 228, lists the bare "fundamental types of judgments upon which all natural scientific knowledge rests, and which cannot be inferred from anything else." This is a very important and imposing list, and is the type of thing so many naïve discussions of the scientific method omit. For metaphysics and epistemology these things which Woodger lists are exceedingly important no matter how much scientisms prefer to ignore them.

5. E. S. Brightman, "The Presuppositions of Experiment," *The Personalist*, 19: 136–143, 1938. In a subsequent issue Brightman was answered but in our judgment not refuted. Oman has also noted this. "The discovery of this order [in the universe] has been the achievement of minds which work by meaning and, therefore, not by mechanism or

anything capable of quantitative measurement. The interests of freedom are the spring of the whole enterprise of science; upon free ideas and free experiments all its methods depend; and only for its uses by freedom has measurement or mechanism any value." John Oman, *The Natural and the Supernatural* (1931), p. 111.

6. Bertrand Russell, *Human Knowledge* (1948), p. 33.

7. *Ibid.*, p. 41.

CHAPTER III

THE FUNDAMENTAL PROBLEMS OF CHRISTIANITY AND SCIENCE

I. THE LANGUAGE OF THE BIBLE WITH REFERENCE TO NATURAL THINGS

GENUINE relevant thinking cannot be accomplished in the realm of Bible-and-science until the nature of Biblical language has been deeply probed. Few books on Bible-and-science treat this point.[1] In those books that do touch on this subject the treatment is usually singularly superficial. Guided by expediency, logic, and analysis, science has built up through the centuries its special language. The language of the Bible is that of ancient Palestine and Greece. To correlate the two languages requires an understanding of both of them. When the scientist uses such words as "atom" or "law" or "theorem" or "logical construct" or "convention" or "curved space" we must know our philosophy of science to understand precisely what these terms mean. The word atom has had a long history and the concept of an atom has varied immensely from Newton to de Broglie. The philosopher of science wishes to know which concept of the atom a writer is employing. Further, the philosopher of science knows that it is forever impossible to see an atom because the size of an atom is several thousand times smaller than the ability of the eye to perceive smallness. Popular understanding of the word atom is usually very different from the technical understanding.

If it is necessary to read lengthily in the tomes on philosophy of science to know what logical constructs or conventions or intervening variables are, it is also necessary to dig deeply to understand the precise nature of Biblical language. Much hyper-orthodox literature on the subject is extremely wooden in its approach. At times its writers have been accused of being too literalistic, but the trouble is deeper than that. The approach seems to rest on the unwritten assumption that if a record is inspired its meaning is *always* obvious, and if we seek any subtlety in the meaning or in the literary form of the narrative we are accused of trifling with the inspiration of the Bible. But after poring over the literature on the subject of Bible-and-science, the author is assured that no real grappling with the

[1] For notes see page 79.

issues is possible till one has worked out his own theory as to the nature of Biblical statements about natural matters.

A. *The language of the Bible with reference to natural matters is popular, not scientific.* By popular we meant what the etymology of the word implies, "of the people." Popular language is the language in which people converse.

It is the language of the market-place, of social gatherings, and of the chance conversation. It is that basic vocabulary and style which the masses use to carry on their daily communication. By scientific language we mean that jargon (in the good sense of the word) developed in the history of science around the various sciences, which enables men of that science to communicate more accurately, conveniently, and economically. Hence scientists use their terms without lengthy definitions of the terms each time they are used. Their fellow scientists know exactly what the terms mean.

Both languages serve their purpose. The scientist writes his essay for his technical journal in the jargon of his speciality, and this jargon is a most valuable tool for the communication of his ideas. When he chats with his neighbour as they meet in some social gathering the scientist prudently recourses to the vocabulary of popular speech.

The Bible is a book for all peoples of all ages. Its terms with reference to Nature must be popular. Perhaps in the medical and nautical language of Luke there are some technical terms, but most of the vocabulary of the Bible with reference to Nature is popular. It is therefore highly improper for scientists to seek technical terminology in the Bible. It is also reprehensible for exegetes to try to find recondite references to modern scientific terminology in the Bible. The first is *unfair* in expecting a popular treatise to speak the language of science, and the second is *undiscerning* in making the Bible speak that which it does not propose to say.

B. *The language of the Bible is phenomenal.* By phenomenal we mean "pertaining to appearances." The Bible uses a language that is not only popular but restricted to the apparent. For example it speaks of "the four corners [wings] of the earth" (Isa. 11: 12) because the division of something into quarters is a frequent human operation and a convenient method of indicating place. To this day it is not uncommon to hear in popular speech such expressions as "from every corner of the earth" or "from all quarters of the globe." Such expressions are neither scientific nor anti-scientific, but the popular and phenomenal expressions of daily conversation. Consider the language of Gen. 1. Astronomically, it speaks of the earth, the sun, the moon, and the stars. It does not mention asteroids, comets, nebulae or planets. The astronomical classification of Gen. 1 is phenomenal. It is restricted

to that which greets the eye as one gazes heavenward.   The same
is true of the biological and botanical terms of Gen. 1.   It speaks of
fish, fowl, cattle, and birds; of grass, herbs, and fruit trees.   It
does not classify amphibians or sea-going mammals.   Gen. 1 is the
classification of the unsophisticated common man.

The opinions of Pratt, with which we heartily agree, are so
excellent, and so well stated, that we shall quote him at length in
reference to the nature of Scriptural language:

> [The Bible] speaks intelligibly because it speaks in such matters
> according to appearances . . .   The method of describing a pheno-
> menon by appearances is as correct as any other method.   There are
> two ways in which a phenomenon in nature may be described; either,
> first, with reference to the principles and laws of nature involved in
> the phenomenon: or, secondly, with reference to the facts or the
> results which an observer beholds.   The first is called the scientific
> description; the second, the description according to appearances, or
> what is seen.   These are equally real and equally true.   The first is
> intelligible only to the scientific; the other can be understood by all
> in every age.   The latter method, then, is the one which Scripture
> adopts . . .   In matters of ordinary observation Scripture speaks the
> language of *sense*, not of theory: it uses the words of everyday life:
> it describes natural objects as they appear.   It adopts the terms which
> the most scientific use in the ordinary intercourse of life, and not
> only so, but often even in their scientific writings, which would other-
> wise be encumbered and obscured with the most tiresome circumlo-
> cutions . . .   The terms [sunrise, sunset] are, I conceive, equally
> true, whether the Ptolemaic or the Copernican system be adopted.
> They are the description of the phenomena strictly according to appear-
> ances, that is, according to what is seen, and involve, as I hope now
> to show, no assumption whatever regarding the sun or the earth being
> the centre of the system . . .   It is clear that the words, *rise, set, fall,
> ascend, descend,* and suchlike are RELATIVE terms, and do not by any
> means indicate of necessity ABSOLUTE motion in the body spoken of . . .
> It would be a hazardous thing to trust, even in ordinary popular
> language, much more in Scripture phraseology, to scientific descrip-
> tions when reference is made to natural phenomena: for the theory
> may in the end prove to be false, or not sufficiently general to explain
> new phenomena, and will therefore require remodelling and restating;
> whereas the description, recording appearances, or what is seen, will
> stand, so long as men's senses remain the same.[2]

To this may be added the excellent judgment of Dawson:

> Perhaps there can be no surer test of a true revelation from God
> than to ask the question, Does it refuse to commit itself to scientific
> or philosophical hypotheses, and does it grasp firmly those problems
> most important to man as a spiritual being and insoluble by his un-
> assisted reason?   This non-committal attitude as to the method of
> nature and the secondary causes of phenomena is, as we shall see,
> eminently characteristic of the Bible.[3]

C. The corollary to the previous point is that *the language of the Bible is non-postulational with reference to natural things.* By this we mean that *the Bible does not theorize as to the actual nature of things.*[4] Contrary to the erroneous interpretation of Heb. 11: 4, there is no theory of matter in the Bible. Although it has been proposed that the word "moved" in Gen. 1: 2 suggests the undulatory theory of light, this must be judged as fantastic exegesis. It is a strange logic which can associate the brooding of the Spirit over the waters with de Broglie's undulatory theory of matter. The Bible is silent as to the "inmost constitution of visible things" to use the wording of the Biblical Commission of Leo XIII. Nor is there a theory of astronomy taught in the Bible. Gen. 1 does not defend Aristotle or Ptolemy or Copernicus or Newton or Einstein or Milne. It does not decide between Newton's theory of universal gravitation or Einstein's geometrical field theory of gravitation.

The Bible is singularly lacking in any definite *theorizing* about astronomy, geology, physics, chemistry, zoology, and botany. These matters are dealt with according to popular and phenomenal terms and are free from scientific postulation. We cannot but agree with the judgment of W. B. Dawson when he wrote:

> A remarkable point in Biblical references to nature, is that we find no definite *explanation* anywhere of natural things. The writers of the Bible do not go beyond the description of what they actually see around them, and the correct way in which they describe what they do see is beyond praise . . . The writers of the Bible show more than severe self-control, and must indeed have been divinely guided, in thus keeping to description and avoiding theoretical explanations of natural things.[5]

D. *The language of the Bible employs the culture of the times in which it was written as the medium of revelation.* This is one of the most important problems of the entire problem of Christianity and science though it is one of the least discussed. Does the Bible speak the language of science, or does it speak in terms of ancient cultures? Does the Bible speak truth in literal terms when it speaks of things scientific, or does it speak theological truth in the garb of ancient cultural modes? At this point two positions are wrong. (i) The position of the radical critic or modernist is wrong who imagines that the Bible is filled with errors and mistakes of these ancient cultures, and so scientifically the Bible must be considered as filled with blunders. (ii) The hyper-orthodox is wrong who expects the Bible to contain modern science. In that the Bible is inspired, the modernist is wrong, because the restraint of the Holy Spirit upon the writers of the Bible preserved them from the errors of their day. In that inspiration came through the mould of the Hebrew culture, the hyper-orthodox is wrong.

It will be admitted by all that the Bible came to us in human languages written by human beings and employing familiar human concepts and symbols. *If God spoke through Hebrew-speaking prophets and Greek-speaking Jews, what He had to say was to a degree limited by the natures of the Hebrew and Greek languages.*

Language cannot be disassociated from culture, for language and culture are profoundly intertwined. If God spoke through the Hebrew and Greek languages, He also spoke *in terms of the cultures in which these languages were embedded.* The eternal truths of the Hebrew-Christian religion are clothed and garbed not only in the Hebrew and Greek languages but also in the cultural moulds of the times of the composition of the Bible. The radical error of the modernist is to write off the supernatural character of the Bible by a destructive theory of accommodation. The radical error of the hyper-orthodox is his failure to see that there is a measure of accommodation. *We believe that the true position is that the revelation of God came in and through the Biblical languages and their accompanying culture.* Coming through these cultures it became meaningful and relevant; and being inspired of God, the writers were restrained from error. In view of what we know of pre-scientific cultures, ancient and contemporary, it appears miraculous that the writers of the Bible are free of the grotesque, the mythological, and the absurd. As Shields observes:

> Although scientifically the Hebrews did not make the advances that the Assyrians or Egyptians or Greeks did, nevertheless, the Hebrews were free from the grotesque absurdity which disfigures the astronomy or geology of their contemporaries as found in the sacred books of the East or even in the more artistic mythology of the Greeks.[6]

Nor can the judgment of Smith be controverted without getting our doctrine of the inspiration and infallibility of the Scriptures into grave difficulty when he wrote:

> We have thus seen it placed beyond the possibility of a doubt, that it is *the manner* of the Scriptures, and most copiously in their earliest *written parts, to speak of the Deity, his nature, his perfections, his purposes, and his operations, in language borrowed from the bodily and mental constitution of man, and from those opinions, concerning the works of God in the natural world, which were generally received by the people to whom the blessing of revelation was granted.*[7]

Although we are not the first to broach such a view, it is certainly the keypoint of the entire approach to the problem of harmonizing the Bible and scientific knowledge, and the point with which the hyper-orthodox will take most serious issue. We will therefore consider the matter more closely.

1. The vocabulary for *time* in both the Old Testament and the New Testament is not strict scientific time but the time-reckoning methods and units of the cultural period of the Bible writers.[8] The light and darkness mark out the day; the phases of the moon, the month; and the cycles of the seasons with the movements of the stars, the years. The day itself is divided into watches or hours. For the general routine of life such measurements are adequate. The refined units of time as current in modern civilization were unknown to them. They repeatedly had to amend their calendar as the period of the rotation of the earth around the sun involves a fraction, and they had no means of detecting nor accurately measuring that fraction. It would be impossible to perform the technical experiments of modern science with the popular time reckonings employed by the writers of the Bible.

This does not argue that there is something radically wrong with the time reckonings of the Bible. The time reckonings of the Bible are the popular, accurate-within-limits methods of the people of ancient times. These methods are not comparable to modern scientific methods, especially with the atomic clock wherewith time is kept phenomenally accurate by the vibrations of electrons in certain crystals.

2. The *psychological terms* of the Bible are terms of ancient cultures and not the terms of strict scientific psychology.[9] The Bible uses such terms as heart, liver, bones, bowels, and kidneys in its psychology, attributing psychic functions to these organs. It is a physiological psychology. Can the heart actually believe (Rom. 10: 9–10)? Can our liver be greatly distressed (Lam. 2: 11)? Does Paul actually have his spiritual love in his bowels (Phil. 1: 8)? Are the kidneys part of our psychical structure (Jer. 11: 20; Rev. 2: 23)? Are we to gather from the New Testament that we each have a soul, a spirit, a mind, a heart, a strength, a body (*sōma* and *sarks*)?

If we insist that the psychology of the Bible is to be taken in a strict literalistic sense then there is no other conclusion than to confess that the psychology of the Bible is not capable of rational defence. But if we agree that the truth of the Bible is expressed in terms of the prevailing culture of the times during which the Bible was written, then we have no problem. Our task is to decipher from the Bible its basic theological psychology. The heart and kidneys are physiological ways of representing our deep emotional and volitional life, experiences and feelings.

3. Consider next the *medical language* of the Bible. Much has been made of Luke's medical language being the medical language

of the doctors of his day.[10]   But is the medical language of Luke modern *scientific* medical language?   It was the medical language of the men of medicine of that place and period when Luke wrote, but it is not the language of modern medical text-books.   It would certainly be a rash effort to try to get modern medicine to use the medical language of the Bible on the grounds of its supposed inspired scientific impeccability.

4. The *mathematics* and *measuring systems* of the Bible are those of that prescientific era and not modern scientific methods of counting and measuring.   Numbers were frequently used in the same way we use the words *many, some,* or *few*.   Three stood for few; seven, ten, and one hundred stood for completeness; ten in other connexions meant several; forty meant many; seven and seventy meant large but uncertain numbers.   Round numbers were used for exact numbers.   Any Bible dictionary will have a chart of the distance measurements of the Bible as well as weight measurements and liquid measurements.   *It is to be carefully noted that as the culture shifts from Old Testament Semitic to New Testament Graeco-Roman the systems change.*   Which is the inspired and infallible system—the one in the Old Testament or the New Testament? If we believe that the inspired truth of God came through cultural mediums we will affirm that the question is meaningless.   God never gave infallibility to the measuring systems of the Bible. They were used in the Bible because they were the customary and familiar units of the people of that time.

5. The *geographical terms* of the Bible are the usual, customary terms of the culture of the time.   It speaks of mountains, valleys, plains, rivers, streams, lakes, seas, and coasts.   It has a *theological geography* of heaven, earth, and hell, but this is not to be converted into literal geography.   The Hebrew Old Testament and the Greek New Testament used the terms common to their cultures to describe geographical matters.[11]

The opinions of E. C. Rust expressed in *Nature and Man in Biblical Thought* (1953) may be noted, as they offer a variant interpretation of what we have stated here.   It is our position that the Biblical writers do not teach any cosmological system or follow any cosmogony, ancient or modern.   Rather their writings are prescientific and phenomenal or non-postulational.   As far as their vocabulary and method of speaking are concerned they use the culture terms and expressions of their time.   The Spirit of God restrained them from any use of the polytheistic or fantastic.   Rust believes that the writers of the Bible not only used the terms and expressions of their culture, but that they also entered into their erroneous ideas of cosmology and anthropology.   With this view we disagree.   Rust clearly says:

Biblical cosmology, zoology, and ethnology are not binding [upon Christian faith].[12]

But the theological truths expressed in these outmoded scientific notions are inspired and part of the Biblical witness. The truth remains the same, GOD IS ALMIGHTY CREATOR, whether we picture the creation as the ancient Babylonians did, or as Copernicus did, or as Einstein did. Therefore Rust is willing to defend the *theological* world view of the Bible, if we may so define it, while admitting the erroneous nature of its *scientific* world view. This is certainly a great improvement over liberalism, but we feel the case has never been conclusively made, *viz.* that the writers of the Bible actually adopted Babylonian cosmology.

E. *Conclusion.* In conclusion, we note that the language of the Bible with reference to natural things is *popular, prescientific,* and *non-postulational.* It is the terminology of the culture prevailing at the time the various books were written. It is a matter of the Spirit of God speaking through these terms so that (i) the terms are not themselves thereby made infallible science, and that (ii) the theological content is in no wise endangered.[13]

There are certain great advantages that accrue from this view of the inspired language of the Bible.

1. Because the language is popular and non-postulational it forms a *meaningful* revelation. Who, even today, would understand a book written in the terminology and concepts of *final science* ? A man who objects to the Bible because it is not in the accents of the latest science knows not what he asks. If the Bible were in the language and concepts of *final* science it would not have been understood by the millions of readers in pre-scientific periods of the past and in pre-scientific cultures of the present. In that the Bible is in popular terminology it is adapted to man as he is. It is therefore *understandable and meaningful.*

2. Although the Bible is not in scientific language it is not in *anti-scientific* language. It is *pre-scientific* language. Men of science to this day speak of the rising and setting of the sun. To the human eye the sun does rise and set, and it does appear to move across the sky. A theory of the solar system attempts to account for our observations. We do not actually see the earth moving around the sun. As far as human observation is concerned, the sun rises and sets. We are not theorizing or postulating any theory of the solar system. Popular or non-postulational language, while not scientific, is not explanatory of Nature and is therefore *pre-scientific,* not *anti-scientific.* Or, as Shields well states it:

In a word, it is because the Bible, though non-scientific, is not anti-scientific, that it is as true for our time as it was true for its own time, and is likely to remain true for all time to come.[14]

3. Because the Bible uses pre-scientific terms it is a Bible for all ages and is adapted to all stages of human progress. No better choice could have been made for the propagation of the Bible through the centuries of church history. Smith taunts those who would wish the Bible in scientific language. A Bible peppered with scientific jargon would be most inappropriate for the religious instruction of humanity. It would be cold, unattractive and most difficult to understand. Smith continues:

> [Try the experiment of using scientific language in religious matters on the peasantry] or even the best educated children of our own families. The style of a Moral Philosophy school would arouse no attention, would leave scarcely any impression: the simple imagery of Scripture is instinct with life, and touches every chord of feeling.[15]

F. *How do we tell what is cultural and what is trans-cultural?* This is one problem remaining over from our discussion which needs further elaboration. For example, a typical religious liberal would negate most of the theological structure of the New Testament on the grounds that its theological structure is that of the world view of ancient antiquity. Vicarious atonement would be negated on the grounds that New Testament writers thought in terms of blood sacrifices or bargaining with God, or were influenced by Mithraism with its blood baths. That is to say, *they write too much off as cultural.* Francis Pieper is so strict in his view of inspiration that he makes no room for the cultural, and so *makes too much of the cultural binding.* He writes:

> But remember: when Scripture incidentally treats a scientific subject, it is always right, let "science" say what it pleases; for *pasa graphē theopneustos.*[16]

The truth is somewhere between the two, *and no simple rule can be devised to divide one from the other.* We propose then the following *general* guide: (i) Whatever in Scripture is in direct reference to natural things is most likely in terms of the prevailing cultural concepts; (ii) whatever is directly theological or didactic is most likely trans-cultural; and (iii) by a clear understanding of the trans-cultural element in Scripture, and by a clear understanding of the sociology of language (*pragmatics*), we can decipher what is trans-cultural under the mode of the cultural.

Let us take for an example Biblical psychology. We have already indicated its physiological character. Furthermore, there is no treatment in the Bible of psychology that compares with the systematic treatment of the resurrection body in I Cor. 15. We must decipher from Scripture its psychology. We have on the one hand to deal with physiological conceptions of psychology, and on the other with the obvious fact that the Bible has no systematized treatise on psychology. The statements about internal organs possessing psychical properties we immediately assign to the prevailing culture as its method of expressing certain psychological data. The statements about the nature of the soul or spirit—its power to worship, its being in the image of God, its immortality, its power to think—lead us to the conclusion that there is a *spiritual entity* within man's body. Having formulated a correct notion of this spiritual entity we re-read the Scriptures and note how this notion of ours makes clear all the psychological passages of the Bible. We may then proceed to those references that are physiological of nature and re-translate them into our trans-cultural concepts.

Because the Scriptures are inspired, the truth of God is there in the cultural, but not obviously so. The truth under the cultural partakes of the binding character of inspiration, not the cultural vehicle. Therefore, our guide in such matters are those passages of Scripture which are clearly didactic, theological, and hence, trans-cultural.

This proposal is nothing new but is the standard procedure in treating the classics. In reading Plato, Aristotle, Augustine and Aquinas, we frequently find items that are purely of the culture of the time. But this does not prevent us from laying bare the essential metaphysics of Plato or Aquinas; nor do these purely local, temporal, cultural items disqualify the basic metaphysics of these great thinkers. By taking as our guide those clear trans-cultural statements of Greek and Medieval authors, and adding to this a knowledge of the culture of their times, we can readily thread our way through their writings to determine what is essential metaphysics and what is not. Further, there is no clear, precise rule for the classicist to tell what is cultural and what is trans-cultural. That is an art, and a skill developed from his learning.

Similarly the Biblical theologian (i) knowing that some of the Bible is in terms of the prevailing culture, and (ii) that some of it is evidently trans-cultural, and (iii) also knowing from research much of the cultural surrounding of the Old and New Testaments, is able to formulate his Biblical theology, and to see what is trans-cultural under the mode of the cultural. When the Psalmist praises God with his bones, the theologian realizes that in theological language this means praising God from the depths of the sincerity of the human soul. Sincere praise to God is binding truth; psychic function of the bones is not.

II. THE BIBLICAL VIEW OF NATURE

One of the mistakes of unbelievers and of religious liberals in criticizing the Bible is a failure sympathetically to understand the Biblical view of Nature. Governed by anti-supernatural beliefs, and convinced that Israel's religion was an emergence from surrounding religious beliefs, they identify the Biblical view of Nature with the beliefs of the surrounding peoples. But there is a chaste, wholesome, refreshing view of Nature in the Bible that is richly theistic. If men like Pascal, Kierkegaard and Barth had reflected more sympathetically with the Biblical view of Nature they would not have defended a type of theism which so negates the strong Nature-theism of the Old Testament.

J. W. Dawson, among all the writers on Bible and science, has put the most thought into this problem. He gives four reasons why the Biblical references to Nature are so remarkably free from error, and form the natural basis of a pure theism.[17] (i) The Hebrews were not great artists or readers of literature, and were therefore more concerned directly with Nature. They did not draw from art or literature for their illustrations but from the phenomena of Nature. (ii) The Hebrews were remarkably free from theorizing about Nature and in forming any sort of scientific hypotheses as to how Nature actually worked. They attributed all effects in Nature to the will of God. In this they were providentially protected from making a host of scientific theories which no doubt would have been proved erroneous by later science. (iii) Because the Hebrews were intense monotheists they were free from mythology and superstition so uniformly connected with the religions of peoples with reference to the objects of nature. This is one of the most amazing things of the Bible. Animal mythology and plant mythology accompanied by superstitious and fantastic notions were characteristic of all the peoples surrounding Israel, and of the Greeks and Romans, and of western culture even to this moment of writing. It is rampant among all contemporary animists and polytheists and is seen clearly in their totemism. Only a small part of educated humanity is free from it. (iv) The Hebrews considered Nature the creation of God and did not worship Nature, but did have a high regard for it as God's handiwork. Nature was the "material expression of the power of God, and therefore as in a sense sacred."[18]

Although there is no formal presentation of a Biblical view of Nature in the Bible itself, there is a basic set of attitudes which permeate the Scriptural references to natural things and to Nature. Much of this has been obscured by radical and sceptical views of

Biblical cosmology which we shall discuss later.   But there is a
very distinctive Biblical attitude towards Nature which apologists
in the circle of Christianity have not always fairly reckoned with,
and which attackers of Christianity have not always taken the pains
to learn.

A. The first feature of the Biblical view of Nature is that it is a
very frank *creationism. God is the Almighty Creator of heaven and
earth*.[19]   Therefore, Nature exists fundamentally for spiritual
purposes, and is capable of *teleological* explanation.   This frank
creationism is found in both Testaments.   It is a theme that is
constantly on the lips of the prophets.   To the Hebrew prophet
Nature was not neutral in regard to the existence of God.   Nature
was a glorious tribute to the power, majesty, wisdom, splendour and
benevolence of God.   No Biblical writer would concur with Pascal
and Kierkegaard that God was secretly present in his works.   To
the Biblical writers Nature is theistically committed.

The attacks on the science of the Bible, and the attacks on the
cogency of the theistic proofs have greatly weakened the orthodox
Christians' appreciation of the frank creationism of the Bible.   It
is not uncommon to hear in orthodox circles that Christianity rests
solely on "faith" or "experience."   *Not so to the prophets of God!*
One of the *differentiæ* of the true and living God is that He is the
Maker of heaven and earth.   False gods are powerless and this is
proved because they are not creators.   The Lord God of Israel is
the Creator of the heavens and the earth and is the true and living
God!

According to Scripture the vast universe around us both in its
minutiæ and in its greatness; in its immense inorganic stretches,
and in the world of life; in the starry sky above, and in the lily of
the valley, is the creation of the one God exhibiting to the eye and
to the mind of the beholder the power, wisdom, and goodness of
God.   Any weakening, enervating, softening, hedging or compromising of the creationism of the Bible is not true to the Bible,
and already is a crack in the wall which unbelief will smash open
into a huge crevice.

If this universe is the creation of God then teleological judgments
of numerous kinds cannot be denied, for they logically follow.
There is purpose in Nature because Nature is ordered by a Personal
Intelligence.   Kant's problem with his *Critique of Teleological
Judgment* is that he had no strong theistic creationism to give it the
adequate metaphysical support it so desperately needed.   Grass is
for animals, and the earth's foodstuffs are for man.   Various conditions necessary for life are not accidental but purposed.   The
universe which is one vast, meaningless, mechanical, blind series
of diverse systems to the unbeliever is the great creation of God to

the believer. The Scriptures describe a universe filled with tokens of divine purpose and providence. It is meaningful, spiritual, and purposeful.

Kant's struggle is pathetic. Here is a man who realizes that to have a moral order one needs a spiritually interpreted universe. He does everything he can to bring purpose into the universe, striving not to be naïve or traditional in so doing. But this purposive interpretation is granted only *regulative* (as it were, *als ob*) status. Constitutive status is reserved only for transcendental aesthetic and the categories of the *Critique of Pure Reason*. His bride dies on the honeymoon! But no such dilemma is faced by the writers of Holy Scripture. The God of Creation is the God of Preservation, and the God of Providence is the God of the Moral Law and the God of the Moral Law is the God of Redemption. Teleological judgments are *constitutive* because God is the *world-ground* of Nature, of morality, of redemption, and of reason.[20]

B. The Biblical view of Nature also clearly maintains that *the universe is maintained by the providence of God*. Biblical theism is unfriendly to deism and pantheism. It refuses to identify God with His works and it refuses to bar God from His works. God is *world-ground* of all things to Biblical theism, and He sustains not only the physical order but the moral and spiritual orders too. The providence of God is deeper than critics of Biblical supernaturalism realize. God's providence is His working all things to their destined goal. In co-operation with the redemption of God it forms the basis of the Christian philosophy of history. In that God works through the natural and the human, providence applies to Nature. The possibility of miracles, and the possibility of answered prayer, are deeply involved in the Biblical doctrine of providence. And in turn providence is deeply involved with the Biblical doctrine of Nature and God's relation to His creation. The God of the Bible is not manacled to the causal laws, nor is He a prisoner in His own creation. The liberal and neo-orthodox doctrine of the providence of God and the relationship of God to Nature is extremely faulty and anti-Biblical. Biblical theism with its unalloyed creationism will not tolerate the metaphysics of religious modernism or of neo-orthodoxy. The providence of God demands the freedom of God in Nature. The Bible is just as frank about its providence as it is about its creationism.

C. In keeping with the consistent creationism of the Bible is the constant prohibition by the Bible of *any worship of any part of the creation*. The worship of the created is forbidden, by implication, by the first verse of the Bible, and is expressly forbidden in the Ten Commandments, which prohibit any material representation of God. Paul in Rom. 1: 25 identifies *the lie* about God with idolatry.

In addition to these rather pointed references are the numerous references throughout the Bible to the intent that (i) the universe and all that is in it is a creation of God, and is not God or part of God; and (ii) that any form of idolatry, a worship of the created, is forbidden.

In contrast to the Judeo-Christian tradition are the religions of the world with their animism or polytheism and universal idolatry. Only in Sacred Writ is there such a positive, uncompromising, lucid creationism, and it is this strong creationism which caused all the writers of Sacred Writ to condemn idolatry so consistently and in all its forms.

D. The Bible clearly teaches that the *regularity of Nature is the constancy of God, and the laws of Nature are the laws of God*. This is in keeping with the powerful, penetrating, direct creationism of the Bible. Of course we must translate the Biblical vocabulary into our vocabulary. Much of the wonderful Biblical view of Nature is lost to many readers because they fail to make this translation.

The *uniformity of Nature* is a Biblical notion and not the sole creation of modern science. Nature as a vast, orderly, law-abiding system was deeply imbedded in Hebrew thought. Only because the Hebrews used a different vocabulary is this idea lost to so many modern readers of the Bible. For example, Robinson remarks:

> The Hebrew vocabulary includes no word equivalent to our term "Nature." This is not surprising if by "Nature" we mean "The creative and regulative physical power which is conceived of as operating in the physical world as the immediate cause of all phenomena." *The only way to render this idea into Hebrew would be to say simply* "God."[21]

The concept of order or regularity or uniformity in Nature is a Biblical concept already before modern science, and it stems from the Bible's strong and frank creationism.[22] All of life produces its young in orders (Hebrew, *min*). Entirely apart from the debates about evolution or species, it must be recognized that the plants and animals of this world produce according to order, and the science of genetics is discovering the *laws* of that *order*. The millions of new creatures born each spring are born according to their *min*. In Gen. 8: 22 God promises the regularity of seed time and harvest, cold and heat, summer and winter, day and night, *i.e.* all such shall be regular and in order. In Gen. 9: 1–17 God vows that Nature will be held in constancy and that never again will such a flood take its toll of human life. Jer. 5: 24 attributes the constancy of rain and harvest time to God. Jer. 31: 35–36 affirms that the sun, moon, and stars fulfil their function because they function according to the *ordinances* which God controls. The regularity of night and day is called a *covenant* of God which cannot be broken (Jer. 33: 20). Job 28: 26 indicates the *regularity* of rain and lightning by speaking of a *decree* for rain and a *way* for lightning and thunder.

Job 38: 8–11 and Prov. 8: 29 indicate that the ocean is held in its place by the will of God. The ocean is under the *commandment* of God, indicating its ordered place in Nature. Jer. 5: 22 adds to this by saying that the sea is under *perpetual decree*. The mountains and the valleys find their place in Nature, for God has set a *bound* for them (Psa. 104: 8–9). Psa. 148 speaks of the sun, moon, stars, the heavens, and the waters above the heavens, and tells us that these things were *established* for ever and are *under a decree which shall not pass away*. By no stretch of inference we presume that Jeremiah attributes the instincts of birds to the inner wisdom of God (Jer. 8: 7). The wisdom of the birds in knowing their appointed times is contrasted to the people of God who know not the Law of God.

Prov. 8 is the famous wisdom chapter. Whatever be its fuller possible Messianic application, certainly this much follows from the passage. First, when God created He created *intelligently, i.e.* by wisdom. Wisdom is here presented as existing before creation, and being with God in creation. Creation is performed by, through, and with *wisdom*. Consequently, there is a plan, a purpose, a uniformity, a regularity in creation because *wisdom* partook in Nature's creation. Second, wisdom saw to it that Nature was made orderly. The mountains were *settled;* the heavens were *established;* the skies were made *firm*; the sea was given its *bound*, and the foundations of the earth were *marked out*. These terms must be translated into our language. They affirm that Nature is orderly, law-abiding, and trustworthy. This is the *uniformity of Nature* in the rich, graphic, theistic language of the Bible.

Furthermore, as already indicated, there are God-given laws of Nature, although the Hebrews expressed such by such terms as *ordinance, decree* or *commandment*. Differences in terminology must not blind us to identity of thought. Another set of Scriptures in Hebrew imagery declares that the secondary or causal laws of Nature are God's laws. God causes the mists to rise, the lightning to break forth, the rain to fall, and the winds to blow (Jer. 10: 13). God makes the grass to grow and feeds the beasts of the field and the birds of the trees (Psa. 147: 8–9). God sends the snow, the frosts, the hail, and the warm winds to melt them (Psa. 147: 16–18). The animals wait for God, for He feeds them in due season (Psa. 145: 15; 104: 27). God sends *His* rain upon the earth and lets *His* sun shine upon men (Matt. 5: 45). It is God who feeds the birds and clothes the lily (Matt. 6: 26–30). God gives man his daily bread (Matt. 6: 11). God sends the bountiful harvest as the witness of His goodness (Acts 14: 17).   It is God Who gives life and breath and all things that His creation might continue (Acts 17: 25).[23] It is God in Whom we live and move and have our being (Acts 17: 28).

E. C. Rust has a beautiful section on our Lord's view of Nature. He has gone through the Gospels and selected those verses which reveal how our Lord viewed the natural order, and the results are very remarkable.   He indicates that: (i) Jesus believed God is Almighty Creator and Sustainer, so that this world and all that is in it is the creation of God.   This is especially true of man and woman.   (ii) In the tradition of Job and Jeremiah, Jesus viewed the regularity and orderliness of Nature as a proof of the care and steadfastness of God toward His creation.   (iii) Jesus believed that the laws of Nature were but the expressions of the activity of God, for it is God Who clothes the lilies, and makes *His* sun to shine, etc. Further, in this regularity and in this care Jesus sees the love of God shining through.   (iv) Jesus taught that man had a body and a soul, a material and a spiritual part.   Man is thus part of the natural order and of the spiritual order.[24]

Here in the teachings of Jesus is reflected the pure theism of the Old Testament in a beautiful form.   We note with pleasure the complete lack of the fantastic, absurd, mythological, or superstitious elements common to most peoples even to this day in the twentieth century.   There is nothing in the view of Nature which Jesus Christ held that is offensive to the most critical scientific mind, if that mind will but see the world through the lens of the wonderful Old Testament theism.

We mortals of the twentieth century think so disjunctively! We suppose we have to choose between God or natural law.   When we speak the language of a strong theism we pass over natural law and proceed directly to the Author and Creator of law, and we attribute all things to God.   But as Rust writes:

> We cannot find in the Old Testament the fondly drawn distinction of later days between the natural and the supernatural, for the whole of the natural order is so directly linked with God that its conservation must be regarded as a kind of continuous creation, quite as dependent on God's creative Word as when first the heavens and earth were made.[25]

When we so speak we are speaking religiously, theologically, metaphysically, and teleologically.   We do not deny natural law. When we speak of the laws of Nature we speak empirically, scientifically, and phenomenally.   If the language of theism does not deny the existence of natural law, natural law does not deny the existence of theism. Modern man may set them antithetically, but the strong theistic faith of the Bible does not do so.

We speak constantly in the analogy of the theism of the Bible. When we assert: "The dentist drilled out the decay in my cavity," we mean that the drill actually did the digging, but we also understand that the drill was under the direction of the dentist. Both expressions ("the dentist did it," or "the drill did it") are correct. The expression "The cook baked the ham" in no manner contradicts "The oven baked the ham" or "the heat baked the ham." Neither is it contradictory to affirm "God sends the rain" and "it rains according to natural law."

Here again we see the profundity of the Biblical theism. Religious modernism utterly failed to develop a genuine working theory of the relationship of God to creation, providence and prayer. By locking the hands of God with its impersonal uniformity of Nature, modernism prevented any transcendental activity by God in providence and prayer. All its proclamations about what God was doing in the world were actually what man was doing. How could God do anything if He were shackled to the impersonal uniformity of Nature? All prayer had to be confined within the realm of attitude and inner spiritual disposition. No matter how desperate man may be, no matter how fierce a trap holds his leg, modernism prevents God from any transcendental activity in answering the prayer of a trapped or desperate man.

Biblical theism is not forced into such a hopeless confusion of God, Nature and providence. With its strong theism it provides all we need for the uniformity and regularity of Nature. With providence working with the theistic view of Nature, a normal, natural, credible doorway was left open for God to answer prayer, work the miraculous, and even send His Son into the world with all the attendant supernatural activity the incarnation and resurrection involved. It is a Christian man of science and not a theologian who has so expertly stated this:

It is a common but groundless and shallow charge against the Bible that it teaches an "arbitrary supernaturalism." What it does teach is that all of nature is regulated by the laws of God, which like Himself are unchanging, but which are so complex in their relations and adjustments that they allow of infinite variety, and so do not exclude even miraculous intervention, or what appears to our limited intelligence as such . . . But if natural laws are the expression of the divine will, if these laws are multiform and complicated in their relations, and regulate vastly varied causes interacting with each other, and if the action and welfare of man come within the scope of these laws, then there is nothing irrational in the supposition that God, without any capricious or miraculous intervention, may have so correlated the myriad adjustments of His creation, as that, while it is His usual rule that rain falls alike on the evil and on the good, He may make its descent at particular times and places to depend on the needs and requests of His own children.   In truth, belief in law is essential to the philosophical conception of prayer.   If the universe were a mere chaos of chances, or if it were a result of absolute necessity, there would be no place for intelligent prayer; but if it is under the control of a Lawgiver, wise and merciful, not a mere manager of material machinery, but a true Father of all, then we can come to such a Being with our requests, not in the belief that we change His great plans, nor that any advantage could result from this if it were possible, but that these plans may be made in His boundless wisdom and love to meet our necessities.[26]

Neither Kant in his great *Critiques* nor religious liberalism in its dualism of science and religion, has achieved the unity of Nature and religion, law and providence, uniformity and redemption, which is achieved in the strong theism, frank creationism, and clear teaching of providence found in the Holy Bible.   The God of Creation is the God of Prayer and the God of Providence and the God of Redemption, and in His wisdom, and in His power, and in His knowledge the diverse threads of science, religion, miracle, and providence are woven into a credible, intelligible, meaningful pattern.   The Greeks failed in this; the Romans failed in it; and certainly religious modernism failed in it.   Due to a distaste for orthodoxy, a proclivity for radical Biblical criticism, and a complete capitulation to the uniformity of Nature impersonally conceived, religious modernism became hopelessly blind and could not see the beautiful theism of the Sacred Writ.

E. *The Biblical outlook on Nature is that Nature is temporal.*   This is an assertion of both fact and value.   It is *factual* in that it asserts that the universe was created by God in the past, and will be concluded by God in the future.   The fiat creation of Gen. 1: 1 precludes its eternal duration in time past, and the clear affirmations of Rev. 21 and 22 tell of its end in the future.   In the glorious theism of the Bible only God is eternal self-caused Being and Reality.

The temporality of the universe is also a value judgment.   Paul writes that "we look not to the things that are seen but to the things that are unseen; for the things that are seen are transient, but the things that are unseen are eternal" (II Cor. 4: 18, RSV). This means that the physical and natural things exist in their own right, have a genuine reality, but that their existence is *instrumental* to higher purposes.   The Christian is not a gnostic attributing evil to matter; nor is he a materialist or naturalist attributing reality in its most primary meaning to Nature or matter.   Certainly, the spiritual is now *in and through* the material and the physical.   The gnostic is wrong in identifying sin and error with matter. Just as mistaken is the naturalist and materialist who make Nature ultimate reality.

The Biblical theistic view demands that Nature or creation be given its rightful place. But the very same theism affirms the temporality of the visible universe. If we capitulate to the gnostic, then the visible universe becomes a burden to our theism and theology. If we surrender to the naturalist we drop all meaning out of life. The Biblical insistence on the first-class reality of the spiritual and its attendant moral values preserves genuine significance to human existence. The easy way in which ultimate significance and meaning for humanity has been given up in modern philosophy is one of the clearest indications as to how terribly sick we are. The price for a nice, neat, uniform causally-operated universe is precisely our own soul's eternal welfare. Better to grant a few miracles here and there than to hang ourselves with this paper rope.

F. *The Scriptures consider Nature a realm of probation and judgment.* God did not say that creation was perfect, but that it was good. In Scripture it is heaven which stands for perfection. The earth is the scene of man's probationary existence, and it is good but not heavenly perfect. Creation is a *system* which involves certain features, and necessarily so, which appear to us as dysteleological (diseases, storms, tornadoes, etc.). Both Augustine and Aquinas wrestled with this problem, and in comparing passages in the *City of God* with sections in the *Summa Theologica* we see how much Aquinas borrowed from Augustine with reference to this problem. In that Aquinas' treatment is the more systematic we shall follow his exposition.[27]

Creatures differ from each other and it is the wisdom of God which makes these creaturely distinctions. These distinctions are twofold: formal distinction is the distinction of species from species, and material distinction is the distinction of one creature from another within a species. Formal distinction is the more important. In the hierarchy of species *there must be inequalities* for species are arranged in degrees of being and perfection. Aquinas writes:

> Therefore, as the divine wisdom is the cause of the distinction of things for the sake of the perfection of the universe, so is it the cause of inequality. For the universe would not be perfect if only one grade of goodness were found in things.

The universe must contain all possible ranges of goodness. One of these grades of goodness is that it can fail in goodness. On the one hand a human soul is immortal and has an incorruptible goodness, but an animal is perishable and has a corruptible goodness.

The system of creation or the perfection of the universe requires that which is corruptible and that which can fail in its goodness. Creation is not the best in every single part for, as indicated, animals are not immortal. But this is the best creation when seen as a whole, an entirety. If there were nothing corruptible, or if there were no evil men, many good things would be missing in this universe. The lion lives because he can kill the ass and eat it. Avenging justice could only be praised if there were injustice; and patient suffering could be a virtue only in the presence of injustice.

Picking up some strands in Augustine, we note his saying that the goodness of a thing must be judged by its own *nature and use*, not its abuse.[28]   Sand on the seashore is part of the system of Nature, but in one's eye it is an irritation.   Sand must be judged when it is on the seashore as to its goodness, not when it is in the human eye.   Bacteria destroy the carrion of the earth for Nature's own good, but unfortunately the same bacteria can kill a living creature.

Augustine also argues that the world as seen in its entirety, not piece by piece, is a wonderful good.[29]

> [Fire, frost, and wild beasts are all injurious to] this thin-blooded and frail mortality of our flesh [but in their own place] how excellent their own natures, how beautifully adjusted to the rest of creation, and how much grace they contribute to the universe by their own contributions as it were to a commonwealth.

But, Augustine continues, *it is our obligation* to discover the utility of things in Nature.   We are to "use them with a knowledge of their fit adaptations."   God does not ask us foolishly to ignore Nature but to investigate it with care.   We may learn to take poisons and use them as medicines; and we must be careful that we do not take good things and convert them into ills, as is the case of the glutton who gets indigestion from eating good food.

There is a profound thought in this section of Augustine, namely this: *it is part of our probation to learn the secrets of Nature; if we do not, even in our innocency, we pay the price*.   If we ignore the properties of metals we will have no modern industry.   If we ignore chemicals and the study of disease we will have no chemical cures of our ills. If we will learn the nature and utility of the things of creation we shall profit our own well-being.

The entire system of Nature involves tigers and lions, storms and high tides, diseases and parasites.   It is part of our probation to learn how to capture or control the tiger and the lion; to learn how to protect ourselves from storms and tornadoes; to learn the mysteries of chemicals and bacteria for the healing of the body.

If we fail in this probation innocent and sinful suffer alike. The baby dies of infection and the mother of fever; the young man of appendicitis and the prophet of pneumonia.

But the Scriptures add to this the use of Nature in judgment. Man was not created in Paradise, but created and then placed there to know the marvellous place he was to inhabit. We cannot speculate too freely as to the nature of that existence, but we presume it was sheltered existence from the necessary violences of the system of Nature. His expulsion from the Garden back into the general system of Nature was a great judgment. The tiger, the thistle, the storm, and the plague are now problems directly in the lap of man. The imperfections of being in Nature now become part of the judgment upon man. Further, in special dispensations of God's judgment God could—and did—call to the service of judgment the earthquake or the plague or the hail or famine.

The above exposition adds something to the plenitude-of-being theory which it needs, and which is overlooked. It is not a matter of having sheer good in the whole through evil in the parts. Why then, is it asked, could it not have been arranged with much less suffering for the parts? The answer is that Nature is also for (i) probation, and (ii) judgment. There is more to "evil" in Nature than sheer plenitude of being is invoked to explain.

III. BIBLICAL COSMOLOGY

A. In discussing the Biblical cosmology we must return to our general position defended earlier in this chapter: *the references of the writers of the Bible to natural things are popular, non-postulational, and in terms of the culture in which the writers wrote.* This principle applies directly to Biblical cosmology. The language of the Bible with reference to cosmological matters is in terms of the prevailing culture. Biblical cosmology is in the language of antiquity and not of modern science, nor is it filled with anticipations which the future microscope and telescope will reveal.[30] We do not agree with over-zealous expositors who try to find Einsteinian and modern astro-physical concepts buried in Hebrew words and expressions. We also disagree with the religious liberals who object to Biblical cosmology because it is not scientific. We object to the over-zealous because it was not the intention of inspiration to anticipate modern science, and we object to the modernist because he sees too much in what is to us a truism. We concur with Calvin, who taught that Gen. I is a record of the creation of the world in the language of the common man and from the viewpoint of common sense. His actual words are:

C

For to my mind this is a certain principle, that nothing is here treated of but the visible form of the world. He who would learn astronomy and the other recondite arts, let him go elsewhere . . . It must be remembered, that Moses does not speak with philosophical acuteness on occult mysteries, but states those things which are everywhere observed, even by the uncultivated, and which are in common use.[31]

B. *The cosmology of the Bible is not systematized and is not postulational.* It is neither for nor against any of the current and ancient theories of the universe except where they might be polytheistic or in conflict with basic Christian metaphysics. But the Bible does not support Aristotle or Ptolemy or Copernicus or Descartes or Newton or Einstein or Milne. Certainly, the Bible works as a *negative* criterion in telling us that dualisms and pantheisms and materialisms are wrong, but it gives us no *positive* cosmology.

We must consider the efforts of radical critics to impose a cosmology on the Bible as an artificial, stilted and abortive effort. The pseudo-Biblical cosmologies will be found in various Bible dictionaries, encyclopædias, and commentaries. The work of Schiaparelli has been of considerable influence. The radical view has been put in one paragraph by Fosdick:

> In the Scriptures the flat earth is founded on an underlying sea; it is stationary; the heavens are like an upturned bowl or canopy above it; the circumference of this vault rests on pillars; the sun, moon, and stars move within this firmament of special purpose to illumine man; there is a sea above the sky, "the waters which were above the heavens," and through the "windows of heaven" the rain comes down; within the earth is Sheol, where dwell the shadowy dead; this whole cosmic system is suspended over vacancy; and it was all made in six days with a morning and an evening, a short and measurable time before. This is the world view of the Bible.[32]

One of the sharpest critics of this cosmological imposture has been Warren (*The Earliest Cosmologies,* 1909, pp. 24–32). He claims that writers of articles on the subject of cosmology in Bible dictionaries ape each other and do not return critically to the concrete data of the Scriptures. Warren claims that their approach to the cosmology of the Bible is so wooden, artificial, and literal that the Bible writers would not recognize such a cosmology if it were handed to them written out on a piece of paper. If, he continues, you follow this wooden and artificial approach to the Bible you would have the Bible writers believing in a heaven made of wax or silk or goatshair! Critics have underestimated the extent of astronomical knowledge among the ancients. Warren is especially critical of the work of Schiaparelli (*Astronomy in the Old Testament.*

1903). Warren accuses Schiaparelli of using an impossible literalism in his constructions and constructing a universe that Solomon, for example, would never recognize. Schiaparelli does not do the Bible justice.

Dawson claims that it is absurd to "fasten upon the sacred writers, contrary to their own words, the views of a school of astronomy which probably arose long after their time, when we know that more accurate ideas prevailed nearer their epoch."[33] In another work he claims that the radical critical view of Biblical cosmology is "abhorrent from the general tenor of Scripture."[34] Let the reader keep in mind that Dawson was a first-rank geologist, and a life-time student of Sacred Scripture.

Orr writes:

> The error is to be avoided of forcing the language of popular, often metaphorical and poetic description, into the hard-and-fast forms of a cosmogony which it is by no means intended by the writers to yield. It is true that the Hebrews had no idea of our modern Copernican astronomy, and thought of the earth as a flat surface, surmounted by a vast expanse of heaven, in which sun, moon and stars were placed, and from whose reservoirs the rain descended. But it is an exaggeration of all this to speak, as is sometimes done, as if the Hebrews were children who believed[35] [that the sky was a solid vault, etc.]. Language is not to be pressed in this prosaic, unelastic way.[36]

Gaenssle, a Semitic scholar, takes the radical critics to task likewise for imposing on the Bible a stilted, artificial cosmology that is nowhere clearly and systematically taught in Scripture.[37] He singles out two basic ideas of this reconstruction of the radical critics to show that their contentions are baseless. (i) He examines the word *raqia* (firmament) which critics have taken to mean a solid something and indicates that its basic idea is that of *thinness* or *tenuity*. Citing Isa. 40: 32; Psa. 104: 2 and Isa. 34:4, he asks:

> Can anyone with these texts before him seriously and honestly believe that the writers of these words entertained the crude inept notion of a metallic canopy above their heads?[38]

The best meaning of *raqia* is *expanse* or *atmosphere*. (ii) He also attacks the notion that the world floats on a vast subterranean ocean. Dealing especially with Schiaparelli, Gaenssle shows how forced his exegesis must be to make the Bible teach that there is a vast subterranean ocean underneath the earth. As for the word *under* in the phrase "under the earth" the Hebrew word *tachath* means not only *under* but *lower*. In our own day we speak of lowlands. Water in the form of seas is always in lower places. He concludes:

Consequently, when the earth is said to be founded on the seas and spread out upon the waters, there is no reason to assume that the Psalmist is singing of an invisible ocean, on which the earth rests or is spread out, but only of earthly waters on which the earth touches and over which it is elevated.[39]

Analyzing all the significant verses in which the Hebrew word *tehōm* is used Gaenssle shows how only by a forced exegesis can it be made to support a subterranean ocean and he concludes:

The upper, terrestrial ocean satisfies all requirements, and it lies below or beneath in the same sense as the Dead Sea lies under Mount Pisgah and the land of Moab.[40]

Maunder has an excellent treatment of the entire problem of Hebrew cosmology.[41]   He disagrees sharply with Schiaparelli's reconstruction.   Maunder believes that such verses as Job 22: 14; Isa. 40: 22; Prov. 8: 27 and Job 26: 7 amply prove that the Hebrews thought of the earth as round and suspended in nothing.   The unaided eye itself sees the horizon as circular, especially the horizon of the sea.   The sphericity of the sun and the moon and the roundness of the stars would suggest to an astronomically alert people the sphericity of the earth.   The expression "He stretched out the north over empty space, and hangeth the earth upon nothing" (Job 26: 7) is taken by Maunder to mean the northern circumpolar constellations which stretch out indefinitely.   The notion that the earth rests on something is impossible and the only conclusion is that the earth hangs on nothing.

The pillars of the earth (Job 9:6), Maunder continues, are the rocks that bear up the surface of the earth.   The *raqia* is the space above the earth in which the clouds float and the heavenly bodies pursue their courses.   The Greek translation of *stereōma* gives the implication of solidity, followed in the Latin by *firmamentum* and then in the English by *firmament*.   Maunder disagrees with the Greek and Latin translations as well as the Ptolemaic concept of crystalline spheres.   The belief that the heavens actually had windows he considers erroneous.   The windows of heaven are not sluice gates or flood gates but *lattice work*.   In contrast to the literalistic interpretation of what is an obvious metaphorical term Maunder notes many other verses in the Old Testament about rain, clouds, dew, and mist which are in keeping with natural science.

The word *tehōm* means ocean and is presented in the Bible as one body of water.   He takes Psa. 136: 6 and 24: 2 to mean that the earth is stretched out *above* the water, that is, the earth stands out of the water.   The association of the Hebrew word *tehōm* with the Babylonian *Tiamat,* the she-dragon of chaos, simply proves the

Hebrew account to be the original, for "the natural object, *tehōm*, the sea, must have preceded the mythological personification of it."[42]

It is improper to construct a so-called modern or scientific cosmology from the Biblical evidence; and it is also improper to try to model one after Babylonian concepts. In that there is no systematic exposition of a cosmology in the Bible, and in that the Bible abounds with either popular expressions or poetic expressions, it is not capable of a systematic construction with reference to a cosmology. The best we can do is to (i) indicate the freedom of the Bible from mythological polytheistic or grotesque cosmologies; (ii) note the general hostility of the Bible to cosmologies which are antitheistic; and (iii) clearly present the *theocentric* view of the Bible towards Nature.

It is typical of radical critics to play up the similarity of anything Biblical with the Babylonian,[43] and to omit the profound differences or gloss over them. When the Biblical account is set side by side with any other cosmology its purity, its chasteness, its uniqueness, its theocentricity are immediately apparent.

> No stronger proof could be afforded of the truth and sublimity of the Biblical account of the origin of things than is given by the comparison of the narrative of creation in Gen. 1–2: 4, with the mythological cosmogonies and theogonies found in other religions.[44]

IV. A CHRISTIAN PHILOSOPHY OF NATURE

By a Christian philosophy of Nature we mean a broad, comprehensive method and system of the interpretation of Nature, receiving its orientation from Christian theology. It would correspond to a philosophy of science as adopted by a naturalist or a materialist. We prefer a larger concept than philosophy of biology or philosophy of science, and that is why we call it *a philosophy of Nature*. A Christian philosophy of Nature will involve three things: (i) It will involve the Biblical data about God and Nature or creation. This we have already outlined in this chapter (*II. The Biblical View of Nature*). All that was said there, now directly applies to a Christian philosophy of Nature. (ii) It will involve elements from the philosophy of science. It will be a larger task than setting forth the Biblical view of Nature for it must relate itself to the larger problems of philosophy of science. Philosophy of science discusses the implied metaphysics and epistemology of science. There are, further, definite schools of philosophy of science, *e.g.* the realists, the conventionalists, the positivists, the pragmatists. The Christian must use the method of the *dialectical yes/no* as he picks his way around in the philosophy of science and the philosophy of biology.[45] (iii) It will concern itself with the reliable data of the sciences. It will willingly face the data of the sciences as the data which must be worked into a Christian philosophy of science. It is not only a matter of facing facts, but it is absolutely necessary to be acquainted with facts to be able to form any sort of intelligent Christian philosophy of Nature. Fosdick cannot be gainsaid when he wrote: *A religion that is afraid of the facts is doomed.*[46]

A. *The necessity of a philosophy of Nature.* If there is to be any intelligent *rapprochement* between Christianity and science there must be clearly delineated a Christian philosophy of Nature. This is not a luxury but a necessity. Too many books on Bible and science have been written completely naïvely on this issue. The larger implications of science are too complex to be treated by a scientist, Christian or non-Christian, who is an amateur in philosophy of science. Scientific training may qualify a man to make an intelligent decision about data within his field, but seldom is routine scientific training broad enough to enable the scientist to express himself in philosophy of science and the larger meanings of science. An effort to set forth a Christian philosophy of Nature is therefore imperative. The reasons are:

1. The approach of the Bible to Nature is essentially *religious* and *theological.* The Bible tells us emphatically *that* God created, but is silent as to *how* God created. It informs us that the stars, and the flowers, and the animals, and the trees, and man are creatures of God, but how God produced them is nowhere a matter of clear affirmation in Scripture. God made the mountains and the oceans, but the Bible has not a chapter on geological processes. *For man's religious and spiritual needs what the Bible says about Nature is ample.* We need no more. There are two chapters in Genesis devoted to creation and more than a dozen to the life of Abraham. Religious experience needs more counsel from the life of Abraham than from the creation of the universe. For the construction of a philosophy of Nature we need more data about Nature than that which we have in Sacred Scripture. The straightforward theological perspective of the Bible is central in formulating a Christian philosophy of Nature, but it is not sufficient in itself for such a theory.

2. Science, rich in empirical findings, is unable to deal with the large problems of epistemology, metaphysics, and theology. If science is a Goliath on the *how* of Nature it is a Mephibosheth on the *why* of Nature. With all due honour and gratitude for the numerous empirical findings of science and the marvellous technological advances it has brought us, we must realize that science

cannot handle the problems it suggests. These problems can be treated only by the broader disciplines of metaphysics and epistemology. A Christian philosophy of Nature, from our vantage point, is the discipline which can provide the solutions for the problems that science raises but cannot solve.

3. In agreement with Shields we believe that the domains of Bible and science need as umpire a philosophy of Nature.[47] A Christian philosophy of Nature will incorporate into its structure all that the Scriptures say of God and creation. It will acquaint itself with the study of the philosophy of science in its various departments. It will learn all it can of the empirical findings of science.

The Catholic scholars working with the framework of the philosophy of Aquinas have a working basis for a philosophy of science. They have constructed a neo-Thomistic philosophy, and with it a Catholic philosophy of science and biology. Whether it be right or wrong does not invalidate the observation that they have been able to effect a reconciliation and harmonization of *their* theology and science. The author must do a measure of pioneering here and suggest such a solution for Protestants. The author is by no means the first to break ground on this problem but he feels that some good contemporary efforts are needed.[48] Too many books on Bible-and-science have no remarks on this subject and the result is usually an artless product. The following *suggested* Christian philosophy of Nature is not offered in any spirit of dogmatism or finality, but it is an *explorative* adventure, a *heuristic* adventure, to try to bring evangelical Protestantism to develop a Christian philosophy of Nature.

B. *Elements of a Christian philosophy of Nature.* The Christian commences with precisely the *Christian* perspective. In Christian theology and Christian philosophy he finds his first great affirmation for a Christian philosophy of Nature, namely:

1. *God is world-ground to Nature.* The relationship of God to Nature has received classic treatment in the writings of Augustine and Aquinas, and Protestant theology has imitated these theological giants in this regard. Both of these men taught that God is *world-ground* to Nature, although the expression "world-ground" is later than their times. In modern philosophy *world-ground* means that Reality lying behind all phenomena, supporting it, directing it, and explaining it. To a materialist, matter is world-ground; for to him matter lies at the basis of all experience, all phenomena, all processes of Nature. To a pantheist, God the One Substance is world-ground; and to a naturalist, Nature is world-ground. To the theism of the Bible, *God is world-ground*. Both Aquinas and Augustine assert this in their own way.

Both assert that God is the Author of all being as Divine Creator. Aquinas writes:

> It must be said that every being in any way existing is from God . . . all things . . . are caused by one First Being, Who possesses being most perfectly.[49]

God is not only the Creator and Author of Being, but He has imparted to creatures their nature or manner of being and their goodness. Whatever is necessary for the existence of each level of Nature, God supplies. Further, the Trinity, as world-ground teleologically, orders all things. He fits Nature together for His purposes, for as Aquinas writes "the will of God is the cause of things."[50] It is this will of God that is behind the laws of astrophysics and gravitation, laws of chemical affinity and reaction, laws of matter and life, laws of mental and moral and spiritual life, and it is this will which maintains creation and moves all things to their *appointed* ends.

Both Augustine and Aquinas believe that *God is in touch with Nature* in such a way as to proclaim that all Nature depends on the eternal God for its life, existence, or character, yet not in such a way as to involve Christianity in any form of pantheism. The Creator-creature relationship so jealously guarded in Scripture is also maintained by Augustine and Aquinas. Augustine writes in a graphic paragraph describing the all-sustaining relationship of God to creation:

> Whatever bodily or seminal causes, then, may be used for the production of things, either by the co-operation of angels, men, or the lower animals, or by sexual generation; and whatever power the desires and mental emotions of the mother have to produce in the tender foetus, corresponding lineaments and colours; yet the natures themselves, which are thus variously affected, *are the productions of none but the most high God. It is His occult power which pervades all things, and is present in all without being contaminated,* which gives being to all that is, and modifies and limits its existence so that without Him it would not be thus, and would not have any being at all.[51]

Although God has rested from creation (*ex nihilo*) God does not rest in the *administration* of creation, continues Augustine. God's administrative activity is summed up in three words: *gubernare* (govern, control, steer, pilot, direct, manage); *movere* (move, stir, set in motion, cause, occasion); and *continere* (hold, keep together, preserve). These verbs tell us that God preserves His creatures, He maintains them in their existence and nature, He moves them to their goal of goodness decreed by His will.

Under the caption of "God in all things" Aquinas maintains the same truth.[52] In that the Scriptures teach that God works all things *God must be in all things.* But Aquinas makes it clear that this word *in* is not to be given a pantheistic interpretation, for God in all things *does not mean that God is part of their essence nor accident,* but God is in all things "as an agent is present to that upon which it works."[53] God is in all things *innermostly, i.e.* deeper than essence or accidence. God is in all things as (i) efficient cause and as (ii) operator on all things to their ends. Aquinas concludes:

> Therefore God is in all things by His power, inasmuch as all things are subject to His power; He is by His presence in all things, as all things are bare and open to His eyes; He is in all things by His essence, inasmuch as He is present to all as the cause of their being.[54]

According to the Biblical view, pantheistic identification with Nature is wrong, God is not Nature, but *world-ground* to Nature, as both Augustine and Aquinas taught. Modernism is equally astray from Biblical theism, for modernism has too clear a difference between religion and science. In religious modernism God is in Nature, but not in His sovereignty and freedom nor in the sense of *gubernare, movere,* and *continere.* It is God in all things in their *innermost* which enables Biblical theism to unite *fact* and *value* (science and religion) which are separated in religious modernism.

God is at the beginning of Nature; at the end of Nature; above Nature; and in Nature. This is not a universe operating at the natural level or material level as if there were no God, but God is world-ground to *all* of Nature. God as world-ground means a spiritual universe, creation to consummation, earth to heaven, matter to spirit, animal to man, time to eternity. The *how* of Nature is supplied by science, but this *how* of Nature is but the manifestation of the *that* of God who is in all things.

2. *The Spirit of God in Nature.* If there is a potential philosophy of Nature and biology in the Bible it would be in connexion with the Old Testament teaching about the Spirit of God. The general affirmation: "God is in all things," is particularly: "the Spirit of God in all things." The Spirit of God is the immanental member of the God-head in creation and preservation. Several verses in the Old Testament indicate this. Job 33: 4 states that the Spirit of God "has made me, and the breath of the Almighty hath given me life." Two interpretations are possible of this verse. Both agree that the first part of the verse means that God made man, but they disagree as to the meaning of the second part. One view is that this is Hebrew parallelism so that both clauses mean the same thing; and the other view is that the last clause means "God has inspired me." Even so, the creative activity is assigned to the Spirit

of God. Job 34: 14–15 teaches that if God should take His Spirit back to Himself all flesh would perish and man would return to dust. This is an extremely powerful verse setting forth the immanental work of the Holy Spirit, and indicating that Nature, to Biblical theism, is under the constant and immanent penetration of God. Psa. 104: 27–30 speaks of animal life looking to God to be fed. When God gives the animals food they eagerly gather it in, but when God hides His face, *i.e.* does not send food, the animals are dismayed. When God takes their breath away they die. But when God sends His Spirit forth again they are created (come to life from near starvation?) for God renews the face of the earth (with grass and foliage). Here too is the immanental work of God in feeding the beasts of the field, and their complete dependence upon God for existence and the Spirit of God for food. Psa. 33: 6 informs us that the heavens and its hosts were made by the Spirit or breath of God, another ascription to the Holy Spirit of creative activity. Isa. 40: 13 asks "who hath directed the Spirit of the Lord?" In the context we have God measuring the waters in the hollow of his hand, marking off the heavens with a span, measuring the dust of the earth and the mountains of the earth. *But who can measure GOD?* "Who can search out His Spirit (*mind*) wherewith He searches out and accurately adjusts all things?"[55] This is another reference to the immanental activity of the Holy Spirit in Nature. Gen. 1: 2 pictures the Spirit of God brooding over the watery abyss. On this word *moved* or *brooded* Lewis remarks:

> No word could have been better adapted to the idea intended in this place of an inward, life-giving power, rather than a mere mechanical outward motion.[56]

Of the presence of the Spirit in creation Lewis remarks further:

> From this place onward and throughout the whole Scripture, the spirit of God is the single formative principle evermore presenting itself with personal attributes in all the divine creative constitution, whether of the earth, of nature, of the theocracy, of the Tabernacle, of the Church, of the new life, or of the new man.[57]

Theologians from Augustine to modern times have recognized the importance of the doctrine of the Spirit with reference to Nature.[58] However, the clearest expression of this doctrine comes from the pen of Abraham Kuyper. Among the relationships of the Trinity it is the power of the Holy Spirit to perfect.

> Thus to lead the creature to its destiny, to cause it to develop according to its nature, to make it perfect, is the proper work of the Holy Spirit.[59]

It is the goal of the Spirit to glorify God and this is done supremely in the children of God. For the Spirit to do this work of glorification He must touch all the universe and so He sustains an important relationship to Nature.

> If sin had not come in [the work of the Spirit in creation would have been] first, *impregnating* inanimate matter; second, *animating* the rational soul; third, *taking up His abode* in the elect child of God.[60]

But sin entered and other activities were added to the Holy Spirit in redemption. But still it is the purpose of the Spirit to glorify God, and still the Spirit has a relationship to Nature. The great visible universe has an invisible background. The intangible forces of Nature are supported by a life.

> [This life] underlies all. Even through the apparently dead trunk sighs an imperceptible breath. From the unfathomable depths of all an inward, hidden principle works upwards and outward. It shows in nature, much more in man and angel. And what is this quickening and animating principle but the Holy Spirit?[61]

God has an inward, invisible touch on all creation. It is this touch which sustains and preserves us and without it we could not even exist.

> [It is] the Holy Spirit . . . whose office it is to effect this direct touch and fellowship with the creature in his inmost being, it is He who *dwells* in the hearts of the elect; who *animates* every rational being; who sustains the *principle of life* in every creature.[62] [It is the purpose of the Spirit to lead creatures to their destiny which means to bring forth hidden life], to cause the hidden beauty to reveal itself, to rouse into activity the slumbering energies.[63]

One of the persistent problems of biology is to find the hidden intelligence of Nature. What is it that directs an ovum through a series of embryonic changes till the baby is born, and then continues its inward course till an adult is produced? How do we account for the wisdom of the brute creation? Perhaps in the Old Testament doctrine of the Spirit of God we have the beginnings of a solution, with these reservations: (i) The Holy Spirit cannot be related to Nature so as to involve us in pantheism; (ii) the Holy Spirit does not efface the imperfections of creatures in their gradation of being and in their deficiency of goodness (*e.g.* He does not keep animals alive forever, nor prevent the leaves of trees from turning brown and falling off); (iii) the Holy Spirit does not rearrange what has been disordered (*e.g.* He does not stop a plague caused by an open sewer system); (iv) the Holy Spirit does not contravene that which is for the probationary experience of man; (v) the Holy Spirit does not do that which we can do for ourselves (*e.g.* we must *drink* water, *eat* food, *keep* warm). But the Spirit of God, within these limits, is *The Divine Entelechy of Nature*.

3. *Progressive creation.* We must now deal with what we consider to be the fundamental pattern of creation. This pattern we gather indirectly and analogically from Scripture and Nature. In Gen. 1 the pattern is a development from vacancy (Gen. 1: 2) to the finished creation at the end of the sixth day. In *manufacturing* the pattern is from raw materials to finished products. In *art* the pattern is from unformed materials to artistic creation. In *life* the pattern is from the undifferentiated ovum to the adult. In *character* the pattern is from random and uncritical behaviour to disciplined and moral behaviour. *We believe that the fundamental pattern of creation is progressive creation.*

At the risk of over-simplification we may assert four patterns of thought in reference to the origin of the universe; (i) fiat creationism; (ii) progressive creationism; (iii) theistic evolution; and (iv) naturalistic evolution. Much of Bible-and-science has been plagued with an oversimplification as if the only alternatives were fiat creation or naturalistic evolution. The hyper-orthodox have as a group been very uncharitable toward both the progressive creationists and theistic evolutionists. Progressive creationism tries to avoid the arbitrariness of fiat creationism and preserve its doctrine of the transcendence of God in creation; and it has tried to avoid the uniformitarianism of theistic evolution, and preserve its sense of progress or development.

Fiat creationists have urged two objections against progressive creationism. (i) They have asserted that it is disguised theistic evolution, and theistic evolution is not to be tolerated. This accusation is careless and is a failure to understand a position. (ii) They have asserted that unless we believe in fiat (instantaneous) creation we insult the majesty and power of God. No one has argued more dogmatically for fiat creation than Higley. He writes:

> No true servant of God would knowingly rob the Creator of his glory by regarding creation as a mere process instead of a miracle.[64]

Those who disagree with Higley are thus branded as "not true servants of God." Higley's position is saturated with *a priorisms*. He reasons that creation was absolutely instantaneous. Why? Because only in sin does God use time, as God's usage of time is a manifestation of His patience in human redemption. Further, if one man can do a job in one unit of time, then two men can do it in one half the time and three men in one-third the time, and *n* men in 1/*n*th the time. If we attribute infinity to the power of God and, following the above reasoning, divide time by infinity we get the amount of time it took God to create, namely, *zero*. One (standing for the unity of time) divided by infinity (standing for the power of God) equals zero (standing for the time consumed in creation). He announces: *The Time is Inversely Proportional to the Power*.[65] We will let the reader himself judge the cogency of this mathematico-theological gerrymandering.

The present author sternly resists any effort to dogmatize about the time involved in creation, and any effort of fiat creationism to reduce progressive creationism to evolution or to impiety, as if progressive creationism questioned the omnipotence of God. "For he spake, and it was done; he commanded, and it stood fast" (Psa. 33: 9) has been one of the verses repeatedly used in the history of Bible-and-science to refute science, and yet the fiat-heliocentric interpretation of this verse has been continually put to rout. The verse asserts nothing about *time* in creation, but it does assert the *certainty* with which Nature obeys the divine will. The command of a great and powerful general is faithfully and obediently carried out. The amount of time consumed in carrying out the will of the general is dependent on the task, and a task which takes a long time is no depreciation of the general's authority, as a task which takes a short time is no necessary tribute to his authority.

Progressive creation was taught as early as Augustine.[66] Progressive creationism believes in two types of creation, the seeds of which we find in Augustine. He taught original *ex nihilo* creation, and subsequent formation, or creation and formation (*formatio*). In his system we have: (i) Creation *ex nihilo* exhibited in the creation of the matter of the world, and in miracles of divine grace; (ii) and creation as *formation* or *administration* in which the matter of creation *ex nihilo* has form imposed upon it. In the second type of creation we have matter impregnated with the *rationes seminales* and subject to *immanent laws of causation* or *secondary laws of causation* and thereby in process over a period of time realizing the preordained forms in Nature. The first type of creation is *creation potential*; the second is *creation actual*. Mivart also taught two types of creation: primary and secondary or derivative.[67]

Mivart also taught that two fundamental laws guided the progression in derivative creation: (i) the movement in Nature comes from the law of cosmical evolution which is a principle of continuity; (ii) the direction comes from the law of final causality.

[By these two laws taken together] the whole phenomena of the universe—physical, biological, political, moral, and religious—may be explained and understood as a *continuous* evolution towards a preordained end.[68]

C. *Summary*.   We are now ready to put together in a summary form our philosophy of Nature.   God is world-ground.   Nature depends upon Him for her origin, character, and movement to her destined ends.   The Spirit of God is God's *innermost* touch on Nature seeing that it complies with His will, and imparts to Nature the spiritual energies the material world needs for its preservation. Progressive creation is the means whereby God as world-ground and the Spirit of God as world-entelechy bring to pass the divine will in Nature.

1.   There is the *concept* in the mind of God, the idea, the form, the plan, the purpose.   Both Augustine and Aquinas believed that "Ideas . . . are *the master forms, which are contained in the divine intelligence*"[69] and were the exemplars of God in creation.   These forms correspond to the blueprints of the construction engineer.   They may be of a clover leaf, or a star, or man.   These forms are the *ultimate* sources of intelligence, wisdom, power, design, and order in Nature—namely the mental activity of God anterior to creation which is the blueprint of creation.

2.   This is followed by a sovereign and fiat act of creation by God *at the level of vacancy or null and void*.   We believe Gen. 1: 2 is not referring to ruin and destruction but to *vacancy awaiting the imposition of form*.   It corresponds to the assembling of the raw materials by the manufacturer or the collecting of the oils, easel and canvas by the painter or the selection and setting up of the marble block by the sculptor.   We believe in several acts of fiat creation in the history of the earth, and this clearly differentiates this view from theistic evolution.

3.   After this comes the *process, or derivative creation*.   God creating directly and sovereignly *outside* of Nature now brings to pass that creation through the Holy Spirit who is *inside* Nature.   The Spirit, the Divine Entelechy of Nature, knows what is the divine blueprint and *through process working from the level of vacancy* realizes the divine form or intention in Nature.   If dry land is to appear, the Spirit sets those laws of geology to work which will produce dry land.   If the seas are to swarm with fish the Spirit initiates whatever is necessary for that to be realized.   In the process of time, the Spirit working through-and-through Nature, *the command of God is fulfilled*.   The laws of Nature, under the direction of the Holy Spirit, actualize over a period of time and through process, the plan of God.

This is the law of Nature and life and creation as we understand it.   First comes the plan, the structure, of any creature in the chromosomes and genes of the ovum and sperm. But the plan is in void and vacancy, the undifferentiated protoplasm of the ovum and sperm. There is the moment of actualization—fertilization. This is followed by *process,* and process is guided by *plan*. Process guided by plan arrives at realization—the fully-developed organism. *The completed product is at the end of process and not at the commencement.*

Conservative Christianity is caught between the embarrassments of simple fiat creationism which is indigestible to modern science, and evolutionism which is indigestible to much of hyper-orthodoxy. It is the conviction of at least this one evangelical that the only way out of the impasse is through some form of progressive creationism which we have imperfectly sketched here. For some reason or other, progressive creationism or developmental creation has been violently rejected by a great many theologians. But progressive creation is *creation by law*. Quite a change has taken place at this point in orthodox thinking. It was the attempt of Chambers, *Vestiges of the Natural History of Creation,* to show that *creation is by law,* and that law is developmental and progressive. Now it is true that Chambers rejected any distinct creative acts once the world was made, and with this view we disagree. But almost all evangelical works on science now concur with Chambers as against his critics, namely, that God works in an orderly, systematic, and progressive way in Nature. As James Dana said:

> The idea of gradual development pervades the Mosaic narrative from beginning to end.[70]

Progressive creation according to law seems to make the most sense out of the numerous facts of Nature.

NOTES

1. The best treatment on this subject we found is that of J. H. Pratt, *Scripture and Science Not at Variance* (1872), p. 24 ff. Another excellent one is Tayler Lewis, *The Six Days of Creation* (1879), Chapter II, "Biblical Interpretation," and Chapter III, "Phenomenal Language." The author, Lewis and Pratt all concur as to the nature of the Biblical language.

2. Pratt, *op. cit.,* pp. 24–29. Italics are his.

3. J. W. Dawson, *Nature and the Bible* (1875), p. 22. In substantial agreement is F. Bettex, *Modern Science and Christianity* (1903), pp. 187–188.

4. This is also the position of the Biblical Commission organized by Leo XIII, as well as the encyclical *Providentissimus Deus* (Nov. 18, 1893). See also Canon Dorlodot, *Darwinism and Catholic Thought* (1923), I, 7 ff., for exposition of the encyclical and the decrees.

5. W. B. Dawson, *The Bible Confirmed by Science* (n.d.), pp. 32–33. Italics are his. In agreement here are Pratt, *op. cit.*, p. 24 ff; Shields, *The Scientific Evidences of Revealed Religion* (1900), pp. 27, 202–203; Bettex, *Modern Science and Christianity* (1903), pp. 187–188; J. P. Smith, *Genesis and Geology* (1840), p. 225; J. W. Dawson, *Nature and the Bible* (1875), p. 22; Angus and Green, *The Bible Handbook* (1907), p. 130. James Orr, ("World, Cosmological," ISBE, 5: 3108) writes that the Bible writes "without consideration of what the afterlight of science may throw on its [the world's] inner constitution, laws and method of working."

6. Shields, *op. cit.*, p. 27.

7. John Pye Smith, *op. cit.*, p. 225. Italics are his. The point of these last few paragraphs is also made by a Christian anthropologist. Cf. Smalley's remarks in Everest, editor, *Modern Science and Christian Faith* (second edition; 1950), p. 159–160. Smalley too says that language and culture *cannot* be separated.

8. H. W. Robinson, *Inspiration and Revelation in the Old Testament* (1946), p. 120, contains a list of the terms used in the Old Testament for time measurements. For New Testament terms for time cf. K. Bornhäuser, *Zeiten und Stunden in der Leidens- und Auferstehungsgeschichte* (1921), reviewed in *The Evangelical Quarterly*, 24: 241 ff., Oct., 1952. See also articles in Bible dictionaries. Very informative is Horne's discussion of Jewish-time reckoning in his *An Introduction to the Critical Study and Knowledge of the Holy Scriptures* (2 vols., 1848). The Jews had watchers on the mountains to signal the phases of the moon and so tell when the new month commenced. Cloudy weather made this difficult! Months were so regulated that periodically a whole month had to be added to their year to bring the calendar into alignment again.

9. Cf. Robinson, *op. cit.*, p. 72, for remarks about the physiological nature of Biblical psychology.

10. Classically defended by Hobart, *The Medical Language of St. Luke* (1882); and attacked by Cadbury, *Style and Literary Method of St. Luke* (1920). Most scholars think the truth is somewhere between Hobart and Cadbury.

11. Cf. Angus and Green, *Cyclopedic Handbook to the Bible* (1907), pp. 296–297 for the peculiarities of terminology in Hebrew geography. Perhaps we can make our entire point clear this way: We expect theologians to conform to the theological truth of Sacred Scripture, and we expect Christian philosophers to create their systems within the confines of the Christian religion. But we do not expect physicists, chemists, geologists, and geographers to take the various systems of natural things taught in the Bible and teach all these sciences in these terms, concepts, and standards of measurement. Or to put it even another way: we believe in the inspiration of the Old Testament, but we would never take seriously the liquid measuring system of the Old Testament as the eternal standard for all time and ask all scientists and commercial activity to conform to the Old Testament system of liquid measurements. Why not? Because the message is in and through these matters; these matters are not themselves the message.

12. Rust, *op. cit.*, p. 17.

13. Dana, in speaking of the fact that the Bible was a necessary accommodation to the situation of man, wrote: "Accordingly, the terms or word by which the ideas in the Bible cosmogony are expressed must necessarily, although these ideas were divinely communicated, bear some impress of want of knowledge or comprehension." James Dana, "Creation: or, The Biblical Cosmogony in the Light of Modern Science," BS, 42: 206, 1880.

14. Shields, *op. cit.*, p. 208.

15. John Pye Smith, *op. cit.*, p. 212.

16. *Christian Dogmatics* (1950), I, 317. The Greek refers to II Tim. 3: 16. The exact opposite of Pieper is of course Bultmann who says that the *entire* New Testament (in his case) is prescientific and therefore mythical.

17. J. W. Dawson, *Nature and the Bible* (1875), pp. 23–25. For parallels between the Bible view and that of modern science—which are remarkable and astounding when the time-period in which the Bible was written is considered—see pp. 31–40; and in his *The Origin of the World According to Revelation and Science* (1877), pp. 73–82. Other important literature on the Biblical view of nature is: H. W. Robinson, *Inspiration and Revelation in the Old Testament* (1946); Charles E. Raven, *Natural Religion and Christian Theology* (Vol. I, 1953); E. C. Rust, *Nature and Man in Biblical Thought* (1953). Both Raven and Rust admit indebtedness to Robinson.

18. Dawson, *op. cit.*, p. 24.

19. The great classic treatises on creation are: Augustine, *Confessions* (Books XI, XII, and XIII), and *The City of God* (Books XI and XII). Aquinas, *Summa Theologica* (Part I, Questions 44–49, "Treatise on Creation"; and Questions 65–102, "Treatise on the work of the Six Days."

20. God as *world-ground* is a far richer and more satisfactory concept than God as First Cause. The latter is the originating link in a chain of events. The former is God continuously at work in his universe—not only as First Cause but as cause of ethics, morality, and religion, and as Sustainer and Provider and Rationale. The O.T. presents God as *world-ground*, not just as First Cause. With reference to Kant, he certainly felt the *Critique of Practical Reason* embodied man's real reasons for existence, but the structure of his very system leaves one unimpressed.

21. H. W. Robinson, *op. cit.*, p. 1. Italics are ours. The Greek N. T. uses such terms as *panta* or *ta panta* or *hoi aiōnes* or *kosmos* or *ktisis* for the universe or Nature or creation. We admit indebtedness to Robinson for much which follows.

22. Both John Baillie (*Natural Science and Spiritual Life*, 1952) and A. N. Whitehead (*Science and the Modern World*, 1925) admit that the idea of the uniformity of Nature is a notion propounded by the scholastics who in turn derived it from the notion of the constancy of the Biblical

God as it expresses itself in Creation.   In truth, Baillie strongly insists that without this undergirding, modern science would not even have arisen.   He says: "It is quite clear to me, then, that modern science could not have come into being until the ancient pagan conception of the natural world had given place to the Christian," p. 25.

23. Grk: *autos didous pasi zōēn kai pnoēn kai ta panta.*

24. Rust, *op. cit.,* p. 161 ff.   This numbering is our own, not Rust's. Rust documents his claims with extensive references to the Gospels. Cf. also, Francis J. Handy, "Jesus and the Natural World," *Religion in Life,* 22: 392–399, Summer, 1953.

25. Rust, *op. cit.,* p. 69.

26. J. W. Dawson, *The Origin of the World According to Revelation and Science* (1877), pp. 74, 75, 172, 173.

27. *Summa Theologica,* I, 42, 2.

28. *City of God,* Bk. XII, 4 and 5.   The solution of Aquinas and Augustine is known as the *plentitude of being, i.e.* for a full or complete universe every sort of creature is necessary.   This plentitude of being involves imperfect creatures.   Strict Calvinism simply leaves the problem with the *sovereignty of God,* feeling that in the last analysis that is where the problem ends up anyway.

29. *City of God,* Bk. XI, 22.   This passage contains the essentials of the section of the *Summa* we summarized.

30. Cf. James Orr, "World: Cosmological," ISBE, V, 3106.

31. John Calvin, *Genesis,* I, 79 and 84.

32. H. E. Fosdick, *The Modern Use of the Bible* (1924), pp. 46–47. E. W. Maunder ("Astronomy," ISBE, I, 314) says that such a view of Biblical cosmology is "in reality based more upon the ideas prevalent in Europe during the Dark Ages than upon any actual statements in the Old Testament."

33. J. W. Dawson, *The Origin of the World According to Revelation and Science* (1877), p. 62.

34. *Nature and the Bible* (1875), p. 59.

35. Orr, *op. cit.,* V, 3106.

36. *Loc. cit.*   Orr follows this with a list of Scriptures which are completely out of harmony with the radical critics' reconstruction of Biblical cosmology.

37. C. Gaenssle, "A Look at Current Biblical Cosmologies," *Concordia Theological Monthly,* 23: 738–749.

38. *Ibid.,* p. 743.   He also demonstrates that the expression "windows of heaven" is metaphorical.   Some scholars object to this on the grounds that we would not translate *raqia* as space or atmosphere unless we were aware of the facts of modern science.   But Saville silences that argument by showing that the greatest Hebrew scholar of the fifteenth century,

Paginus, writing well before modern science, translates *raqia* by *expansionem*. B. W. Saville, "On Heathen Cosmogonies Compared with the Hebrew," JTVI, 10: 274–275 (1877). Incidentally this essay of Saville's is one of the finest summaries we encountered of ancient cosmological systems.

39. *Ibid.,* p. 747.

40. *Ibid.,* p. 749.

41. Maunder, *op. cit.,* p. 314 ff.

42. *Ibid.,* p. 316.

43. Conservative Christianity explains Babylonian and Biblical parallels by the theory of *cognateness* (not of dependence, nor of purification). See Orr, *op. cit.,* p. 3107; and especially J. McKee Adams, *Ancient Records and the Bible* (1946), p. 249 ff.

44. Orr, *op. cit.,* p. 3107. Cf. words to the same intent in C. M. Walsh, *The Doctrine of Creation* (1910), p. 7; and George Barton, *Archaeology and the Bible* (seventh edition, 1937), pp. 297–298.

45. This *dialectical yes/no* is Tillich's idea that in interacting with any thinker we should not speak an uncritical yes nor a dogmatic no, but must be able to detect what is worthless or erroneous and discard it; and be able to salvage what is a genuine contribution. Cf. Paul Tillich, *Systematic Theology* (1951), I, 25.

46. H. E. Fosdick, *The Modern Use of the Bible* (1924), p. 178.

47. C. W. Shields, *The Final Philosophy* (1877), p. 435 ff.

48. The author admits the most stimulating writer on this general subject has been the great Catholic biologist of the nineteenth century, St. George Mivart (*Lessons from Nature as Manifested in Mind and Matter,* 1876). It was a pleasure to note how much space Fothergill gave to Mivart in his epochal work. Fothergill considers Mivart a model for those who would mix biology and philosophy and remarks that "Mivart carried out a large amount of historical research on the subject and his views remain sound and lasting, in fact they have scarcely been improved upon." *Historical Aspects of Organic Evolution* (1952). Cf. also R. Voskuyl, "A Christian Interpretation of Science," *Modern Science and Christian Faith* (second edition; 1950); Abraham Kuyper, *Calvinism* (Fourth Lecture, "Calvinism and Science"); and H. Bavinck, *The Philosophy of Revelation* (reprint, 1953).

49. *Summa Theologica,* I, 44, 1. For Augustine we are making use of C. J. O'Toole, *The Philosophy of Creation in the Writings of St. Augustine* (1944); and William A. Christian, "Augustine on the Creation of the World," *Harvard Theological Review,* 46: 1–25, January, 1953.

50. *Summa,* I, 46, 1. Also: "We must hold that the will of God is the cause of things; and that He acts by the will, and not, as some have supposed, by a necessity of His nature." I, 19, 4.

51. *Confessions,* XII, 25. Note carefully how Augustine ascribes the source and preservation of all being to God, and that the natures of all

being, the teleological order of all being, and the laws of nature or being *are of God yet without contamination, i.e.* without pantheistic involvement. Italics are ours.   Note it is also *occult, i.e.* hidden, not anything you find as a thing or substance in Nature, hence supersensible and not in the obvious sense "scientific."

52. *Summa,* I, 8, 1–4.

53. *Ibid.,* I, 8, 1.

54. *Ibid.,* I, 8, 3.   Cf. the remark of E. C. Rust (*op. cit.,* p. 66): "For the Hebrew, nature was shot through and through with the divine activity.   He had no idea of chains of causality and secondary causes. Everything depended directly upon God Himself, and His control of the life of His creatures was immediate."

55. *Isaiah,* JFB.

56. *Genesis,* LANGE.

57. *Loc. cit.*

58 Augustine taught that the Spirit introduced form into the formless matter, and even entertained the idea that the Spirit of Gen. 1: 2 might be the *world-soul.* O'Toole, *op. cit.,* p. 20 and p. 51 ff.   Aquinas speaking of creation wrote: "But to the Holy Ghost, Who has the same power from both [the Father and the Son], is attributed that by His sway He governs, and quickens what is created by the Father through the Son." *Summa,* I, 45, 6.   Bishop Moule speaking of the connexion of the Holy Spirit with Nature wrote: "It is one among the many suggestions in the divine Word that matter has for its immediate basis the absolute immaterial will and power of God; that in this respect as in others *la dernière raison des choses, cest Dieu.*" *Veni Creator* (1895), p. 46.   E. C. Rust comes to a similar conclusion.   The increasing emphasis on the transcendence of God led to an emphasis of the mediatory activity of the Word (or Wisdom) and the Holy Spirit.   By post-exilic times the *ruach* (Spirit) of God came to mean "*the cosmic life-principle which upholds and sustains the whole order of creation.*" *Nature and Man in Biblical Thought* (1953), p. 133.   Italics are ours.

59. Abraham Kuyper, *The Work of the Holy Spirit* (1900), p. 21.

60. *Ibid.,* p. 24.   Italics are his.

61. *Ibid.,* p. 25.

62. *Ibid.,* p. 26.   Italics are his.

63. *Ibid.,* p. 31.

64. A. A. Higley, *Science and Truth* (1940), p. 69.

65. *Ibid.,* p. 32.   Italics are his.   It is true that Augustine believed in instantaneous creation, but he made room for a derived or secondary "creation" through the development of the *rationes seminales* planted in matter.   Cf. *infra.*

66. Cf. O'Toole, *op. cit.,* and Christian, *op. cit.*   It is not necessary to believe with Augustine that (i) the first act was to create prime matter, or that (ii) all things were created at once, or (iii) in much of the angelical and figurative interpretation he placed upon Genesis' six days.

67. Mivart, *op. cit.,* p. 371.

68. *Ibid.,* p. 359.   Italics are his.

69. *Summa,* I, 44, 3.   Cf. also, I, 44, 4.

70. James Dana, "Creation; or, The Biblical Cosmogony in the Light of Modern Science," BS, 42: 219, 1880.

CHAPTER IV

ANTICIPATION OF SCIENCE IN SCRIPTURE

I. INTRODUCTION

ARE there any anticipations of modern science in Sacred Scripture? Few works on Bible and science wrestle with this significant question: Does the Spirit of God convey the final facts or theories of science in inspiration? As we discussed the problem in Chapter III we indicated our belief that the Spirit of God did not convey the inner constitution of things to the authors of the Bible, but that the infallibly inspired theological truth is conveyed in the cultural terms of the cultural period of the writer. We also noted in the same chapter how pure and free the Israelitish culture was from those elements which contribute to either a mythological or fantastic view of natural things. If we believe that the Spirit of God did not teach the writers of the Bible final science (how do we know modern science is *final* science?) we shall not go hunting through the Bible for so-called marvellous anticipations of modern science.

On the other hand, in that the Hebrew people had such a magnificent view of Nature due to their revealed knowledge of God, and because they were observant and conversant with Nature, we can expect some of their inferences and statements to accord with modern science.

II. AN EXAMINATION OF SPECIFIC PASSAGES

In that many writers profess to find modern science tucked away in various verses of the Bible we need to examine such claims in detail. In Rimmer's opinion:

> *It is possible for the careful student of science and Scripture to discover literally scores of such anticipations* [of modern science].[1]

A. It has been suggested that the word *moved* of Gen. 1: 2 anticipates the modern undulatory theory of matter.[2] To unravel Sanden's paragraph is difficult, for with no warning he moves from undulation in physics, to John 1: 32 where the Spirit descends like a dove, to the modern undulatory theory of light and sound, and

[1] For notes see page 94.

concludes with a reference to undulations in the stratosphere.   In Gen. 1: 2 the Spirit is seen brooding over the waters.   Certainly Sanden does not wish to attribute undulation to the Spirit of God, and it would be meaningless to attribute the undulation to the waters.   This so-called anticipation is groundless.

B. Job 38: 35 reads: "Canst thou send lightnings, that they may go, and say unto thee, Here we are?"   Sanden claims that this is a prediction of wireless telegraphy.[3]   In this context God is informing Job that God can control Nature, and Job cannot.   Part of God's proof of His control over Nature is His control over lightning. God can send lightning where He wishes to send it.   It goes, and in fulfilment of the will of God by personification says "Here we are."

Sanden's notion that communication of thought is here implied is a mistake for such a notion is foreign to the meaning of the verse. To make this anticipatory of modern wireless telegraphy, we must violate the essential meaning of the passage and take a personification with a crass literalism.   It is not God nor Job that says, "We are here."   It is the lightning which says this in its perfect obedience to the will of God.   In spite of Rimmer's glowing statement ("What a marvellous Book, that anticipates this triumph of man's ingenuity some four thousand years or more")[4] we must reject this as an anticipation of wireless telegraphy.

C. Sanden claims that James 1: 17 refers to a parallax.[5]   Here again it is hard to decipher what is meant.   He says that James uses the word *paralogia* whereas James actually uses the word *parallagē*, and whereas actually the Greek word for parallax is *parallaxis*.   A parallax in astronomy is the angle subtended by observing a star from the periphery and from the centre of the earth or the sun.   An unabridged dictionary will usually illustrate this with a diagram.   If Sanden means that James refers to a parallax his Greek is faulty at this point.   Further, the idea of God's having a parallax is absurd.   In our observations it is our observations which vary, not the fixed star.   James is referring to two different astronomical phenomena.   *Variation* refers to the constant changing of the position of the sun in contrast to the constancy of God.[6] A shadow cast by turning means a shadow caused by a revolution. In no case is James referring to parallax, but as claimed by Maunder:

> James is using astronomical technical terms for these same apparent movements [rising, setting, moving, its solstices] of the sun.[7]

D. In answer to the question, "Does the Bible throw light on nuclear physics?" Sanden answers in the affirmative by citing Heb.

11: 3 (tangible objects are made of invisible atoms) and Heb. 1: 3 (where "upholding all things" is paraphrased as *binding together*).[8] Taking Heb. 1: 3 first, the verb *pherōn* means *directing,* as any good commentary will reveal.   There is no idea of *binding,* either in the verb or in the phrase.   Further, such an interpretation would make nonsense out of the passage for it would then mean that all things were held together by atomic binding power.   The structure of an atom may be held together by some mysterious binding power, but the *everything* of Heb. 1: 3 includes everything in the physical world, and perhaps even more directly the moral and spiritual history of humanity.

A number of men have appealed to Heb. 11: 3 as proving that the writer of Hebrews anticipated atomic theory, *e.g.* Sanden, Rimmer, and Chesnut.   Their interpretation is that by faith we understand that the visible universe is composed of invisible atoms. Such an interpretation must be vigorously rejected.

If this is the correct interpretation it means that all scientists who believe in the atomic theory *have the faith of Heb. 11*!   Belief in protons, photons, positrons and electrons is put on the same level as faith in God's power and promises.   It is absurd to assert that an atheist's faith in atomic theory is the same faith as that of Heb. 11.

The exegesis such an interpretation puts on this verse is indefensible.   The verse affirms that the visible universe was made by the spiritual and invisible word of God.   The great physical universe has a spiritual cause for its origin and continued existence. The things which appear were created *de novo*—they were not refashioned from previously existing material as both Plato and Aristotle believed.   *Ex nihilo* creation is distinctly Biblical and foreign to Greek thinking, and it is *ex nihilo* creation which we perceive by faith.   To assert then that the "things which do not appear" refers to invisible atoms, and not the *word of God* (the divine agency of creation) *is to contradict directly the teaching of this verse.*   It would make the verse mean: God created the world from previously existing invisible atoms.   *But that is precisely what the passage seeks to deny* for it seeks to tell us that the visible universe was brought into existence *ex nihilo* by a spiritual God and a spiritual power, namely, the word of God.

Rimmer accepts the Pauline authorship of Hebrews and praises Paul as follows:

> We merely cite this to call attention to the fact that the atomic theory was apparently first discovered by Paul the Apostle.   *The best statement of the atomic theory that literature contains* is found in the eleventh chapter of Hebrews, in the third verse . . . Dr. Millikan

received the Nobel prize of almost two score thousand dollars for proving this theory. Paul the apostle did not receive so much as a dime for anticipating the discoveries of Millikan by eighteen centuries.[9]

Any standard work on the history of philosophy, or the history of science, or the history of atomic theory, will indicate that the atomic theory first adumbrated in the invisible seeds of Anaxagoras was fully propounded by the Greek atomists, Leucippus and Democritus, several centuries before Paul was born! Modern atomic theory dates from the corpuscular theories of Newton and Descartes, and has a detailed history from Dalton (1766–1844) through Wollaston, Fraunhöfer, Brown, Young, Fresnel, Mendelyeev, Roëntgen, Planck, Thomson, Bohr, Heisenberg, de Broglie, etc. Millikan is not noted for discovering or proving the atom or atomic theory. He is noted for his famous oildrop experiment (1922) in which he proved that the so-called weight of the electron and its electrical charge were identical, and was able to measure and observe the influence of presumably one electron as it contacted an oil drop. This was a decided experimental improvement over the Wilson cloud chamber. No serious student of science would take Heb. 11: 3 as a better or more accurate definition of an atom than, shall we say, de Broglie's or Dirac's.

To appeal to Heb. 11: 3 as affirming atomic theory is actually to contradict what the verse is saying, namely, that the visible universe does not have a physical origin but a spiritual one.

Sanden finds more atomic physics in Gen. 1: 3 where he calls light the common denominator of all substance;[10] in Gen. 1: 4 where dividing day and night is made an anticipation of nuclear fission; and in Isa. 34: 4 and Luke 21: 25–28 which he interprets as meaning a final chain reaction. All of these references in their simple, obvious meaning have nothing to do with nuclear physics, and such an interpretation put upon them can only be called grotesque exegesis.

Sanden ventures into relativity theory by citing Isa. 40: 22 as an anticipation of the expanding universe (God "stretcheth out the heavens"). The theory of the expanding universe is not as yet a fully established theory, and there is no possible connexion between the oriental imagery of stretching a curtain and pitching a tent and modern astrophysics and its retreating galaxies.

E. In a most peculiar article it is argued that Joel 2: 3–4 anticipates motor-cars;[11] Isa. 31: 5, aeroplanes; Rev. 9: 1–11, submarines; Eccles. 10: 20, radio; and Rev. 11: 3–12, television. First of all, Beirnes cites Joel 2: 3–4 and actually quotes Nahum 2: 4. But Nahum 2: 4 was fulfilled thousands of years ago in the destruction of Nineveh, and it is impossible of sober exegetical defence to lift that verse out of context and make it refer to automobiles.   Nineveh was destroyed by the Medes and Chaldeans in 612 B.C.

At the danger of invasion by Sennacherib, the king of Judah wished to make an alliance with Egypt.   But the prophet Isaiah warned against it and said that God is the Protector of Judah, not the Egyptians.   The KJ has "as birds flying so will the Lord of hosts defend Jerusalem," but the ARV and RSV both have *hovering*. God will come down and hover over Jerusalem like a hen over her nest, and so protect Jerusalem.   Therefore to refer this to aeroplanes is misinterpretation.   Further, the passage does not refer to the end times but to Judah's immediate future.   Rimmer thinks that Isa. 60: 8 refers to aeroplanes.[12]   A check of the commentaries will disclose that the passage refers to boats with white sails coming into harbour, giving the appearance of white doves coming into their nest.   Again, any reference to aeroplanes is misinterpretation.   Beirnes' references to submarines, radios, and television are impossible of any serious exegetical defence.

F. Job 14: 17–19 ("But the mountain falls and crumbles away, and the rock is removed from its place.   The waters wear away the stones; the torrents wash away the soil of the earth." RSV) has been taken as suggestive of modern geology.   Most of the commentators consulted viewed this verse as a reference to the processes of erosion which any sensitive observer would notice as happening in the world around him.   Anyone who has been around mountains notices the piles of chips and rocks, and the slides, all of which indicate that the face of the mountain is wearing away.   The water sweeping away tons of earth as it pours down as rain over the landscape and then finds its way to the sea in muddy streams is again a matter of general knowledge.   The verse appeals to nothing more than what any intelligent observer would note as he considered such processes in Nature.   There is nothing profound here in the nature of genuine geological theory.

G. Job 22: 14 ("Thick clouds enwrap him, so that he does not see, and he walks on the vault [circuit, KJ] of heaven" RSV) has been appealed to as proving the sphericity of the earth.   The basic meaning of the verse is that Eliphaz contends that God does not take cognizance of human affairs.   God is up in the sky walking around, he jeers, and is not noticing what is happening to Job. None of the standard commentaries consulted made much of this verse as indicating anything spherical about the earth.

H. Job 26: 7 ("He stretcheth out the north over the empty place [void, RSV], and hangeth the earth upon nothing" KJ is a far more controversial passage.   Critics have challenged this verse as proving that the earth hangs suspended in space on the grounds that (i) the word *north* means the mountains in the northern part of the earth, not the north part of the sky; and (ii) although there is no apparent connexion between the earth and the sky above, the verse says nothing about the lack of support *underneath* the earth.[13]

With reference to the word *north* Delitzsch strongly rejects the interpretation that it refers to mountains in the northern part of the earth, and insists that it refers to the northern part of the sky.[14] (i) The writer would hardly refer to the mountains of the earth in the first part of the verse, and then refer to the entire world in the second; (ii) the expression used here is never used of the earth but is the stereotyped word for the sky; and (iii) one expects a reference to the sky with mention of the earth.

With reference to the interpretation that rejects the idea that the ancients had no notion of a sphere floating in nothing, two things may be said. (i) If a cosmology of the Bible like Schiaparelli's has already been adopted, then verses like Job 26: 7 are fitted into a predetermined mould. But if such a reconstruction is rejected then we are not bound to interpret this verse within the confines of such a theory. (ii) The astronomical sense of the ancients is not always fully appreciated. Who needs modern astronomy to give him the idea of a freely floating sphere when both the sun (especially when its silhouette can be seen through fog, clouds or smoke) and the moon give such obvious examples of the same? Would it be totally impossible for a man of that age to make such an induction about the earth? As a child, before he knew a word of astronomical theory, the writer often thought of the earth as sailing through space just like the moon, which was so clear and bright on a wintry night.

Gibson sees nothing in the verse but ancient Babylonian cosmology modelled after the thinking of Schiaparelli.[15] However, such men as Fausset, Cook, and Leathes, are very strong in their statements that this verse through divine inspiration gives us a hint of the world being suspended in nothing, as modern astronomy teaches.[16]

I. Job 28: 25 refers to God as giving the winds a weight and measuring out the waters. Most of the commentators take this to refer to God's wisdom in ordering and regulating Nature. Winds and waters are measured so as to fit into Nature in their allotted place and way. Zöckler interprets it as meaning that the winds and waters must be kept in due proportion.[17] The interpretation that this teaches us that air has a weight and is not a nothing as previously thought, is incorrect. The writer was not referring to the air but to the wind; and he was not referring to the weight of the wind, but to its proportioned function in the system of Nature.

J. Job 36: 27-28 ("For he draws up the drops of water, he distils his mist in rain, which the skies pour down and drop upon man continually." RSV) has been appealed to as proving that the Bible teaches a cycle of rain from evaporation to cloud formation to rain. The crucial factor is the meaning of the verb *draw*. The verb has been interpreted as meaning (i) evaporation or (ii) God's power in drawing the rain to Himself or (iii) God drawing the drops away from the clouds and letting them fall. Most commentators take the third interpretation. Much of the debate over this verse is as to whether the ancients had any notion of evaporation as fitting into the world's water cycle. The central meaning of the verse is clear: the fall of the rain in light drops or misty vapour from huge, heavy clouds is one of the miracles of God's wisdom and providence. If the verb *draw* means to draw up from the earth, as Fausset believes,[18] then we do have here a cycle of water in Nature; but if it means that God draws the water from the clouds in little droplets, then it does not.[19]

K. Prov. 8: 27 refers to God as setting a "circle upon the face of the deep" (ARV). Does this teach the circularity of the earth? Or does it refer to the circularity of the heavens above? The best interpretation seems to be that of taking the verse as a reference to the sphericity of the ocean. This is capable of two interpretations. (i) This verse actually teaches the sphericity of the globe, *e.g.* Fausset says:

> It is striking how the sacred writers, whilst not rudely offending the conceptions of their age respecting cosmography, yet use language which harmonizes with the later discoveries of science.[20]

However, we prefer the interpretation of Delitzsch.[21] First of all he rejects the interpretation that the ocean girdles the earth, as the radical critical scholars have so imagined. He claims that this is an importation into the text without the sanction of the Old Testament. Next, he says that the meaning of the verse is that God has set a boundary to the extent of the ocean. To set a circle is to draw the boundaries for the ocean beyond which it is not to come. So interpreted the verse does not refer to the sphericity of the earth, but to the divinely drawn boundaries of the ocean.

L. In Eccles. 1: 6–7 the Preacher argues that part of the monotony of existence is the perpetual cycles of the wind and rain. Both of these assertions are possible by a careful observer even in Biblical times. He needs neither science nor revelation to write these verses. Any adult with a keen mind and observant eye realizes that the wind blows from a variety of directions, and therefore must go through some kind of circuit. We do not think that this verse refers to the great movement of air masses as charted by modern meteorologists nor the wind highways they chart on their weather maps. The verse refers to the constant cycles of the wind as it blows in from various directions.

Far more debate has been made over v. 7 ("All the rivers run into the sea; yet the sea is not full; unto the place, from whence the rivers come, thither they return again" (KJ). Does this verse teach the cycle of water from clouds to rain to rivers to ocean to evaporation to clouds? Or does it teach a seepage of the ocean water back to the springs again?

The general meaning of the verse is obvious. It refers to the monotony of the water cycle in Nature. Water goes through its cycle, so the ocean is never full. Plumptre rejects the interpretation that this verse refers to the regular water cycle as we understand it, as this is reading modern science back into an ancient book.[22] He thinks that the Preacher thought water returned to the springs and sources by seepage. Others like Bullock and Zöckler feel that reading in the concept of a universal subterranean ocean or underground channels is doing an injustice to the Old Testament.[23] Bullock says that Solomon does not tell us *how* the water gets back to its source but that it *does*. Further, such verses as Prov. 8: 28 and Psa. 104: 10, 13 teach that the clouds feed the springs of the earth, and not subterranean water. Zöckler comments:

> The return of the water from the ocean the author [of Ecclesiastes] certainly thinks effected in a way corresponding to the natural course of things; namely, that of exhalations, and clouds, and falling mists, and not by means of secret subterraneous canals and passages.

M. Isa. 40: 22 ("It is he that sitteth upon the circle of the earth") has been cited as a proof for the sphericity of the earth. Few commentators so interpret this verse. The main import of the verse is that God is exalted in the heavens, and when He looks down upon the earth men appear as grasshoppers. If this is the true meaning of the verse then the *circle of the earth* means the hemisphere in which the earth appears as being in the centre, although Fausset does say the expression is "applicable to the globular form of the earth above which, and the vault of the sky around which He sits."[24]

N. It has been urged that our Lord intimated the sphericity of the earth by His references to His second coming. In Mark 13: 35–37 our Lord states that He may come at evening, or midnight, or at cock-crow or at morning. The interpretation is that it will be *all* these times at once when Jesus comes, but that is hardly the point. The point is that it may be *any* of these times when He returns. Luke 17: 34–35 is a similar reference and is similarly misinterpreted.

III. SUMMARY

Our summary is but a restatement of our premise that the Holy Spirit conveyed infallibly true theological doctrines in the cultural mould and terms of the days of the Bible writers, and did not give to the writers the secrets of modern science. It is a misunderstanding of the nature of inspiration to seek such secrets in various verses of the Bible. However, contrary to liberalism, we affirm that the theological does at times overlap the scientific, *e.g.*, matter is not eternal but created; the simple preceded the complex in the order of life; man is the latest and highest creation of God; Jesus was actually born of a virgin; or, the universe will have a demise and make way for the new heavens and the new earth. But to look for relativity theory or nuclear physics or atomic theory is something far different.

NOTES

1. H. Rimmer, *The Harmony of Science and Scripture* (third edition; 1936), p. 87. Italics are his.

2. O. E. Sanden, *Does Science Support Scripture?* (1951), pp. 39–40, and p. 139.

3. Sanden, *op. cit.*, p. 62. Rimmer accepts this interpretation too. *Op cit.*, p. 155.

4. *Loc. cit.*

5. Sanden, *op. cit.*, p. 64.

6. So Mayor, quoted in the *Expositor's Greek Testament, in loco.*

7. E. W. Maunder, "Astronomy," ISBE, I, 302.

8. Sanden, *op. cit.*, pp. 122 and 137.

9. Rimmer, *op. cit.*, pp. 91 and 92. Italics are ours.

10. Sanden, *op. cit.*, p. 139.

11. W. F. Beirnes, "Forecasts of the Advent," *Dawn*, 29: 31–32, Jan. 1951.

12. Rimmer, *op. cit.*, p. 97 ff.

13. So argue Davidson and Lanchester, *Job*, CB.

14. *Job*, KD.

15. *Job*, WC.

16. Fausset in *Job*, JFB; Cook in *Job*, HBC; Leathes in *Job*, ELLICOTT.

17. *Job*, LANGE.

18. *Job*, JFB.

19. Gibson, *Job*, WC, thinks the concept of evaporation was too scientific for Job's time.

20. *Proverbs*, JFB.

21. *Proverbs*, KD.

22. *Ecclesiastes*, CB.

23. Bullock in *Ecclesiastes* HBC; Zöchler in *Ecclesiastes'* LANGE.

24. *Isaiah*, JFB.

CHAPTER V

ASTRONOMY

I. GENERAL SURVEY

THE most judicious essay on astronomy and the Bible is that of E. W. Maunder in ISBE.[1] It is characterized by learning, good judgment, and loyalty to the Holy Scriptures. It is apparently a condensation of his treatise, *Astronomy of the Bible*. The most obvious character of Biblical astronomy is its difference from the astronomy and astrology of surrounding nations. This is to be attributed to the Hebrews' faith in God as the Creator of all. The Hebrews had a purer, more chaste attitude toward astronomical bodies, which were considered as moved by the one Eternal God.

That which the Hebrews saw pre-eminently in the heavenly bodies was order "great, magnificent, and immutable."[2] The regularity of the sun, and the procession of days, seasons and years all indicated that God governed the heavenly bodies by His ordinance. These ordinances had their effects upon the earth, bringing to pass the seasons, and so God asks Job: "Knowest thou the ordinances of the heavens? Canst thou establish the dominion thereof in the earth?" (Job 38: 33).

There is no Biblical record of any astronomical theory as to how the stars actually behave. The lesson which the Hebrews learned from the stars was not any theory, such as the Copernican, but rather the faithfulness of God (Jer. 33: 25–26); and that the glory of God is seen in the heavens (Psa. 19: 1).

The Hebrews used ordinary, simple terms to describe the heavenly bodies. Biblical terminology is free from the grotesque and fanciful terminology of the Babylonian myths. The simplicity of Biblical terminology is its freedom from all myth, personification, and deification of heavenly bodies.

It is the expression of man's earliest observation of the heavenly bodies, but it is real observation, free from any taint of savage phantasies; it marks the very first step in astronomy. No record, oral or written, has been preserved to us of a character more markedly primitive than this.[3]

[1] For notes see page 115.

The purposes of the heavenly bodies are given in Gen. 1: 14, namely, to tell time and to give light. The emphasis given to moonlight must be seen in its ancient setting, for in those times "artificial lights were few, expensive and dim, and the lighting of streets and roads was unthought of."⁴ An added purpose of the heavenly bodies was for *signs*. The eclipse was especially frightening to the pagans and was usually reckoned as an omen of disaster. But Jeremiah, the prophet of the Creator, tells Israel not to be dismayed at the signs in the heavens (10: 2). Eclipses seem to be clearly indicated in Joel 2: 10, 31 and Rev. 6: 12. Both in Revelation and in Joel the moon appears blood-red. When the moon is eclipsed by the earth the only rays which reach it are those filtered through the earth's atmosphere, and the moon appears a dull, copper-red colour.

The sun and moon were to function for man for *seasons*. By an analysis of the usage of the word *seasons* Maunder indicates that it means religious seasons, not the four seasons of the year. The position of the sun indicated the various times for daily sacrifices, and the position of the moon for monthly sacrifices. Seven was very important in the whole Jewish economy and it figured in their astronomy and religious seasons. At the forty-ninth year there was a season of restitution. This forty-ninth year is a perfect lunar cycle lacking just thirty-two hours, but it was exact enough to keep the Jews on their regular cycle. Maunder gives elaborate details here, but they are not germane to our purposes.

With reference to the stars the Hebrew Scriptures emphasized especially their number and height. Verses indicating the vast number of stars are Gen. 15: 5 and Jer. 33: 22. It is a sign of the infinite power and knowledge of God that He knows the names and numbers of all the stars (Psa. 147: 4). Verses which indicate the Hebrew emphasis on the height or distance of the stars are Prov. 25: 3; Job 11: 7–8; Job 22: 12; Jer. 31: 37; and Psa. 103: 11. Paul indicated that stars vary in their brightness (I Cor. 15: 41). Job knew of the morning stars or stars of the twilight which were used by the ancients to mark out the beginning of spring, the coming of winter, the time of ploughing, the time to sow, and the coming of the rains (Job 3: 9; 38: 7). Falling stars might be indicated by Rev. 6: 13; Isa. 34: 4; Rev. 8: 10; and Acts 19: 35.

The Hebrews apparently had the same system of constellations that was developed in Babylonia by 2700 B.C. The most obvious reference to a constellation in the Bible is the reference to the crooked serpent (Job 26: 13). Maunder also finds reference to Draco the dragon or leviathan in Isa. 27: 1. With reference to the so-called "gospel in the stars" he notes that the constellations Scorpio, Ophiucus, and Serpens deal with elements of Gen. 3; and

D

in Argo, Centaurus, Lupus, and Sagittarius, he finds reference to the rainbow set in the clouds in connexion with Noah. But, he admonishes, to find all forty-eight primitive constellations as exhibiting gospel truth is far-fetched. He warns us that this interpretation was founded on the fanciful Arabic etymologies of a certain Miss Frances Rolleston.[5] Job 3: 8 is a reference to certain mythological traditions about the Dragon Head and the Dragon Tail.

Whether there is astronomical significance in Joseph's dream is problematic. The Jews were familiar with the twelve signs of the Zodiac. The sun and moon and eleven stars did obeisance to Joseph. The only connexion here with astronomy is the possibility that some of the twelve tribes adopted Zodiacal signs for their standards. Maunder also thinks that there is a possible reference to constellations in Isa. 27: 1 in which the enemies of God are likened to dragons, and he finds a reference in the phrases of this verse to Hydra, Draco, and Cetus. There is also the possibility that John in Rev. 12 could have obtained some imagery from the constellations Andromeda, Cetus, and Eridanus where we have a woman, a dragon, and a river which the earth seems to swallow up.

The Hebrew word *kimah* evidently refers to Pleiades (Amos 5: 8; Job 9: 9; 38: 31). This is a cluster of six stars, although the tradition has been that there were originally seven. Others, with the naked eye, have counted up to fourteen. Photographic plates taken with modern telescopes reveal thousands of stars "and show the principal stars as enveloped and threaded together by delicate streams of nebulous matter, the stars shining on these filamentous lines of light, as upon a string."[6] Modern telescopic photography bears out what God says to Job when He mentions the cluster or chains of Pleiades. Maunder also thinks that these traditional seven stars of Pleiades might be referred to in Rev. 1: 12, 13, 16, 20, in which the seven churches are likened to seven stars, yet forming one cluster, *i.e.* one body.

The Hebrew *kesil* apparently refers to Orion. It occurs in the three verses mentioned in connexion with *kimah* and in Isa. 13: 10. By comparative linguistics the Hebrew word Nimrod is connected to the Babylonian Marduk. An old tradition associates Nimrod with these constellations, which suggest a gigantic armed warrior. Thus the word *kesil*, indicating a rebellious one, fits in with what is known of Marduk and Nimrod. What was to the Babylonians a hero was a Titan rebel to the Hebrews and to loose the bands of Orion (Job 38: 13) would be the same as asking, "Canst thou bring down out of their places the stars that make up this figure, and so, as it were, set the Titan free?"[7]

The term *mazzaroth* is apparently a reference to the twelve constellations of the Zodiac. That there are twelve such constellations, Maunder affirms, but the *signs* are divisions drawn in the heavens which once roughly corresponded to the constellations, but owing to the stellar movements themselves the signs have pulled away from the constellations.

There is the possibility that the "scatterers" alluded to in Job 37: 9 are the two winnowing fans which are called in North America the two dippers.

II. CREATION

Because astrophysics and astronomy are prime factors in the Christian proof of creation we shall discuss creation under the chapter on astronomy.   We do not propose here to discuss creation as a philosophical problem and therefore we shall have little to say about such matters.   Suffice it to indicate that, as the Old Testament scholar Robinson asserts, the Bible is anti-deistic, anti-dualistic, and anti-pantheistic:

> The creation is so closely linked to the conservation and control [of God] that all dualistic deism is irrelevant, whilst there can be no pantheistic absorption of such a Person in the immanent energies of Nature.[8]

In view of Heb. 11: 3 we feel bound to interpret Gen. 1 as creation *ex nihilo*.   We are convinced that the *ex nihilo* doctrine is affirmed in Genesis even though some scholars believe that such an idea does not occur till II Macc. 7: 28 ("God made them not of things that were").   As Burgon correctly reasons:

> The word in the original does not indeed necessarily imply [creation out of nothing]; but since there is *no* word in Hebrew (any more than there is in Greek, Latin, or English), peculiarly expressive of the notion of creating out of nothing, it need not excite our surprise that Moses does not employ such a word to describe what God did "in the beginning."[9]

We reject the interpretation that is placed upon Gen. 1 making it teach either that (i) creation here stated is limited to part of the universe or even the earth, or (ii) that creation was from previously existing materials.   Our question is this: *what is the evidence from science to support the claims of Gen. 1: 1?*

A. *Proof from design.*   The argument from design is based on (i) the analogy from experience, and (ii) the repugnancy or irrationality of chance.   It is the common experience of men that if order exists it exists only by the concerted, intelligent effort of man, and if things are left to themselves they proceed to a state of deterioration.   A beautiful picture, a lovely garden, a magnificent building, a complicated printing press or a cyclotron are the result of concerted effort and planning.   At least in human experience machines, works of art or mansions are the willed and conscious productions of human intelligence.   Machines left to themselves rust out, abandoned buildings decay, and neglected gardens become weed plots.   The analogy of experience would indicate that the presence of design implies the prior existence of conscious will, mind, and purpose.

Further, the argument from design is based on the repugnance of sheer chance to produce order.   It is admitted that chance may imitate creation and a few such instances are used over and over again in the literature to refute the argument from design, especially Huxley's illustration of the sand, little rocks, and big rocks at the base of a cliff at the ocean shore.   Such examples admitted by both sides are not sufficient to refute the entire scope of data presented in the argument from design.   Nothing in these examples compares with the intricacy of a printing press or the complexity of the human brain.   Would anybody believe a counterfeiter if he asserted that his bills emerged by chance, or would a murderer be let off because of a chance bullet flying through the air fired by no gun?   Our civil laws definitely operate on the principle of the repugnance of chance.

The opponents of teleological thought argue that the analogy from experience is invalid and that chance when divorced from sheer randomness is not repugnant.   The way in which Nature creates and man creates are so different, they argue, that the transference of the principles of creation by man to Nature is improper.   Man works as a creator on the *outside* and Nature works slowly from the *inside,* and if this is true the analogy breaks down.   Further, the concept of chance is not repugnant for (i) the desired event eventually turns up, given enough time and enough chances, and (ii) a very lucky throw, not too uncommon in chance situations, may actually simulate intelligent activity.

The general scheme of the teleological proof of creation is to show the presence of mind in Nature and from that presence infer the Divine Mind.   If we discover a piece of paper with an involved problem in higher mathematics worked out correctly we quite reasonably infer that some mathematician did it.   The possibilities of such configurations occurring on a piece of paper as the sheer chance dabblings of an infant or as remarkable weatherings of the paper are so slight as to be completely written off as possibilities. Mathematical symbols and methods of calculation are too distinct, too highly developed, and too technical to be the result of any chance arrangement.   The problem is: *can we find such a clear case as this in Nature?*

Sir James Jeans is famous for his mathematical-Platonic theory of creation. He reasons that the mathematical nature of modern scientific theory proves that Nature was fabricated by a mathematician. Jeans admits that his argument is similar to that of Plato's.[10] Science reveals Nature not as composed by the artist or the biologist or the engineer but by the mathematician. All previous models of the universe have failed, and therefore our only analogy left is that of mathematics. Therefore the universal applicability of mathematics to Nature and the failure of all other types of mechanical analogy drive us to the conclusion that Nature was fashioned by a Pure Mathematician. This does not mean that we use mathematics in science—an obvious truism—but that scientific knowledge is mathematical in *form*.[11] Thus the universe being mathematically described and mathematical in form is on the order of pure thought, for mathematics is the function of pure thought. Thus the universe is more like a great thought than a great machine.[12]

Teleology has been used to prove creation from the times of the ancient Greeks and Hebrews to modern times. The history of teleology has been traced by Fulton.[13] It received outstanding treatments in Western thought in Paley's *Natural Theology* and in Kant's *Critique of Judgment*. It has been generally assumed among scientists and educated men that Darwin undermined the teleological argument. The human hand, once appealed to as a magnificent organ designed for grasping and handling objects, is now interpreted as the product of an almost infinite number of variations. The hand is "created" by the combined factors of chance, utility, and survival value. Its appearance as a highly manufactured product is therefore deceiving.

Just when the scholars had decided that the teleological argument had been permanently buried it was unceremoniously dug up by L. J. Henderson in his works, *The Fitness of the Environment* (1913) and *The Order of Nature* (1917). In a famous set of books called the *Bridgewater Treatises* (12 vols., 1833–36) some of Great Britain's outstanding scientists banded together to undergird the theistic argument with data from the sciences. Among their arguments is found *inorganic* teleology. Paley's argument is essentially an argument of *organic* teleology. This deals with the design in living creatures. Inorganic teleology deals with those numerous factors in inorganic Nature which are necessary for life. Darwin's work might seriously damage organic teleology but it leaves inorganic teleology untouched. It is the inorganic teleology of the *Bridgewater Treatises* which Henderson professes to bring up to date. The data which Henderson presents is staggering in its wealth. You cannot start citing instances without including the entire book, but we will resist the temptation and take a few things he says of water as an example of the nature of data in his works.   Water has a high specific heat.   This means that chemical reactions within the body will be kept rather stable.   If water had a low specific heat we would "boil over" with the least activity.   If we raise the temperature of a solution of 10° C. we speed up the reaction by two.   Without this particular property of water, life would hardly be possible.   The ocean is the world's thermostat.   It takes a large loss of heat for water to pass from liquid to ice, and for water to become steam quite an intake of energy is required.   Hence the ocean is a cushion against the heat of the sun and the freezing blast of the winter.   Unless the temperatures of the earth's surface were modulated by the ocean and kept within certain limits life would either be cooked to death or frozen to death.   As a solvent, water is universal.   It dissolves acids, bases, and salts.   Chemically it is relatively inert, providing a medium for reactions without partaking in them.   In the blood stream it holds in solution the minimum of sixty-four substances.   Perhaps if we knew the actual number it would be a staggering figure.   Any other solvent would be a pure sludge!   Without the peculiar properties of water, life would be impossible as we know it.

Henderson is an enigma.   After a review of a veritable cavalcade of collocations of inorganic Nature necessary for life, he asserts that (i) this could not be a matter of chance, and (ii) no explanation is forthcoming.   Why he did not see the theistic creation postulate staring him in the face we do not understand.   But Henderson's conclusionless book has not prevented men from using his findings, and Henderson is the greatest name in the contemporary revival of inorganic teleology.

We now notice some of the recent scholars who accept a teleological interpretation of Nature.   Northrop argues that the process of breathing is a cosmic process.[14]   The gases of the atmosphere and their properties, and the needs of the organism, are mutually adapted to each other.   Every act of breathing is a cosmic process and only possible because of inorganic teleology.   Tennant argues for the teleology of collocations or the wider teleology.[15]   Citing Henderson for evidence he notes the innumerable factors necessary in Nature to make life possible.   Buttressing his position with strict, rigid, empirical logic he comes to the conclusion that "the world is comparable with a single throw of dice.   And common sense is not foolish in suspecting the dice to have been loaded."[16]   Even the rejection of teleology by Darwinism he boldly questions. A narrowly conceived teleology might be upset by Darwin, but certainly not a wider teleology.   Further, the variations in Darwinianism are just *givens* with no genuine explanation as to their source.   In a very controversial work, *Human Destiny* (1947), du

Noüy defends a case for *telefinalism*. He affirms that the chance formulation of a typical protein molecule made up of 2,000 atoms is of the order of one to 2.02×10^{321} or practically nil. Even if the elements are shaken up at the speed of the vibration of light it would take 10^{243} billions of years to get the protein molecule for life, and life on the earth is limited in time to about two billion years. The arguments of Wyckoff and Stanley that they have found intermediaries between dead matter and living substance are rejected because the molecular weight of such material is 10,000,000 and the calculus of probability makes such a happening by chance an impossibility. The only explanation of the origin of life is *finalism* or *telefinalism*.

Boodin (in his numerous writings) feels that chance can no longer be referred to as the explanation of everything. Nature has an order and this order is as objective as the periodic law of elements.[17] Order is of cosmic proportions and to assume that the cosmic system emerged from chaos is absurd.[18] The cosmic environment which controls the events of the universe and creates the emergence of order and life is none other than God. The history of the order in the universe is essentially *emergence by guidance,* or in another expression of his, by *controlled emergence*. God is a supreme spiritual field and under His influence order and design are brought into being. Bishop Barnes, who reviewed with a good measure of competence all major divisions of scientific knowledge in his Gifford Lectures, *Scientific Theory and Religion* (1933), accepts the validity of teleological thought. Creative activity is the only explanation of the order of the universe. The pattern of the atom, the success of mathematics in astronomy, the origin of our galaxy, the prevalence of natural law, the order of elements in Mendelyeev's table, are all indications that there is an Almighty God, Creator of heaven and earth. Mention should be made of the collection of essays in Frances Mason's *The Great Design; Order and Progress in Nature* (1934). Here again a series of scientists affirm their conviction of the presence of design in Nature—Aitken on astronomy, Crowther on radiation, Eve on the universe in general, Fraser-Harris on the unity and intelligence of Nature.

We conclude this discussion of the evidence of creation from design with the words of the Regius Professor of Astronomy at the University of Glasgow:

> When we study the Universe and appreciate its grandeur and orderliness, it seems to me that we are led to the recognition of a Creative Power and Cosmic Purpose that transcends all our limited minds can comprehend. In one of his essays Lord Bacon expresses this belief picturesquely as follows: "I had rather believe all the Fables in the Legend and the Talmud and the Alcoran than that this

Universall Frame is without a Minde." Today we have learned very much more about the "Universall Frame" than was known in Bacon's time; nevertheless, to many of us, scientific and non-scientific alike, the belief in a Divine Creator is as necessary now as ever it was. To one astronomer at least "The Heavens are telling us the Glory of God and the Wonder of His Works."[19]

B. *Proofs from the temporality of the universe.* If we were to find a warm stove in a mountain cabin we may assume that sometime before our arrival the fire box was burning fuel. We could take the temperature of the stove, fire the stove up, and wait till it returned to the same temperature it was when we found it. We would then have an approximate idea how long a time ensued between the time some unknown man left the cabin and our arrival. The closer we come to the original conditions of the stove when it was left the more accurately we shall know the elapsed time.

If two cars are racing and we know exactly how much faster one car is than the other—other conditions being equal—we can tell how long they have been racing by measuring the distance between them. If we know the rate of flow of water from a tap we can tell how long the tap has been turned on by the amount of water in the tub.

In such situations we calculate from the present state of affairs backwards to the original state of affairs. The degree of accuracy in each case will depend upon the numerous factors involved, but we can set certain limits. The wood stove cannot have been cooling for a week; the cars cannot have been racing for more than fifteen minutes; and the faucet could not have been on for half an hour. The argument for creation from certain processes in Nature is in effect trying to discover in Nature something like the situations we have described above. Are there any races or stoves or runs ning taps in Nature? If so, how long have they been running?

There are several processes known to physicists that suggest a given time when present events, calculated backwards, reached a certain termination. The usual argument is that this termination is identical with creation. The materialist and atheist will argue that all we can do is to trace back the origin of *the present run of events* of an eternal series. The Christian argues that a universal furnace does not have an eternal stoker and so *this present run of events is the only one there has been.*

Eggenberger has listed the various processes which point to a limited series of events whose origin is a finite time ago.[20] (i) The oldest known rock of the earth's crust is the uraniute of Manitoba, date, 2.4 billion* years ago. The earth must be several hundred million years older than this since the materials which these rocks

---

* Throughout this book the author uses the word "billion" in the American sense of a thousand millions.

were made of were derived from previously existing rock. (ii) An analysis of the lead isotopes (as a function of time) leads to a figure of 3.5 billion years. (iii) U-235 is supposed to be either of the identical concentration as U-238 or in the inverse ratio of their stability. Knowing the rate of disintegration, and knowing that the present relationship of one to the other is 1 to 139, it is possible to calculate a time of the origin of the elements of about several billion years. (iv) The moon is slowly retreating from the earth, and its original point of departure in time was several billion years ago. (v) Meteorites are dated five billion years old. (vi) Calculations with reference to the phenomena of star clusters and binary stars leads to three billion years for the former and three to four billion years for the latter as to the time of their original conditions. (vii) The calculations in connexion with the expanding universe lead to about four billion years. The recent work with the two-hundred-inch telescope of Mt. Palomar suggests 5.5 billion years as the absolute maximum for the age of the earth.

However, the most serious effort to prove the temporality of the universe is in the evidence derived from the second law of thermodynamics, also called the law of entropy. Its validity as indicating the temporality of the universe is maintained by such men as Jeans, Barnes, Boodin, Inge, Urban, Northrop, and Eddington. It is denied any such interpretation by such men as Bridgman, Frank, Russell, and Milne. The second law was developed successively by Carnot (1824), Mayer, Rumford, Clausius, and Boltzmann.

What the law asserts can be illustrated from a self-mixing oleomargarine bag which contains white margarine and a small capsule filled with yellow colouring. When the capsule is broken and as the bag is massaged the colouring is eventually spread throughout the mass of white margarine. If the bag is squeezed indefinitely the distribution of the colouring will proceed till the colouring is perfectly spread throughout the entire mass. No matter how much more we squeeze, we cannot reverse the process and get the colouring back into the capsule. There are some parts of the universe that are much hotter than other parts of the universe. The distribution of the heat is always "down," from the hotter regions to cooler regions. As the heat "flows" from the hot regions to the cool regions it becomes more and more evenly distributed throughout the universe. If the universe is infinitely old, the energy would have already been evenly distributed by now. The fact that there are still hot bodies in the universe means that the furnace was stoked, so to speak, at some measurable time in the past. This would be the moment of creation, or some creative activity.

The most forceful evangelist of the metaphysical significance of entropy has been Eddington.[21] Shuffling, he states, is something

Nature cannot reverse, and the spread of heat is a shuffling process. Once a pack of cards is mixed, the possibilities of getting the factory order again are infinitesimal. A confused order of cards indicates a time factor—this happened *after* the cards were purchased. So entropy, a shuffling process in Nature, indicates a *direction* in Nature or as Eddington calls it a Time Arrow.

The law of entropy, as a proof for creation, is resisted by physicists on the grounds that (i) no real operational definition can be given of entropy as applying to all the universe, *i.e.* it is true of local heat systems, but as to what the status is in all the universe we can make no meaningful statement; (ii) that recoverability is possible on the grounds of chance; (iii) that entropy is relative to the observer and therefore we can make no absolute pronouncements about it; and (iv) Millikan argues that cosmic rays are the result of matters being made in the outer regions of the universe, and therefore, that recoverability is going on in the universe.[22]

Gen. 1 now stands in higher repute than it could ever have stood in the history of science up to this point. We now have means whereby we can point to a moment of time or to an event or cluster of events in time *which date our present known universe.* According to the best available data that is of the order of four to five billion years ago. A series of calculations converge on about the same order of time. We cannot with our present information *force* a verdict for creation from the scientists, although that is not to be considered an impossibility. Perhaps the day will come when we have enough evidence from physics, astronomy, and astrophysics to get such a verdict from the scientists. In the meantime we can maintain that Gen. 1: 1 is not out of harmony with the trend of scientific information.

Let us now note the situation when we bring together all that we have said in the previous pages. Gen. 1: 1 affirms that a great and powerful God created the universe. The unity of the universe is here indicated which is verified by modern science. No time element is here indicated other than the phrase, "in the beginning." Up till the nineteenth century men were aware only of so-called metaphysical or theological proofs for creation. If there were any traces of scientific proof in teleology or of the dependence of the universe upon something other than itself, these traces were obliterated either by Darwinism or by the scientific rationalism of the nineteenth century. But now the situation has radically changed. A good number of competent philosophers or scientists have asserted that teleology is not undercut by Darwin but rests on grounds that are impossible to undercut. The environment might form or mould an organism or act through selection as a creative agency, but no such relations are sustained on the inorganic level.

Added to this are the data which point to an original state of the now known order of things at about four or five billion years ago.[23] Thus, acceptance of creation, while not as yet thoroughly compelling in a scientific sense, is nonetheless on far surer grounding than it has been in the history of science. There is still no statement in science or philosophy as satisfying as the opening verse of the Bible with reference to the origin of the universe. As Lincoln Barnett writes:

> Man has always postulated a Creation, and Genesis speaks with universal accents in its mighty opening phrases . . . In its assault on these uttermost questions modern cosmogony impinges on the ancient realm of religion. The striking fact is that today their stories seem increasingly to converge. And every mystery that science resolves points to a larger mystery beyond itself.[24]

III. THE LONG DAY OF JOSHUA

One of the most widely known and controversial passages in the Bible is the so-called long day of Joshua recorded in Joshua 10. There are four interpretations made to explain this remarkable phenomenon. These interpretations divide over two major decisions. First, we must regard the language as either poetical or literal; second, we must decide whether Joshua asked for more sunshine or for less sunshine.

A. The first interpretation is that the command of Joshua to the sun and moon is poetical.[25] Cooke writes:

> It is better to recognize frankly that the verses are poetry and must be understood as poetry. A literal interpretation cannot avoid forcing an unnatural sense on the language.[26]

It is argued that the people of those days wove astronomy into their speech far more than we do as exhibited by (i) the reference in Judges 5: 20 when Deborah and Barak sing that the stars fought against Sisera, and (ii) the presence of astronomical pictures in prophetic passages as for example in Joel 2: 10, 30–31. The cry of Joshua was then a cry for help and strength. His cry was answered with renewed vigour in his soldiers who then fought so valiantly and were so refreshed that they did a day's work in half a day, and it seemed to them that the day had actually been lengthened.

But if this poetical interpretation be rejected as not doing justice to the text, we must next decide the exact nature of Joshua's command. Was he in a situation where he needed more time, and hence more daylight, to defeat thoroughly the enemy? Or were his soldiers wearied from the sun and in need of relief from its burning heat? If we take the former interpretation we have an actual prolongation of sunlight as the miracle intended; if the latter, the miracle intended is the cessation of sunlight so that the soldiers would be refreshed by shade supernaturally provided.

B. If we accept the miracle as one of the prolongation of light then we may take as one alternative that God stopped the sun or the earth and the moon.[27] By stopping the sun for a period of time sufficient daylight would then be available so the enemy could be pursued and defeated. This, I suppose, is what most interpreters have taken as the meaning of the passage. Sanden apparently supports this interpretation in his recent work.[28]

Serious objections have been brought against this theory since we have greatly increased our knowledge of physics and astronomy. The disturbances on the earth and the solar system would have been enormous. That God *could* do it and keep the solar system and universe together will not be debated by those who admit the omnipotence of God. But that God *would* do it, and that the text demands it, are yet further problems that a reference to the sheer omnipotence of God does not settle. Most students of this problem feel that the record does not call for a miracle of such gigantic proportions.

C. Another alternative we may adopt, if we wish to maintain that the need of Joshua was for more daylight, is to assert that the sun and moon kept on their way, but through a miracle of refraction or through a supernaturally given mirage the sun and moon *appeared to be out of their regular places*. Such an interpretation allows for the solar system to keep on its way, yet provides Joshua with the needed light, and maintains the supernatural character of the record. This is the view advocated by Rendle Short and Butler.[29] Short cites with approval A. F. Fleming's article in the *Proceedings of the Physical Society* (1914, p. 318) that it was a miracle of refraction. He also observes that every day the sun is seen four seconds after it sets, due to the refraction of its light. In a most fascinating article Butler reviews for us the various types of mirages, gives some examples, and the scientific explanations. His own interpretation is that it was a supernaturally given mirage.

> [It was] a special and rare mirage in the Earth's atmosphere which is similar to one or more of the natural mirages, but is of a magnitude, altitude, and character that would be the result of a divine miracle only, and therefore produced for some important purpose.[30]

The miracle did not occur at noontime but late in the afternoon,

giving more daylight for further battle.   He bolsters his view that
this was a supernaturally given mirage by telling us how many
drastic things would happen on the earth if the earth stopped spin-
ning on its axis.

There are two other matters that have been urged as evidence
for a lengthened day and this material the author has not been able
to track down nor confirm to his own satisfaction as to their accuracy or validity.   First, there are Egyptian, Chinese, and Hindu
reports of a long day.   Short makes nothing more than a passing
reference to this.   Harstad, *The Bible Is Reliable,* also makes mention
of these legends.   Second, there is the claim made by Harstad,
Black (*Bible and Science*), and Rimmer (*The Harmony of Science and
Scripture*) that it is common knowledge among astronomers that
one full day is missing in our astronomical calculations and that
Prof. Pickering of the Harvard Observatory traced it back to the time
of Joshua.   Maunder of Greenwich and Totten of Yale are then
supposed to have taken it right back to the time of Joshua, practically
to the year and day.   Then Totten added to this the 10° [*sic*] of
Ahaz' dial to round out the full day.   This I have not been able to
verify to my own satisfaction.[31]

D. Maunder has argued that the request of Joshua was not for
more time but for release from the heat of the day.   He has set
forth his theory in considerable detail in ISBE, "The Battle of
Beth-Horon" (I: 446–449), and in JTVI, "Joshua's Long Day" (53:
120–148, 1921; reprinted JASA, 3: 1–20, Dec., 1951).   He attempts
to prove that Joshua did not ask the sun to stand still but to be
silent, *i.e. keep from shining.*   What Joshua's men needed was refreshment from a burning sun.   Maunder claims that the sun was
overhead at noontime heat and that the moon was on the horizon.
In answer to Joshua's petition God sends a hailstorm which has
the double effect of refreshing his own soldiers and harming the
enemy.   Under such refreshment the soldiers of Joshua did a
day's march in half a day and so reasoned that the day had been
prolonged.   The march of thirty miles to Makkedah was one day's
march and, having covered it in half a day, they reasoned they had
been on the road a whole day.   Maunder undergirds his argument
with various astronomical, geographical, exegetical, and historical
data, the details of which will be found in the articles cited.

A. L. Shute in a remarkable article agrees with this interpretation of Maunder.   He believes the miracle was not a prolongation
of light, but a cessation of light for the refreshment of the soldiers.
But he differs in what the expression "hasted not to go down for
a whole day" means.   Maunder took it to mean that the soldiers
were so refreshed they did a day's march in half a day and so they
figured the day had been lengthened.   But Shute argues from the

etymology of the words of the text that the expression means that the sun did not come out from the clouds till very late in the afternoon. It was cloudy all afternoon and then, just before setting, the sun burst forth again and shone upon the battlefield.[32]

Rimmer's treatment of the subject is confusing because he changes theories in the midst of exposition and so ends with an interpretation that is self-contradictory. In the first place, he accepts Maunder's interpretation that the miracle was that of getting relief from the heat of the day, not in protracting the day. Without documentation he uses the identical data presented by Maunder in the ISBE article. Although it is possible that he arrived at it by independent research or through sources common to both men, it is rather improbable in view of the many similarities between the chapter in Rimmer's book and the data in the ISBE article. But with no documentation, final judgment must be suspended. However, following along with Maunder's explanation for a while, he then switches to the theory that the time was prolonged and makes "be still" mean "go slow." That is to say, he accepts both the Maunder idea that the sun was to be darkened and the traditional notion that time was to be delayed. There was certainly the refreshment from the storm in any case. But either the command of Joshua was to give more time or get relief from the heat. Rimmer makes it both. It was to get relief from the heat and then to slow down the sun. So he concludes his article with the reference to Totten, putting together one day from (i) Joshua's long day and (ii) the retreating shadow of the dial of Ahaz.

There are then, in summary, three live possibilities as to the interpretation of Joshua's long day. Either the language was poetic and the miracle was the physical invigoration of Joshua's soldiers; or it was a supernatural refraction of the rays of the sun and moon, thus giving the soldiers more time (by refraction or mirage); or it was a supernaturally induced thunderstorm giving the soldiers relief from the burning heat. The details may be found in the literature cited. All we need assert is that evangelicalism is not embarrassed for want of a rationale of the long day of Joshua, and even though the author sides with Maunder he would not feel embarrassed if any of the other interpretations was proved to be correct.[33]

IV. THE DIAL OF AHAZ

The return of the shadow ten degrees on the dial of Ahaz (Isa. 38 and II Kings 20) is much like the problem of Joshua's long day. Isaiah comes to Hezekiah when Hezekiah is sick and informs him

that God has heard his prayer. He may ask for the shadow on
the sun-dial to go forward or backwards, or up or down. Part
of the problem here is to determine what sort of sun-dial is meant.
There have been three suggestions. (i) It was a hollowed-out
hemisphere with lines drawn on the inside so that the shaded part
would intersect the various lines and roughly indicate the time of
the day. Pictures of these will be found in various Bible dictionaries. (ii) It was a pillar with steps around it and as the sun moved
across the heavens the shadow of the pillar would fall on different
steps, thus giving a rough estimate of the time of day.[34] (iii) It
was a series of steps leading from east to west. As the sun sank
in the west the shadow would come down the steps. A glance
at the shadow on the steps would indicate how much daytime was
left.[35]

The intention of the phenomenon is obvious. For the shadow
to go ten degrees more on its usual way would not be so mani-
festly supernatural as for the shadow to retreat. A passing cloud
could cause the entire staircase or sun-dial to be overshadowed in
a minute. But for the shadow to retreat would take miraculous
intervention. It is for this latter miracle that Hezekiah asks.
There are several possible interpretations.

A. We may presume that the sun actually backed up in its tra-
jectory to shed more daylight on the ten steps or dial. This was
Rimmer's theory as he expounded it in connexion with the long
day of Joshua. Isa. 38: 8 reads: "So the sun turned back on the dial
the ten steps by which it had declined" (RSV). In actuality all
this verse teaches is that the sunlight fell on the ten steps. If we
take Rimmer's view we are faced with the enormous problem of
accounting for all the disturbances in the machinery of the heavens.
II Chron. 32: 31 apparently restricts the phenomenon to the land
of Palestine. Again, it is not a problem as to whether God could
do it, but whether this is the best interpretation of all the facts
involved.

B. The theory of Butler[36] is that the miracle was a "supernatural
superior mirage of the sun." Lateral images have been known to
shift objects ninety degrees. Butler tells of Martin, one of the
round-the-world fliers of 1924, who crashed his plane in Alaska
because a lateral image moved a mountain ninety degrees out of
place! So, Butler reasons, a superior image of ten degrees would
be no great phenomenon.

C. Annie S. D. Maunder and E. W. Maunder have concurred
in the interpretation of the sun-dial of Ahaz as consisting of a series
of steps (which Josephus teaches in his *Antiquities of the Jews,* X, 2,
1).[37] E. W. Maunder considers it to have been a miracle of lighting
up the steps, and that is all. There is no known astronomical

miracle which will account for it.   Annie Maunder thinks it was
the Shekinah Glory which appeared and lighted up the steps.

Here again are two or three possibilities that are credible interpretations of a possible event (and we think actual) unless the supernatural itself is an embarrassment.   Personally, we feel that E. W.
Maunder's interpretation is the best.

V. THE STAR OF BETHLEHEM

In Matt. 2: 1–11 we have the record of the star which the Magi
followed.   The details as to who the Magi were and the proposed
theological significance of the star we leave to the commentators
and theologians.   Our concern is with the relationship of the star
to the science of astronomy.   The details about the star are: (i)
The Magi saw the star in the east (*en tē anatolē*), which some take to
mean the eastern sky and others the rising of the star.   They called
it *his* star, the *his* (*autou*) being emphatic in its order in the sentence.
(ii) Herod learns of the time (*ton chronon*) of its appearance, so it was
not a customary sight but something that so came into existence as
to be datable.   (iii) The star disappears and then reappears to the
wise men and they recognize it as the identical star they saw in the
east.   It was going before them (*proēgen,* imperfect active) until
(*eōs*) it came and stood over (*epanō*) the place where the child was.
(iv) Then Matthew records that upon seeing the star again the
Magi were exuberant with joy (*echarēsan charan megalēn sphodra,* v. 10).
(v) Next, they were able to go to the very house where the child
was (*elthontes eis tēn oikian,* v. 11).

Those who do not believe in the divine inspiration of Scripture
write this off at the start as legendary, or if the wise men actually
came, there was nothing supernatural in any of the circumstances.
Olmstead considers it a Babylonian, not a Jewish story.[38]   The
language he finds to be Akkadian in point of reference.   Matt. 2: 7
is the technical Akkadian for the rising of the planet.   To see the
star in the east means to see it at its rising.   The going before the
Magi refers to the nightly shift of the planet.   The standing still
over the house is when the star reaches a point of opposition when
"to the naked eye for about four days the planet does not appear
to change its position in the celestial vault."   For those who take
the narrative seriously there are several possibilities.

The first decision is to decide if the phenomenon was genuinely
astronomical or a very special creation of God.   Those who consider it genuinely astronomical have suggested that it was a comet,
a nova, or a conjunction of planets.   The theory of a comet has
little support if for no other reason than that such a tremendous

display would have attracted far more attention. The theory that it was *Nova Cassipeiae* must be rejected, as this is a northern star and the wise men would have travelled to Palestine with the star at their backs!

The most popular view of the phenomenon, first suggested by Kepler, is that the star was a conjunction of Jupiter and Saturn in the constellation Pisces in 7 B.C.

> The two planets went past each other three times, came very near together, and showed themselves all night long for months in conjunction with each other, as if they would never separate again.[39]

From the east Jupiter and Saturn would appear to hang right over Jerusalem. This theory was given considerable undergirding and support by Ideler of Berlin. However, it has been criticized by Pritchard in *Smith's Bible Dictionary,* as well as in the article on "Star" in MS, and by E. W. Maunder, "Star of Magi," ISBE, V, 2849. For example, the same conjunction occurred fifty-nine years before with no stir among the astrologers or Magi. The planets do not actually come together so as to appear as one star. Ideler had to postulate that to weak eyes they would appear as one. Actually the two stars (planets) do not come closer than two times the diameter of the moon.

However, a most interesting interpretation of this is given by Notz.[40] The Magi were astrologers who had worked out a whole series of beliefs about the stars. The rising of a star meant birth. The sun stood for a king, but in that the sun was not seen at night its place was taken by Saturn and Jupiter. Hence, the rising of these stars meant the birth of a king. Now, in that they rose in the westward constellation of Pisces, the astrologers would take this to mean that a king had been born in Palestine.

> The unusually bright heliac rising of the royal star Jupiter, coinciding with Saturn, must have been considered as forecasting the birth of a great king.''

For whatever value such late information is worth Notz cites the opinion of a Jewish savant, Abarbanel, (born 1437 A.D.) that a conjunction of Saturn and Jupiter in Pisces signified the Messiah to Jewish astrologers, and that in the Middle Ages astrologers generally interpreted Pisces as the constellation of the Jewish nation. The wise men, seeing the phenomenon, would then travel to Judea and ask where the great king had been born.

Maunder, in the article cited *supra,* defends the theory that at first the star was a nova. As an evening star it would appear in the west and guide the wise men to Judea. It would keep moving toward the sun and at last get lost in the rays of the sun. The wise men would then be compelled to wait till it reappeared on the other side of the sun. But what they saw the second time was not the nova but Venus. In clear daylight it takes an astronomically trained eye to pick out Venus. However, if one were to look into a well with Venus straight overhead, Venus would be very apparent. Now, writes Maunder, there is a tradition that the Magi knew they were in the city of the Messiah because they looked into a well at midday when they were drawing water and saw the star overhead. They investigated about any newborn baby and found the right one. The star they saw in the well was Venus.

The critical issue here is the apparent *guiding motion* of the star. Was the guidance of the star general or specific? Box defends the position that the guidance of the star was general.[42]

[The expressions about its guidance are not] intended to be understood literally. It is merely a poetical description of the illusion which makes it appear that a luminous body keeps pace and maintains its relative position with the movement of the observer.

If this be the case then the most likely solution to the star of Bethlehem would be the conjunction theory or the nova theory.

However, if the language be more strictly followed, no known astronomical phenomenon could account for a star as near as this star to indicate even the house where Jesus was. Such a notable event would certainly be noticed in extra-Biblical writings, and a star so close would have scorched the populace to death for hundreds of square miles around. The only recourse, if we take the language strictly, is to follow the ancient Patristic interpretation and assert that it was a special luminous manifestation, the sole purpose of which was to guide the Magi to Bethlehem. This was advocated by Augustine in ancient times and Wordsworth in modern times, and we take the language strictly, and so we agree with this interpretation. We believe that it was a special manifestation for the birth of Jesus and that it was seen only by the wise men. Further, we agree with Maunder that the knowledge and meaning of the star was given to the Magi supernaturally, and was not arrived at in any other way—although we do admit that Notz's interpretation is very tempting.[43]

We have now reviewed the major interactions of astronomical science with the Bible and have found two things: (i) the general astronomical remarks of the Bible are chaste, non-postulational, and free from the usual mythological and astrological elements which corrupt all pre-scientific astronomy; and (ii) for those supernatural events with reference to astronomical matters there are one or more credible, reasonable interpretations which should cause no embarrassment to any man with a scientific mentality but also with Christian convictions.

NOTES

1. Vol I, pp. 300–316. We have checked numerous dictionaries and encyclopaedias and this is far superior to all others. Next best, although very sceptical in tone, was T. G. Pinches, "Astronomy," MS, I, 191–194.

2. *Op cit.,* I, 301.

3. *Ibid.,* p. 302.

4. *Ibid.,* p. 303.

5. "The gospel in the stars" idea was greatly popularized by Joseph A. Seiss's work, *The Gospel in the Stars; Or Primeval Astronomy* (1884). Seiss writes of Miss Rolleston: "A more valuable aid to the study of the subject as treated in this volume is Frances Rolleston's *Mazzaroth; or, The Constellations*—a book from an authoress of great linguistic and general literary attainments, whom Providence rarely favoured for the collection of important facts and material, particularly as respects the ancient stellar nomenclature," p. 7. Miss Rolleston led Seiss astray, and Seiss numerous other popular writers. Moral: be careful in making close identifications with Providence and the works of men—and women.

6. Maunder, *op. cit.,* p. 312.

7. T. G. Pinches, *op. cit.,* rejects this association with Nimrod as based on worthless tradition, p. 192.

8. H. W. Robinson, *Inspiration and Revelation in the Old Testament* (1946), p. 21. However, C. M. Walsh, *The Doctrine of Creation* (1910) argues that emanation is not incongruous with the Bible and is the only intelligible theory of creation, pp. 125–126.

9. J. W. Burgon, *Inspiration and Interpretation* (1905), p. 25. Italics are his. Wilhelm Vischer has strongly expressed himself that the word *bara* means *creatio ex nihilo,* but is challenged by R. J. Wilson who cites to the contrary Skinner, Driver, Bennett and Peake. But Wilson *et al.* miss the point of Burgon. Cf. R. J. Wilson, "Wilhelm Vischer on 'God Created,'" *The Expository Times,* 65: 94–95, December, 1953.

10. James Jeans, *The Mysterious Universe* (revised edition, 1944), p. 160.

11. James Jeans, *Physics and Philosophy* (1944), pp. 174, 190.

12. *The Mysterious Universe,* p. 186. Allen completely misunderstands Jeans in calling the universe an illusion. Philosophically speaking Jeans defends *mentalism* (a form of idealism) which does not reduce the universe to an illusion nor does it deny the reality of the universe. It affirms that the universe is ideal not material. Frank Allen, "The Witness of Physical Science to the Bible," *Modern Science and Christian Faith* (2nd edition, 1950), pp. 280–82.

13. W. Fulton, "Teleology," ERE, XII, 215–232.

14. F. S. C. Northrop, *Science and First Principles* (1931), p. 176 ff.

15. F. R. Tennant, *Philosophical Theology* (1937), II, Chapter IV.

16. *Ibid.,* p. 87.   For a strict philosophical analysis of cosmic teleology and a shrewd defence, Tennant is, to this writer, unsurpassed.

17. J. E. Boodin, *Cosmic Evolution* (1925), p. 22.

18. *Ibid.,* p. 33.

19. W. M. Smart, *The Origin of the Earth* (1951), p. 235.

20. Delbert Eggenberger, "Methods of Dating the Earth and the Universe," JASA, 3: 1–3, March, 1951 (Dr. Kulp has suggested some changes in these figures). Cf. also, Roy Allen, "The Evaluation of Radioactive Evidence on the age of the Earth," JASA, 4: 11–20, December, 1952; H. D. Holland, "Recent Concepts of the Origin and Evolution of the Earth," JASA, 4: 23–28, December, 1952; and *A Symposium on the Age of the Earth* (edited by Kulp; contributors being Ramm, Icke, Everest, Rex, Lammerts, and Stoner, 1948).   This symposium contains an excellent bibliography of the present scientific knowledge of the radioactive method of dating the strata of the earth.   For the dating of the age of the universe from astrophysical studies being now set at five billion years, cf. George Gamow, "Modern Cosmology," *Scientific American,* 190: 54–63, March, 1954.

21. A. S. Eddington, *The Nature of the Physical World* (1929), p. 64 ff.

22. R. A. Millikan, *Science and Life* (1924), pp. 27–28.

23. Reviewing the evidence for the age of the earth from radio-activity, salt in the ocean, stellar, combustion, and galactic movements, Lincoln Barnett concludes: "all indicate a beginning, a creation in a fixed time." *Life,* 33: 89, December 8, 1952.

24. *Ibid.,* p. 85.   "Perhaps, here, we may ask legitimately if in probing, in the deepest sense, the mystery of Creation science has *really* been more successful than the poetic expounder of Hebrew cosmogony; the answer seems to be emphatically 'No,'" is the belief of one of England's greatest living astronomers, W. M. Smart, *The Origin of the Earth* (1951), p. 8. Italics are his.   George Gamow indicates that the figure reached by the geologists and physicists for the age of the earth (five billion years) is now the same as determined by astrophysicists for the age of the universe. The two independent means of calculation converge.   Gamow states that the phenomenon of retreating galaxies points to a time-series beginning five billion years ago beyond which we cannot go.   He does not admit creation in so many words.   "Modern Cosmology," *Scientific American,* 190: 54–63, March, 1954.

25. So Fay in LANGE, and apparently the view of Davis-Gehman in *The Westminster Dictionary of the Bible,* "Sun," pp. 583–84.

26. G. A. Cooke, CB., p. 91.

27. Ecclesiasticus 46: 4 and Josephus, *Antiquities of the Jews,* V, 1, 17, favour the lengthening of the day.

28. O. E. Sanden, *Does Science Support Scripture?* (1951), pp. 63–64; R. A. Torrey, *Difficulties in the Bible* (1907) believes that the sun was slowed down, p. 53. For a variety of other minor views see "Joshua," MS, IV: 1025–1032.

29. A. R. Short, *Modern Discovery and the Bible* (1942), p. 117. J. Lowell Butler, "Mirages are Light Benders," JASA, 3: 1–18, December, 1951.

30. Butler, *op, cit.,* p. 9. S. Kinns, *The Harmony of the Bible with Science* (1881), p. 475, believes that it was a miracle of refraction and observes that in the polar regions the sun is seen for several days after it has actually gone below the horizon.

31. Harstad, Rimmer, and Black give 40 minutes as the time reversed on the sun-dial, but Butler gives 80 minutes. *Op. cit.,* p. 13. Dr. Kulp has tried to check this theory at Yale and in England, and has found nothing to verify it.

32. A. Lincoln Shute, "The Battle of Beth-Horon," BS, 83: 411–431, 1927.

33. Robert Dick Wilson accepts the view of Maunder apparently with no knowledge of Maunder's view. Wilson shows that the words used in the Joshua account are technical astronomical words in their Babylonian counterparts. The root DM in Babylonian astronomy meant "to darken," and "in the midst" meant "in the half of." The prayer of Joshua was a prayer for darkness, not for the prolongation of the day. He concludes: "I confess to a feeling of relief, as far as I myself am concerned, that I shall no longer feel myself forced by a strict exegesis to believe that the Scriptures teach that there actually occurred a miracle that involves so tremendous a reversal of all the laws of gravitation." "What Does 'The Sun Stood Still' Mean?" *Moody Monthly*, 21: 67, October, 1920.

34. So W. S. Caldecott, "Ahaz," ISBE, I, 81–82.

35. So article on "Dial," MS.

36. Butler, *op. cit.,* p. 13.

37. Annie S. D. Maunder, "The Shadow Returning on the Dial of Ahaz," JTVI, 64: 83–101, 1932 (reprinted in JASA, 3: 21–32, September, 1951). E. W. Maunder, "Dial of Ahaz," ISBE, II, 841–842.

38. "Star," WD, p. 580.

39. "Star," MS, IX, 991. This article contains the basic bibliography on this question as discussed in the nineteenth century. Trench's important work, *The Star of Bethlehem*, we have not been able to locate.

40. William Notz, "Star of Bethlehem," BS, 73: 537–545, 1916.

41. *Ibid.,* p. 543. Other interesting works he mentions are H. H. Kritzinger, *Der Stern der Weisen* (1911); F. X. Steinmetzer, *Der Stern von Bethlehem* (1913); and G. H. Voigt, *Die Geschichte Jesu und Der Astrologie* (1911).

42. G. H. Box, "Star," *Dictionary of Christ and the Gospels,* II, 675. Cf. also S. J. Andrews, *The Life of Our Lord* (revised edition, 1891,

pp. 6 ff) for a review of the problem and its bearing on the date of the birth of our Lord.

43. E. W. Maunder, "Star of the Magi," ISBE, V, 2848–2849.   C. R. Lenski, *The Interpretation of Matthew* (1943), argues too that it was no known star "but a miraculous phenomenon, vouchsafed to the magi by God in order to lead them to Jesus," p. 60.

CHAPTER VI

GEOLOGY

I. INTRODUCTION

GEOLOGY deals in particular with the history of the crust of the earth. It is the scientific effort to recover the past of the rock formations of the earth. The majority of practising geologists believe that about three billion years ago the surface of the earth was in a molten condition. It gradually solidified and cooled off, eventually forming land masses, oceans, and atmosphere. Physical and chemical conditions operating over vast periods of time produced the record of the rocks. This vast period of time is divided by geologists into *eras, periods,* and *epochs.* For example we are now living in the Cenozoic Era or the age of mammals; in the Cenozoic Period or the age of new forms; and in the Recent Epoch. Although there is no exact verbal agreement by all geologists as to their terminology, there is a wide agreement. As I write I have a British and an American geological chart before me and the differences are of no great moment.

The geologists date the beginning of the earth four to five billion years ago. The period in which fossils of the major forms of animal life suddenly appear is called the Cambrian Period, dated about 500 million years ago. Two-thirds to three-fourths of all geologic time passed before this period. Evidence for simple plant life goes back at least one billion years ago, and recently Barghoorn of Harvard, and Tyler of the University of Wisconsin, claim to have found fossil algae and fungi dating back to two billion years ago. The next observation is that the fossil record reveals a complexity of life passing upward through all the various forms of life till it reaches the higher vertebrates and finally man. We are not trying to simplify geology nor write a treatise on it at this point but trying to present the most general scope of the geological record.

Looking in the pages of Holy Scripture we find Gen. 1: 1 declaring the creation of the heaven and the earth; Gen. 1: 2 stating that the earth was in an unformed condition. In Gen. 1: 3 ff. we have a narration of six days in which the earth is formed, and plant, fish, bird, and mammal life is created, consummated by the creation of man. There is no date nor time element in the record except the expression "in the beginning." The account is simple, brief, majestic, and monotheistic.

The central problem is: If we accept the divine inspiration of Holy Scripture, what are we to think of the relationship between the story geologists tell and the one the Bible tells? In order to be fair to all opinions and to present part of the historical struggle with this problem we shall pass in review some of the outstanding views of the relationship between Genesis and geology. We must decide what to think of the Genesis record and the geological record. Before we commence our discussion one thing must be kept in mind. We must realize precisely what the Bible says and cannot say; and what science says and cannot say. Due to the very nature of the Biblical language and the very nature of the situation it is difficult to disentangle acts of immediate or direct creation from mediate or progressive or indirect creation. This means that *reverent* science will admit the creatorship of God, the activity of God in Nature, and the validity of a teleological aspect to Nature. This also means that *intelligent* faith will *grant ample room for the legitimate inquiries of science* and will not theologically dogmatize outside of its domain. The details of creation can be told only by the co-operative efforts of the theologian and the scientist.[1] Furthermore, evangelicals must grant wide latitude among themselves as they seek out possible interpretations of the Scriptural and geological accounts. For as Pohle observes:

> Since the true interpretation of the Hexaemeron with regard to the origin of the universe is uncertain, theologians and scientists are free to adopt whatever theory they prefer, provided only it be reasonable and moderate, and not evidently opposed to Scripture.[2]

Before we begin our actual discussion of this problem let us note the wonderful tribute paid to Gen. 1 by one of the world's greatest living archaeologists:

> The account of Creation is unique in ancient literature. It undoubtedly reflects an advanced monotheistic point of view, with a sequence of creative phases so rational that modern science cannot improve on it, given the same language and the same range of ideas in which to state its conclusions. In fact, modern scientific cosmogonies show a disconcerting tendency to be short-lived and it may be seriously doubted whether science has yet caught up with the Biblical story.[3]

II.   CREATION: THE SIX DAYS

A. *Naïve-literal view*. The majority of Christian people have believed that the world was created about 4000 B.C., in six literal days. Such a view would be prompted by the simplicity of the record coupled with a complete ignorance of the data of science. It must be kept firmly in mind that the science of geology did not reach a state of maturity till the nineteenth century. William Smith, the founder of English geology, died in 1839, and Lyell, the great systematizer of geological knowledge, died in 1875. Although most evangelical Christians have long ago given up the date of original creation as 4000 B.C. or so, many non-Christian scholars—even such as the famous Bertrand Russell and H. F. Osborn—suppose that conservatives believe in creation at 4004 B.C. The date of 4004 B.C. was tagged on to the Bible well before the founding of modern geological theory. This date goes back to the work of James Ussher (1581–1656), an Irishman and Archbishop of Armagh. Working with the genealogical tables in Genesis plus the other data of the Bible he deduced that there were about 4,036 years from the creation of the world to Christ. He followed through with a chronology for the entire Bible. These dates of Ussher have been almost canonized as they have been printed in many English Bibles as part of the sacred page for centuries. Lightfoot (1602–1675), famed Hebraist of Cambridge, followed through with Ussher's work and figured out that creation took place the week of October 18 to 24, 4004 B.C., with Adam created on October 23 at 9.00 a.m. forty-fifth meridian time. Brewster sarcastically remarks:

> Closer than this, as a cautious scholar, the Vice-Chancellor of Cambridge University did not venture to commit himself.[4]

Fossils, until modern times, were great mysteries to people, and many fantastic theories were propounded as to their meaning. For example, some said that God commanded the earth to bring forth life and as living forms came forth from the earth some got stuck behind rocks and there fossilized; or they were created by God, said others, to tempt our faith; or by the Devil to deceive us.[5] The writer himself had a man learned in the languages of the Bible and trained in the universities of two continents solemnly say to him that he believed the Devil created fossils to destroy our faith in the Word of God. Today, even among the strictest fundamentalist circles, such an opinion is an intellectual oddity. Others said that fossils were due to the plastic power in Nature, or from Nature's effort to produce something which was an abortive effort and never rose above the mineral level of existence. Still other theories were that they were products of fatty matter set into fermentation by heat; or products of lapidic juice or the seminal air or a tumultuous movement of terrestrial exhalations or sports of Nature.[6] Voltaire thought the fish fossils discovered in the mountains were fish skeletons thrown there by the Crusaders on their way

to Palestine.   Most Christians, however, thought fossils to be
relics of the flood of Noah, and this notion still has a wide hearing
in some circles.

White records the tragic case of Johann Beringer, a professor
in the University of Würzburg, who believed that fossils were
special stones hidden by God in Nature for His own glory.[7]   Certain students baked sham fossils out of clay and imitated plants,
reptiles and fishes.   But they even imprinted on some of them the
name of God and other inscriptions in Hebrew and Syriac.   Being
planted where Beringer hunted for fossils they were discovered by
Beringer.   With great joy he announced his find and at great cost
had a book printed with twenty-two plates of facsimiles of these
finds.   A premature exposure did not deter him, but when the book
was published its fraudulent contents were unmistakable even to
Beringer.   He spent his fortune in buying back these copies and
died in chagrin over it.

There is only one thing necessary to make impossible a view
which holds that creation was in one ordinary week about 4000 B.C.,
and that is to show that the earth has been here considerably longer
than that.   We have already indicated in our discussion of creation
that there is substantial evidence admitted by men of Christian faith
and scientific ability that the earth and the universe is at least four
billion years old.   We shall discuss radio-active dating of the rocks
in more detail later but for the present we observe that radio-active
methods of dating rocks in the earth yield figures running from
five million years for the Pleistocene epoch up to 500,000,000 years
for the Cambrian.[8]   Now it used to be argued against the geologists
that they dated the rocks by the fossils, and the fossils by the rocks,
and so argued circularly.[9]   But with radio-active methods—as well
as many other—such a traditional accusation is no longer valid.
Although there is some difference between the older methods of
dating strata and the radio-active results the general order and proportion of time are about the same.

For those unfamiliar with radio-activity a word of simple explanation is in order.   A material is radio-active if it gives off small
atomic particles which fly away from the active substance at great
velocity.   Radium and uranium are the most commonly known of
such substances.   The atomic bomb and allied studies in atomic
physics have made the public very conscious of radio-active phenomena.   As uranium gives off high-speed particles it disintegrates
till eventually it becomes lead.   The speed of this process of disintegration is known and is the same no matter what temperatures
or pressures the substance is subjected to.   Pressures and temperatures have been applied in the laboratory to these substances of
greater intensities than are found in the crust of our planet, and

the process is neither accelerated nor retarded. Hence physicists can tell how long a sample of uranium has been disintegrating by finding out its atomic weight. For example, the number of inches the weights of a pendulum clock have fallen will indicate how long the clock has been running. By measuring how much petrol we have left in the tank we have an idea how many miles we have driven. By such similar methods of reasoning and calculation physicists can tell how old a uranium sample is and thereby get some idea of the age of the strata in which it was found. We trust that the learned reader has not been too greatly vexed by this over-simplification of the method of radio-active dating of rocks.

However, it is certainly obvious that if there is any truth at all in the time processes indicated by modern geology then creation at 4004 B.C. is an impossibility and we either must admit a straight contradiction between Genesis and geology or (i) try to overturn geology completely or (ii) seek a different interpretation of Genesis.[10] We believe the evidence of the antiquity of the earth from all geological methods of measurement to be overwhelming, and we certainly seek another interpretation of Genesis.

B. *Religious-only theory.* Another approach to the problem of Genesis and geology is to affirm that Genesis states the origin of the universe in religious or theological terms, and that it is the province of science to declare *how* it happened. Part of the spirit behind this theory is the conviction that all efforts at reconciliation between Genesis and geology have collapsed as, for example, was affirmed by H. E. Ryle when he wrote:

> No attempt at reconciling Genesis with the exacting requirements of modern sciences has ever been known to succeed without entailing a degree of special pleading or forced interpretation to which, in such a question, we should be wise to have no recourse.[11]

This view of Genesis is that Nature is the creation of a powerful, wise, and good God and with this much it is satisfied. The scientific view of Nature is the effort to find out the precise causes or factors or processes which brought Nature to her present state. This religious-only theory would assert that the theologian who tries to derive science from Genesis is as much in error as the scientist who sees nothing of God in Nature. It would assert that it is not necessary to try to harmonize geology and Genesis for it is impossible to do so with theological utterances on the one hand and scientific ones on the other. Scientifically considered Genesis is perhaps purified Babylonian cosmology; religiously it is inspired with typical religious insights of the Hebrews. Genesis is theologically a true view of Nature; but scientifically it is of no moment.

The virtue of this position is to remind us that Gen. 1 is primarily a *theological tractate*. Its perspective is theological. There are no secondary causes mentioned. The only causation stated is the omnipotent speech of God. We must never lose sight of the *theocentric* nature of Gen. 1, nor try to press its structure into a hard and fast scientific mould. The vice of the theory is that if this much concession is made to the view of science it will be difficult to maintain any theological validity for the record at all. Such theory smacks too much of deistic thinking. The Biblical view of Nature is such that God is *over, in* and *through* His creation. To have a consistent theism we must have theism constantly. The theological must definitely impinge upon the scientific in this problem. But when the theological and the scientific are separated as widely as the theory indicates, then it is not long before the theological is deemed irrelevant. If we can work without the theological then why need we ever have recourse to it? Therefore, such a sharp separation of the two as advocated in this theory is fatal to the well-being of the theory itself. It may make an apparent peace with geology but usually such a peace ends with the irrelevancy of theology, so that the very disease the theory seeks to avoid is the one to which it succumbs and by which it is destroyed.

C. *Flood geology.* In the sixteenth, seventeenth, and eighteenth centuries various investigators of geological data were bringing to light the fact that a world of animal and vegetable life was buried in the strata of the earth. The interpretation put upon these data was that these data represented the tell-tale results of the flood of Noah. The caves filled with skeletons of animals, the diluvia on the face of the earth, and the occurrence of fossils were all taken as proof of the flood. With the steady growth of geological science in the latter part of the eighteenth century and the early part of the nineteenth century, this interpretation had to be given up. Geologists showed that all the phenomena of the geological record could not have happened in one event, but that they represented forces at work over a great period of time. Flood geology is essentially a geology of catastrophe, and the evidence that much of the geological record was to be spread out over millions of years made a geology of catastrophe difficult if not impossible to maintain. As we shall see, the restitution or gap theory replaced the flood geology. But a new form of catastrophism appeared in the works of Cuvier and Agassiz. We shall review their works later, but now we shall pass on to the great revival of flood geology in the twentieth century. This revival was carried on principally by the Seventh-Day Adventist apologists and was termed the new diluvialism or the new catastrophism to distinguish it from the older views of Cuvier and Agassiz. Can the flood of Noah be the source of all geological phenomena and thus be the means of harmonizing Scripture with geological science?

One of the strangest developments of the early part of the twentieth century was that George McCready Price, a Seventh-Day Adventist with very limited professional training, became American fundamentalism's leading apologist in the domain of geology. Even this had a most peculiar quirk, because most fundamentalists accepted the gap theory as taught in *The Scofield Bible,* a theory which the Seventh-Day Adventists vigorously reject. At any rate, the influence of Price is staggering. In preparation for this book we searched through the issues of several decades of *Bibliotheca Sacra, The Bible Champion,* and *Christian Faith and Life.* These journals were the defenders of orthodoxy in those trying years. Price contributed articles to all of these journals in an unceasing stream, and Whitney also contributed many articles. It is not at all uncommon to find the most laudatory praise by fundamentalists of Price's *The New Geology* (1923). It forms the backbone of much of fundamentalist thought about geology, creation, and the flood. Byron Nelson's *The Deluge Story in Stone* and A. M. Rehwinkel's *The Flood* are deeply indebted to Price, and adopt his major premise. Another disciple of Price has been H. W. Clark, who expressed his views in *The New Diluvialism* (1946).

The flood geologists believe that the world was created not too long ago. Perhaps the earth itself might have been created millions of years ago, but at any rate the six days of Genesis deal with a not too distant past. At the flood God through direct or indirect means (such as an approaching astronomical body) flooded the earth and sent huge waves at a thousand miles an hour rushing over the surface of the waters. These waves picked up the various forms of life and carried them along, and then as the waves lost their velocity they deposited the mud, dirt, animals, and other debris as huge strata. Under the pressures of the water and other strata laid down on top of them the mud strata hardened into rock. The various strata with their fossil content represent the ecology (distribution) of plants and animals before the flood. Man, who fled to the highest hills, was caught last and so is found only in the highest strata of the earth. The geological strata represent the various waves of the flood and the plants and animals fossilized in them represent the part of the earth or level of the land swept over by the various waves. The strata of mud hardened into rock under the terrific pressures. What geologists have spread out over three billion years all took place during a flood of little more than a year's duration. Somebody is very sadly mistaken if the range of possibilities is from one year to three billion years.

The so-called strength of Price's work is his effort to poke holes into the uniformitarian geology of Lyell as it is taught in standard books on geology.[12]   We must be careful of a logical fallacy at this point.   To show the logical fallacies of another theory does not automatically prove ours to be right.   It is admitted that the geological record is not completely lucid, and that there are problems.   Suppose that 80 per cent of the geological record makes clear sense when interpreted from the Lyellian point of view, and that 20 per cent remains a problem to uniformitarian geology.   We have our choice of taking the 80 per cent as established and going to work on the 20 per cent; or, of taking the 20 per cent as normative, and trying to dissolve the 80 per cent.   Price adopts the latter procedure.   The author does not know what the actual percentages are, but he is sure that he is generous to Price in the choice of the above percentages.   If by analogy Price's principle were followed *in other sciences* it is obvious that chaos would result.   Medicine would be impossible of serious practice if doctors conducted their practice on the guidance obtained from the exceptions rather than from the averages.   Physics, chemistry, physiology and psychology would all be impossible.   Price is popular for one reason alone—that he strode forth like David to meet the Goliath of modern uniformitarian geology and that even though the giant has not fallen Price has been slinging his smooth stones for more than forty years.

Dr. J. L. Kulp has given this theory a very sharp criticism.[13] Due to the author's own lack of technical training in geology certain of Dr. Kulp's criticisms are beyond his grasp, but the main drift of them is as follows: Price has not had an adequate training in geology. He has had two years at Battle Creek College in classics and theology and a teacher's training course at the Normal School in New Brunswick.   The other writers in the Flood tradition are mostly men with no degrees listed, a few with an M.D., and one with a Ph.D.   Kulp concludes:

> None of these men have done any professional geologic field work such as mapping or studying paleontological or structural sequences.[14]

Four basic errors in flood geology are indicated by Kulp.   (i) The flood geologists confuse evolution with geology.   This is a very important point.   It is true that evolutionists appeal to the geological record for support, and that geologists presume evolution. But the geological record—its sequence and its time periods—can be constructed independently of the evolutionary hypothesis. Much fundamentalist opposition to both evolution and geology errs at this point.   It has been assumed that uniformitarian geology and biological evolution are logically related and that we cannot have one without the other. Evidently we can.

(ii) Flood geologists assume that we now live in a zoologically impoverished world. When we compare the number of forms represented by the fossils, and the number of forms alive today, we realize a tremendous number of them have dropped out of existence, and the flood geologists attribute this to the flood. But if these fossil forms were spread out from the Cambrian period till now our present earth population of animals is not in an impoverished state.

(iii) The flood geologists do not understand the physical and chemical conditions under which rocks are formed and later, under stress, folded.

(iv) Price wrote before some very significant geological laws were formed, but persists in teaching a theory of geology which is not possible in view of these subsequent discoveries.

Kulp affirms, and we believe correctly so, that uniformitarianism has been wrongly attacked by the hyper-orthodox. Confusing evolutionary biology with geological continuity they have felt it necessary to believe in catastrophism in geology, or discontinuity. To the contrary, the entire roll-call of earth sciences is built on the uniformitarian principle. These hyper-orthodox expositors, inadequately versed in the philosophy of science, opposed more than they ever should have when they objected to uniformitarianism in geology. To continue Kulp's exposition, the past is like the present because we can imitate the past in our laboratory.

Further objections from such knowledge against flood geology are:

(i) The amount of material carried by a stream of water varies with the sixth power of the velocity of the stream. There is little deposit far out on the continental shelf, where a few feet may represent thousands of years of deposits. Flood geology has no means of accounting for this.

(ii) Hedberg has shown that river mud needs at least one mile of sediment on top of it to form it into rock. Wherever we have this type of rock lithified we know that once upon a time it was a mile underground. Unusually long processes are necessary for mud to be formed into rock, be lifted to the surface of the earth, and then undergo a measure of weathering. Flood geology has no room in its theoretical structure for such a lengthy process as this.

(iii) The huge amount of material carried out of the geosynclines is of such proportions that it is impossible to account for the missing material by a flood of one year's duration.

(iv) It takes a hundred feet of loose vegetable matter to make one foot of coal. There was not enough vegetable matter in the entire world to make a tiny fraction of the coal beds of the earth at the time of the flood.   All the vegetation from the central United States multiplied by ten would not be adequate to supply coal for the thirty significant coal horizons of that region.   Further, most of the coal was actually formed by the successive growth of vegetation upon itself building up a great layer of material, but according to flood geology coal would have been formed by the deposit of debris.

(v) We may now observe the process of fossil formation which duplicates that which is known from past geological periods.   Further, the geologist does not reason in a circle by dating strata by the fossils, and then fossils by the strata.   The evidence for the ages of these strata is so monumental that any vestiges of reasoning in a circle are now eliminated.

(vi) In discussing orogeny or the science of mountain formation, Kulp shows that mountain formation can be duplicated in small-scale laboratory models.   A universal flood would have mixed everything up but the laboratory models using soft clay or shoe polish can duplicate earth formations which show that the current geological theories are on the right track and that Price is not. Further, the fact that many of these formations are made *without the presence of water* is fatal to Price's theory.   Kulp also shows how juvenile is Price's claim that thrust-faulting is a geologists' invention to save their tottering theory.

> 70 years of additional detailed mapping in the Canadian Rockies has thoroughly confirmed the thrust faults—on physical not paleontologic [fossil] grounds.[15]

(vii) Any genuine demonstration of a long period of time in some geological process would be fatal to flood geology, for flood geologists must account for all phenomena in a flood of one year's duration about three thousand years before Christ.   In the Yellowstone Park are two thousand feet of exposed strata which reveal eighteen successive forests wiped out by lava.   The individual forests had to mature, and then be covered with lava.   Before another forest could appear the lava would have to be weathered to form soil for trees to grow in.   The amount of time involved is far more than the few thousand years flood geologists are able to allow.   Gypsum and salt deposits are formed by the evaporation of sea water.   One thousand feet of water yields 0.7 feet of gypsum. The fastest evaporating body of water known is the Dead Sea which evaporates ten feet of water a year.   The fifteen hundred feet of gypsum in West Texas and New Mexico would then require 5 million feet of water evaporating over 500,000 years.   Here again flood geology is refuted, as it cannot allow this much time.   Finally, the data accumulating from radio-active dating of strata is too well established to be discounted by flood geologists. Flood geologists have done their best to disrupt this method and try to show that it is completely unreliable. It is not a matter of this method being 50 per cent wrong or even 75 per cent wrong. It must be over 99 per cent wrong. In fact if it were 99 per cent wrong (or one per cent right) it would still refute flood geology. Five million years is one per cent of the 500 million years of the Cambrian period.[16]

(viii) Finally, Kulp shows that the positive theory of Price, namely of these one-thousand-mile-an-hour tidal waves, cannot account for the geological structure of the crust of the earth.

We may add to this imposing list of objections one more which will be discussed at length later on, namely, the assumption of the flood geologists that the flood was universal. They must not only (i) tear up geology as taught and practised by the overwhelming majority of the world's trained geologists; (ii) throw the entire processes of geological formations into a flood of one year's duration; but (iii) they must also carry some of the unbearable problems of a world-wide deluge. It has been a matter of deep sorrow to this author to see how great and noble men like Dana and Dawson with their sound, Biblical and scientific approach to Genesis and geology have been ruled out of court or forgotten by the hyper-orthodox and their places taken over by apologists of the flood geology school. The opposition of the hyper-orthodox to the uniformitarian geology has blinded them to the absurdities of flood geology.

A work which all evangelicals who delve into these matters ought to consider is F. E. Zeuner, *Dating the Past: An Introduction to Geochronology* (third edition; 1952). Such a book simply demolishes much of Price's *The New Geology* (1923). Zeuner's book is a thorough compendium of all the methods known to geologists in dating strata. There are essentially seven: tree ring analysis valuable up to 3000 years; varved clay analysis reliable to 15,000 years; radio-carbon dating with a limit of 30,000 years; "per cent of equilibrium method" (a form of radium dating) serviceable to 300,000 years; solar radiation, good to a million years; typical geological methods (sedimentation, denudation, erosion, weathering, and chemical changes) used in all periods; and uranium and radio-active methods giving results up to 3 billion years. In Zeuner's work one will find the painstaking results of the works of geologists all over the world. Further, there is a genuine frankness in Zeuner and he frequently notes that some method is very unreliable, or that certain figures are just plain guesses. *But the intersection of data is fatal to the position of Price.* For example, the chart of the glacial periods conforms very closely to the chart of solar radiation.   Each chart was arrived at independently from the other.   When different researchers using different methods and working on different parts of the earth come to similar conclusions it is difficult to doubt that they are on the correct path.   It is impossible to conceive that the wealth of data in a book like Zeuner's is fictitious, and that the host of world-wide scientists quoted are all close to one hundred per cent wrong.

D. *Successive catastrophes*.[17]   Before geological phenomena were understood mankind could accept Creation as occurring in six literal days a few thousand years ago.   When geological phenomena became known and constituted a problem, these phenomena were accounted for by the flood of Noah.   Later, when the flood of Noah could no longer account for the data of geology, the restitution theory was invoked.   As this theory plays such a vital role in the twentieth century we defer exposition of it till later in this chapter.   However, the sheer request for time in the gap theory or restitution theory did not meet the problems presented by a steadily growing science.   New efforts had to be made to understand the geological record.   This was done by recourse to a *series* of floods or catastrophes with a *series* of new creations.   This solution was propounded by Cuvier, and then modified by Agassiz to keep up with the strides in geological knowledge.

Cuvier, one of the greatest names in the history of science, propounded a theory of successive floods.   He believed that ocean waters shifted about, covering first one territory then another. The flora and fauna would be buried under the drifting sands. When the waters had receded animals and vegetation would again migrate into the region.   Evidence of this on a limited scale has been demonstrated time and time again.   Finally, there was one big flood a few thousand years ago which prepared the world for the now existing geological conditions and flora and fauna.   Cuvier broke with the simple theory of Linnaeus and advocated the disappearance of forms due to these floods.   He also indicated clearly that fossil man was late and was not mixed in with the older fossils. The older fossils accordingly could not be counted as part of the evidence for the flood.

Criticism of Cuvier was maintained on the grounds that: (i) *certain* forms were caught in *certain* strata; whereas if the ocean waters came in, a regular cross section of life should have been caught; (ii) and if all of certain species were eliminated, the entire world would have had to be flooded.   If the entire earth had to be flooded for the elimination of certain species, then re-creation, not migration, accounts for the repopulation of the various tracts of the earth.   This was precisely what Louis Agassiz argued in the light of the problems of Cuvier's theory.   Successive creation would account for the suddenness of the appearance of species; sudden catastrophes would account for their disappearance.

Agassiz took the usual data of the flood and regulated it to glaciation. Agassiz realized that geological processes must take a vast period of time, for he calculated that the coral reefs of Florida took 200,000 years to form. Following Beaumont's *Systèmes de Montagnes* in which a certain theory of orogeny was propounded, Agassiz believed that there were sudden and short catastrophes which blotted out species and raised the mountains. This was followed by another creation and a long period of quiet and a slow building up of deposits. Agassiz less and less found himself able to make any sort of parallelism between Genesis and geology but, as Brewster observes, Agassiz is "the last great naturalist to believe in Special Creation."[18]

Of the two men Agassiz comes closer to the data of geology. Fossils do suddenly appear in the geologic strata. Cuvier's position could not account for the progression in the appearance of fossils. In neither case is there any close parallelism with the Genesis account. These men defend creationism rather than Genesis. Twentieth century hyper-orthodoxy has paid little attention to Cuvier or Agassiz.

E. *Local creation.* In the middle of the nineteenth century those informed in geological science gave up Noah's flood as a solution to the data of geology. We have already seen that some took refuge in the gap theory. But the gap theory soon proved to be inadequate to the problem. We noted the principle of successive catastrophes and creations of Cuvier and Agassiz to account for the geological puzzle. New theories were being constantly propounded and one of the most influential, though least successful, was that of *local creation*.

In a very splendid book, remarkable for its intellectual depth and frankness in facing facts, John Pye Smith (*On the Relation Between the Holy Scriptures and Certain Parts of Geological Science*, 1840) argues for a local creation in Gen. 1 as the method of harmonizing Genesis and geology. Maintaining an original creation as stated in Gen. 1: 1, he accepts the interpretation of the German scholar Dathe that Gen. 1: 2 should read, "But afterwards the earth became waste and desolate." In this connexion he argues that the earth means "that portion of the universe which the Supreme Lord has assigned for the habitation of mankind,"[19] since the term "earth" had no meaning for the Jews beyond a stretch of territory, and they did not have the faintest idea of the earth as a sphere. Hence:

[The six days of Genesis refer to the divine re-organization or rehabilitation of a portion of the earth] lying between the Caucasian ridge, the Caspian Sea, and Tartary, on the north, the Persian and Indian seas on the south, and the high mountain ridges which run, at considerable distances, on the eastern and western flank.[20]

The plants and animals created were those in connexion with man himself.

How does this reconcile Genesis and geology?   It does so, states Smith, by letting geology take over the main history of the earth in the matters of both time and space, and introduces a small variation in the near eastern world some few thousand years ago as a special act of God in keeping with the Biblical record.   Thus geology is given full and free status, and the supernatural is given its due in the remodelling of a small part of the earth.   Geologists cannot object to Genesis because Genesis is not talking of all the world or all of its history; neither can Genesis conflict with geology because it is dealing with a very limited territory which was re-created not too long ago.   Smith is very insistent that the geologist be given his full due, and his advice on this score is good advice to all who would write on Genesis and geology.   Speaking of those who believe that all the practising geologists are mistaken, he writes:

> Upon the former supposition it must appear a strange thing that the persons, who have given such distinguished proofs of their general ability, and of their acuteness of penetration in this particular department of scientific study, who possess the resources of those auxiliary sciences which are the best guides in physical inquiry, and the most stern checks on sanguine minds, to guard them against precipitance or inaccuracy in drawing conclusions—it must appear a strange thing, that such persons should labour under an obliquity of judgment so peculiar and so obstinate that they cannot see the just conclusions from premises which they have obtained by so much expense of time and fortune, of mental and bodily toil.[21]

The strength of this theory of Smith's is that Gen. 2 seems to argue for this very thing.   We shall argue similarly later on but with certain differences.   Smith identifies the earth of Gen. 1 with the Paradise of Gen. 2, and we do not.   The weakness of the theory is that it essentially cheapens Gen. 1.   The majestic language, the chaste and factual terminology, and the celestial-terrestrial scope of the passage lose so much of their import and force if restricted a small patch of the earth.   Rather than having the six majestic acts of creation of the world and all its life, we have a small scale remodelling job.

A second weakness is that it leaves the entire domain of the earth's history and its interpretation completely in a non-Christian or non-theistic setting.   If Gen. 1 deals solely with a local remodelling, what are we as Christians to say of the record of geology? Are we to say it is indifferent to Christian faith? How are we to stave off the geologist from swallowing up even the little bit of territory we have tried to remove out of his hands? We must reject this theory on the grounds that (i) it cheapens the creation account;[22] (ii) it leaves us with no Christian principle for the interpretation of geology; and (iii) its exegesis in connexion with the words "earth" and "was" is not sound, in our opinion.

F. *Pro-chronic or ideal time view.* In 1857 Philip Henry Gosse published *Omphalos: An Attempt to Untie the Geological Knot.* Gosse was a man learned in natural history and not a simpleton nor an arm-chair speculator. He argued that Nature is a circular process and therefore that creation must commence somewhere in the cycle. A building may be commenced from scratch at the foundation but buildings do not have a cyclical existence. You cannot create an organism from scratch. Because all organic life exists as a cycle, creation must start somewhere in the cycle, and hence the created life would appear as if it had already gone through the cycle up to the point where it was created. Gosse lists as his two fundamental theses that (i) all organic life moves in a cycle, and (ii) creation is a violent irruption into the cycle of Nature.[23] He asks what creation is and answers his own question:

> [Creation] is *the sudden bursting into a circle.* Since there is no one state in the course of existence, which more than any other affords a natural commencing point, whatever stage selected by the arbitrary will of God, must be an unnatural, or rather a preter-natural, commencing point.[24]

Omphalos is the Greek word for navel. Did Adam have a navel? Of course he did, argues Gosse. He was created at a given point of the circle of life and therefore was created as if he had gone through the entire cycle. If God created a tree, it would have rings in it. God could create a tree only at a point in its natural cycle.

Every object of creation has two times. That which is before time or instantaneous in coming into existence is *pro-chronic.* That which consumes time is *dia-chronic.* All processes during the course of the world since its creation are *dia-chronic.* All things at the moment of creation were *pro-chronic.* Gosse also uses the terms real time and ideal time. At the moment of creation Adam's *real* time was zero—actually he did not exist till the moment of creation. His *ideal* time was, say for purposes of illustration, thirty years old. A tree in the garden of Eden would appear fifty years old (its ideal time) whereas it had just been created (its real time).

How does this apply to geology? It means that the real time of the universe might be 6,000 B.C. or 10,000 B.C., whereas its *ideal* time might be in millions of years.   Fossils and geological processes refer then to *ideal* or *pro-chronic* time, not to real or historical time. Gosse is not trying to prove any specific date for creation, but he is trying to set a limit to what science can say.   If creation is an irruption into the cycle of Nature then we cannot reckon backward indefinitely.   Nor does this pro-chronic view of geology interfere with the work of the geologists.   The facts of geology remain unchanged and the geologist can do his work unhampered by the theologian.   The only word to the geologist from the theologian is to inform the geologist that he is working with ideal and not real time.[25]

Logically it is difficult to get around Gosse, for he claims that all the evidence for the reality of the fossils, geologic strata, are simply testimonies to the perfection of God's job of antiquating His universe.   Even Brewster misses this point in a most glaring example of failing to follow through the logic of the man he is criticizing. Brewster appeals to half-digested food in fossil finds, or foetuses in fossils as if these were real items, not ideal.   If God antiquated the earth He did a master job in catching the cycle *in situ,* as it were, catching such things as they are, just as Brewster describes them.

There is one commendable feature to Gosse, and even Brewster admits it, namely, that God at creation would have to make certain things appear older than they were.   Certainly in the nature miracles and healing miracles of Christ there would be a real time and an ideal time.   To obtain a calm lake one would have to go back several hours in the course of the weather and follow through the necessary changes from a storm to a calm.   Yet when our Lord spoke, those intervening changes were omitted.   So God in creation started Nature in a given point of a cycle.

The weakness of Gosse's theory is not that we can find some indications of real time, but in the thinness of the theory.   If the earth were perfectly antiquated then it would be impossible to tell the difference between (i) a world which actually went through long processes of aging, and (ii) a world which was *perfectly* antiquated. If the two are impossible of differentiation, common sense prefers (i) over (ii).   If we conduct our science and geology on the grounds of a world having gone through such a process, it would be rather absurd to affirm that it had not really gone through such a process. Such a scheme as Gosse propounds, clever as it is, is a tacit admission of the correctness of geology.   Better sense will state that the ideal time is the real time.   If this is done Gosse offers us no basis of the reconciliation of geology and Genesis and, therefore, we must look elsewhere.

G. *Creation-ruination-re-creation theory—or restitution theory, or gap*

theory.   As we have seen the theologians rested content with creation at 4004 B.C., till the geological studies disturbed this position.
The first theory of harmonization propounded was that all geological
data known at that time could be accounted for by the flood.   We
have seen how this theory was revived in the twentieth century
under G. M. Price.   But as the surface of the earth was studied and
deciphered it became apparent that a flood of one year's duration
could not account for the phenomena of the rocks.   Geologists
had come to the conclusion that these formations occupied thousands if not millions of years for their construction.   *What the
geologists needed was time*.   How could time be found in the Genesis
account?   It was the suggestion of the capable and brilliant Thomas
Chalmers that the time element could be found by a reconsideration
of Gen. 1: 2.   There was a creation (1: 1) followed by a catastrophe
(1: 2), in turn followed by a re-creation (1: 3, ff.).   All the *time* the
geologists needed could be found in Gen. 1: 2.   This theory became
the favourite one of twentieth century hyper-orthodoxy.

Although it has been claimed that the Fathers believed it and
some of the post-Reformation exegetes taught it, its great popularity
dates from the work of Chalmers.[26]   As early as 1791 Dathe
(*Pentateuch*) had argued that the *was* of Gen. 1: 2 should be translated
by *became*.   Other men who gave it standing and prestige were
Buckland (*Bridgewater Treatises*), Sedgwick (*Discourses on the Studies
of the University of Cambridge*), and Pratt (*Scripture and Science not at
Variance*).   If it was Chalmers who first vigorously advocated it
in modern times, it was the work of G. H. Pember (*Earth's Earliest
Ages*, first edition, 1876; frequently republished) which canonized it.
The gap theory was adopted by Scofield in his *Reference Bible* and
so accumulated to itself all the veneration and publicity of that
edition of the Bible.   Scofield ranked Pember (or whomever he
followed at this juncture) over Dana and Dawson, the two greatest
geologists of the nineteenth century in North America.   The gap
theory was espoused by Rimmer, who was hyper-orthodoxy's outstanding spokesman in matters of Bible-and-science till the time of
his death.[27]   As a result the gap theory has become the standard
interpretation throughout hyper-orthodoxy, appearing in an endless
stream of books, booklets, Bible studies, and periodical articles.
In fact, it has become so sacrosanct with some that to question it is
equivalent to tampering with Sacred Scripture or to manifesting
modernistic leanings.

Although the defenders of the gap theory have variations among
themselves in interpretation, the general features of the theory are
held in common by all.   The theory runs something like this:
God created a perfect world as recorded in Gen. 1: 1.   This world
was turned over to Lucifer, who conducted the Temple worship of

God located in a mineral Garden of Eden (Ezek. 28: 13 f.).   The exalted condition of Lucifer was too much for him and in seeking to exalt himself as a god, he and those who consorted with him fell and judgment was passed on them and the earth.   For countless millions of years the earth was left alone and during these years the various geological formations took place.   Some argue that the ugliness of the dinosaurs and the great bed of fossils emerging as vast cemeteries of the past indicate that a judgment for sin had been passed on the earth.   Somewhere around 4000 B.C. God *reconditioned* the earth in six literal twenty-four hour days.   Gen. 1 contains an original creation, a judgment and ruination, and then a re-creation.

This theory is supposed to harmonize Genesis and geology on the grounds of granting a vast period of time in Gen. 1: 2 for all the geological events to take place.   Scofield triumphantly announces:

> Relegate fossils to the primitive creation, and no conflict of science with Genesis cosmogony remains.[28]

In support of this theory we will note the arguments of Pember and Rimmer.   Pember, the more acute thinker of the two, argues that the Hebrew word *asah* does not refer to creation but to re-creation or making over.   The original creation was created; but the things of the six days are made, not created.[29]   *Tohu* and *bohu* (Gen. 1: 2, without form and void) can refer only to something once in a state of repair but now ruined.   These words, *tohu* and *bohu,* express "an outpouring of the wrath of God."[30]   The word *was* (Gen. 1: 2) should be translated "to be made" or "to become." Pember writes:

> Such a meaning is by far best for our context; we may therefore adopt it and render, "and the earth became desolate and void."[31] [Furthermore, according to Isa. 45: 18 God did not create the world *tohu*.   Therefore Gen. 1: 2 can only refer to a judgment passed upon the earth by God and] age after age may have rolled away, and it was probably during their course that the strata of the earth's crust were gradually developed.   Hence we see that geological attacks upon the Scriptures are altogether wide of the mark, are a mere beating of the air.   There is room for any length of time between the first and second verses of the Bible.   And again; since we have no inspired account of the geological formations we are at liberty to believe they were developed in the order we find them.[32]

The reader must note well in this citation that Pember admits (i) that the Bible contributes no formal principle for the interpretation of geology, and (ii) therefore whatever honest and competent geologists tell us about the *geological* record we ought to accept.

In that Jer. 4: 23–26 refers to this ruin we must believe that there were men in the original creation of Gen. 1: 1 and cities too, for Jeremiah speaks of the broken-down condition of the cities. Pember is forced to adopt a pre-Adamite view of man. With reference to fossils Pember believes that they reveal disease, death, and ferocity —all tokens of sins.

> Since, then, the fossil remains are those of creatures anterior to Adam, and yet show evident token of disease, death and mutual destruction, they must have belonged to another world, and have a sin-stained history of their own.[33]

Pember here adopts the principle of *retroactive interpretation.* The millennial conditions in the future tell us from what state the world orginally fell. The conditions among the present cursed Nature tell us what sort of curse fell on the first creation. The millennium with its docile animals tells us how peaceful the original creation was; and the present ferocity of animals informs us of the depraved condition of the brutes after the fall of Satan.

The head of this lost creation was Satan. Ezek. 28 is about Satan and anti-Christ. The mineral garden of Ezekiel is parallel to the New Jerusalem with its precious stones. The fact that there are no fossil remains of man in the ancient fossil beds simply means we do not know the conditions of the destruction. Pember thinks that *the earth may have swallowed them up like the sons of Korah in Numbers* 16.[34]

Rimmer's views are found in his *Modern Science and the Genesis Record* (1937). Although he admits that we cannot prove with finality whether the Hebrew word *yom* means day or period he vigorously argues for solar days. His reasons for taking the days literally are too extended to summarize here, but certain of them are open to much doubt. For example, he asserts that those who believe in the period interpretation of the days must teach that there are periods of darkness 250,000 years long. The age-day theory asserts no such thing. He appeals to instantaneous creation, but instantaneous creation has been one of the chief aggravations between theologians and scientists. He argues that Moses could hardly have had the concept of periods in his mind. The use of terms or ideas which transcend the understanding or meaning of the original writer, he tells us, is only for prophecy. Moses could not have had the idea of a geologic epoch in his mind when he wrote. If this is true, this flatly contradicts all he wrote in *The Harmony of Science and Scripture,* for in that book he points out scores of anticipations of modern science in the Old Testament, such as modern ideas of space, wireless telegraphy, germ theory of disease, and aeroplanes!   His assertion that the age-day theory is a concession made to evolutionary geology is again a typical confusion of evolutionary biology and uniformitarian geology.

In continuing his positive argument he follows Pember in noting the contrast between *bara* and *asah,* which means that Gen. 1: 3 ff. is about reconstruction, not creation.   He appeals to Isa. 45: 8 to prove that God did not make the world a waste.   A world of waste must be a judged world.   He says the *and* of Gen. 1: 2 should be translated *but*.   He appeals to the Septuagint and to the Latin Vulgate.   He claims that the Hebrew had no word for *became,* so *was* must be pressed into service and translated in the sense of *became*.   He appeals to Robert Dick Wilson as affirming that *tohu* and *bohu* refer to "desolation succeeding previous life," but for such a claim from such an important authority he gives no documentation.   Finally, he appeals to Ezek. 28 as the story of Satan's fall, causing the earth to be brought into the condition described in Gen. 1: 2.

The criticisms of this view are many and serious.   (i) It gives one of the grandest passages in the Bible a most peculiar interpretation.   From the earliest Bible interpretation this passage has been interpreted by Jews, Catholics, and Protestants as the *original creation of the universe*.   In six majestic days the universe and all of life is brought into being.   But according to Rimmer's view the great first chapter of Genesis, save for the first verse, is not about original creation at all, but about reconstruction.   The primary origin of the universe is stated in but one verse.   This is not the most telling blow against the theory but it certainly indicates that something has been lost to make the six days of creation anticlimactic.   So entrenched has this theory become in hyper-orthodox circles that they feel as if the foundations are removed if this theory is criticized, whereas the majority of commentators feel that the entire theory has a peculiarity to it in that it makes the great creation chapter the second time round!   Or, in the words of Allis:

> The first objection to this theory is that it throws the account of creation almost completely out of balance . . .   It seems highly improbably that an original creation which according to this theory brought into existence a world of wondrous beauty would be dismissed with a single sentence and so many verses devoted to what would be in a sense merely a restoration of it.[35]

(ii) The Hebrew exegesis of Gen. 1: 2 (after Pember, Rimmer, and Scofield) cannot be adequately maintained on two grounds: grammatical and interpretative.[36]   The *and* of Gen. 1: 2 is the Hebrew *waw* which is used in so many thousands of instances that it is difficult for the author to understand how anything *important* could hinge on it. A word that has had such an enormous usage simply cannot be squeezed into such a definite meaning for this one verse. Rimmer is most untrustworthy at this point. He appeals to the Septuagint and Latin Vulgate for support. However, the Septuagint has *de* not *alla*. In Greek, *de* is one of those little words like the German *gar* or *doch* which are used freely and are usually untranslatable. The strong Greek word for *but* is *alla,* and *de* means *but* only in the *men/de* construction. The Latin has *autem* which is another word like *waw* or *de,* whereas the strong word for *but* in Latin is *sed.*

The effort to make *was* mean *became* is just as abortive. The Hebrews did not have a word for *became* but the verb *to be* did service for *to be* and *become.* The form of the verb *was* in Gen. 1: 2 is the Qal, perfect, third person singular, feminine. A Hebrew concordance will give all the occurrences of that form of the verb. A check in the concordance with reference to the usage of this form of the verb in Genesis reveals that in almost every case the meaning of the verb is simply *was.* Granted in a case or two *was* means *became* but if in the preponderance of instances the word is translated *was,* any effort to make one instance mean *became,* especially if that instance is highly debatable, is very insecure exegesis. This whole matter was debated in JTVI.[37] P. W. Heward defended the Pember-Scofield-Rimmer interpretation of Gen. 1: 2 and F. F. Bruce defended the traditional interpretation. To the author, Bruce is easily the winner of the debate. Gedney informs us that a student writing a master's thesis on "Fundamental Christianity and Evolution" polled twenty leading Hebrew scholars in the United States, asking them if there were any exegetical evidences of a gap interpretation of Gen. 1: 2. They unanimously replied in the negative.[38]

The interpretative objection is this: the entire interpretation of geology and Genesis is made to hinge on *secondary meanings of two Hebrew words.* To indicate that in some cases *waw* may mean *but,* and that *hayah* means *became,* does not give us full warrant to insert these meanings in Gen. 1: 2 and require all geology to conform.[39]

(iii) The appeal to *bara* and *asah* as well as to *tohu* and *bohu* are not at all conclusive. The Pember interpretation makes *bara* a strong word for creation, and weakens *asah* so that it means something like re-make or fashion or construct. But if they who defend this view will face the evidence of a Hebrew concordance and note *all* the occurrences of *bara* and *asah* they will have to admit that (*a*) *bara* is not quite as strong a word as they make it out to be and that (*b*) *asah* is not as weak as they wish it to be.

In the case of *tohu* and *bohu* we would not know that these words

referred to a destroyed creation unless we have independent knowledge of the same.   Surely the line of reasoning is very thin which
seeks to found a theory of a great sin and judgment upon the supposed connotations of these words.   It is equally admissible to
consider these words as referring to the unformed nature of the
earth before God impressed upon it His creative will.   A marble
block and a crumbled statue are both formless.   The former is in
a state which awaits a form and from that formlessness emerges the
image.   When God made the earth He made it like a marble block
out of which He would bring the beautiful world.   Or as Godet
states it:

> The earth did exist, but in the form of chaos . . .   This expression
> does not mean a state of disorder and confusion, but that state of
> primitive matter in which no creature had as yet distinctive existence,
> and no one element stood out in contradistinction with others, but
> all forces and properties of matter existed, as it were, undivided.[40]

Concurring with this interpretation is Flack, who wrote:

> "It would seem, therefore, that the proper interpretation of Gen.
> 1: 2a is that of viewing the universe in an *empty* and *undeveloped* state
> rather than in a confused and chaotic condition.   That is, God created
> the earth with the capacities and potentialities of light and life, but
> at the period in question it was as yet undeveloped . . .   The universe
> did not *become* empty and desolate subsequent to its creation . . . but
> . . . it *was* empty awaiting the further creative work of God."[41]

(iv) The appeals to Jer. 4: 23–26; Isa. 24: 1; 45: 18 are either
totally irrelevant or outright misinterpretations.   Scofield says of
the Jeremiah passage:

> [It] describes the condition of the earth as the result of the judg-
> ment . . . which overthrew the primal order of Gen. 1: 1.[42]

This is certainly exegetical fancy to take a picture of the destruction
of the land of Palestine—not the earth as a globe—under Nebuchad-
nezzar and throw it back to Gen. 1: 2.   What is there in the passage
which introduces the ideas of creation and destruction of creation?
Certainly *in context* the passage is about the destruction of the land
of Judea.   The beholder is certainly Jeremiah, and it hardly makes
sense to have him looking back to a destroyed creation.   If Isa.
24: 1 is taken as referring to the destruction of a pristine creation it
stands completely disconnected with anything in the passage.   In
fact, it would be an oddity to have the verse refer to the destruction
of creation, while the previous verses refer to the destruction of
Babylon and Tyre and the following verses refer to the destruction

of Palestine.   One of our severest criticisms of Catholic exegesis is their procedure of hanging so much on isolated verses.   Isa. 45: 18 settles nothing in the matter, for God has not finished creating till the end of the six days.   When God finished it was a *cosmos*, not a *chaos*, so an appeal to Isa. 45: 18 is improper.

Allis is right when he asserts that a catastrophe of such dimensions and of such great importance (as required by the gap theory) could hardly be stated in one brief sentence.[43]   The elaboration of the gap theorists at this point is beyond all sense of proportion in terms of the actual data they have to work with.

(v) The references to an elaborate theory of angelology and demonology derived from Isa. 14 and Ezek. 28 and *inserted here in the Genesis account* we judge as erratic exegesis.   That there has been an angelic fall is a matter of revelation and this we do not argue. But to interpret Isa. 14 and Ezek. 28 as descriptions of the fall of Satan and his angels we must seriously debate.   Even if this could be demonstrated, *it would yet be insufficient warrant to insert them in the Genesis account.*   Not all commentators are at all agreed that these two passages refer to Satan.   Some who do see truth beyond the mere record throw the meaning into the future as predictions of anti-Christ, not backward to Satan's fall.   Certainly, if conservative and scientific exegesis still considers the Satanic-fall interpretation of these passages as highly improbable, it is not the best procedure for gap theorists to make such a prominent use of them in their interpretation of Genesis.   As we affirmed above, even if the Satan-fall interpretation is a possibility, there is nothing in all the Bible to warrant our placing this fall at Gen. 1: 2.

Typical of the hyper-orthodox exegesis at this point is the work of Baxter.   With reference to the interpretation of Isa. 9: 5, he has three pages devoted to a defence of the *literal* exegesis of the verse.   To spiritualize the passage is branded as "*sheer imposition and distortion.*"[44]   Then, when he discusses Isa. 14 and Ezek. 28 he comes across expositors who wish to stick to the letter of the Scripture and see in these passages only the kings of Tyre and Babylon. Baxter then completely reverses his approach and writes:

> We know, of course, that there are scholars who would limit these passages in Ezekiel and Isaiah simply to Tyrus and Babylon.   But there is a scholarship *which is merely of the letter* [literalism?], and when we think of other passages like Psa. 22 and Isa. 53 (*not to mention many others*) where the same SORT OF LATENT MYSTIC SIGNIFICANCE IS INTERWOVEN WITH THE MORE IMMEDIATE REFERENCE to local and historical happenings of long ago, we cannot but sense that in Ezek. 28 and Isa. 14 there is this deeper reference to Satan.[45]

It is assumed by the Pember school that if you prove the kings of

Tyre and Babylon to be mirrors in which we see the Satan majesty in his fall, then their interpretation of Gen. 1: 2 is verified. But this is not the case, for even if these passages do refer to Satan we cannot by any certain means associate them with Gen. 1: 2.

(vi) The gap theory settles nothing in geology. Pember, as we noted, turns the entire field over to the geologists. In that there is no inspired record of geology we may let the geologist say what he likes. *Is the entire science of geology then to be developed without one ray of Scriptural light?* Was Pember fully aware of the terrifying potentialities of this concession? Such an assertion allows the evolutionist a geological field-day because according to Pember the Biblical record is mute on the subject of geology. In the effort to make peace with geology the gap theory actually spells suicide for any harmony of science and Scripture for it removes any common ground for Genesis and geology. *Harmony with geology is attained by making Scripture irrelevant to geology.* There is no interpretative principle which this theory can give to the geologist.

What has proved very contradictory in the history of the gap theory is that the very cause for the popularity of the theory has been repudiated. The theory since Chalmers received such acclaim because it gave full recognition to the findings of the geologists. It gave the geologists his ages and his time demands. With the coming of Darwin, evolution and uniformitarian geology were made to support each other. To destroy evolution, apologists felt they also had to destroy uniformitarian geology. The very geology which the gap theory is supposed to harmonize with so beautifully must now be routed out as a foe of Christianity! The agreement with geology, once a virtue, is now a vice!

There are other geological problems associated with the gap theory. As we understand it, a beautiful creation gradually became a chaos covered with water. A few thousand years ago that watery shroud was removed and the earth reconstructed. *But the geological record is the exact opposite.* Chaos is at the *beginning* of the earth's history. The geological record does not record a gradual decay ending in a watery grave, but it describes a constant *emergence* of life on higher and higher levels. The "became null and void" of Gen. 1: 2 does not fit the facts of geology. Further, as far as we know, no reputable geologist believes that the earth was completely submerged under water around 4000 B.C. (or earlier), from which watery shroud it emerged in one day. *There is no evidence of such a serious and radical break between the geological record of the past and the situation of the present.* In the judgment of Dawson, a great Christian geologist:

[The gap theory] involves a strained interpretation of the passage, and is contradicted by the fact that no chaotic period intervenes between the human period and the preceding tertiary age.[46]

In regard to geology Rimmer pays due tribute to Price. But this cannot be done with any consistency. First, the gap theory is invoked to account for geological ages.[47] Price invokes a universal flood to account for geological ages. Rimmer *appeals to both*! He even compounds the contradiction by saying that perhaps the days of Genesis could be epochs (although he vigorously defends the literal day interpretation). This makes a triple problem out of Genesis and geology. *First the data of geology are attributed to the catastrophe of Gen. 1: 2, and then to the universal flood of Price's theory, and then to the age-day interpretation of the creative week.* When a geologist does his work he cannot possibly tell to which of these three he is to assign his strata. Certainly, he cannot practice all three theories at on ce. The only conclusion is that the gap theorists have not thought their way through to a workable theory. They are to be credited with the realization that geology must have a say, and that the great time periods must be granted to the geologists. Beyond that their theory has more problems than any true theory can bear.

Allis gives them a most interesting problem to struggle with. Almost all gap theorists believe in pre-Adamite man, but of this man the Bible knows nothing. Further, the gap theorists admit to the geologists vast periods of time, but demand the creation of man in one day. He is then advocating *twenty-four hour anthropology and limitless-time geology*. His only recourse is to make the days into periods, and if he does this he has no need for his gap theory. This again emphasizes the undigested state of the gap theory.[48]

(vii) We shall discuss later the matter of fossils, death, and sin. But the affirmations that: (*a*) *all* death comes from sin; (*b*) fossils are evidence of a judgment; and (*c*) that ugliness of animals as indicated by fossil remains is a result of judgment, are all dogmas which have not been adequately thought through. *The Bible ascribes death from sin to man alone*. Plant life had to die even in pristine Eden. To insist that all carnivora were originally vegetarian is another preposterous proposition. Why such huge teeth and sharp claws? Its application to sea life is impossible, for the large fish could not possibly survive on a seaweed or plankton diet. With reference to fossils, the process of fossilization is going on right now under identical conditions of past geological time. This means that fossilization is an ordinary process of Nature. Again, the aesthetic judgment that ugliness implies a judgment is not capable of defence. Is the peacock uncursed because beautiful, and the dogfish cursed because ugly? Is the majestic lion uncursed and the slinking coyote cursed?

We are not the sole critic of this theory. We have already noted Dawson's rejection of it. Pohle[49] rejects it and says:

> To attribute such a catastrophe to the fallen angels almost verges on superstition.

Tayler Lewis rejects it on the grounds that: (i) it utterly fails to understand the profound nature of the days of Genesis; (ii) it builds the present world on the ruins of a former one, and with no rational connexion between the ages that were and the one which now is; (iii) it is too patently an artificial effort to reconcile Genesis and geology rather than an interpretation growing naturally out of the text; (iv) it makes the heavens of Gen. 1: 1 different from the rest of the passage; and (v) it breaks the connexion between Gen. 1: 1 and 1: 2 for which there is no justification in the text.[50]

Miller examines it and rejects it on the grounds that:

> It virtually removes Scripture altogether out of the field [of geology]. I must confess, however, that on this, and on some other accounts, it has failed to satisfy me.[51]

Gedney criticizes it on the grounds that (i) it calls for an entire re-creation of the animal life of the world in six days; (ii) it fails to explain the orderly progression of the appearance of fossils; (iii) it fails to offer any correlation between definite Biblical statements and geology, for the six days in the gap theory refer solely to a creation of a few thousand years ago; (iv) there is no geological evidence for the catastrophe postulated; and (v) the Hebrew exegesis involved is incapable of defence.[52]

H. *Age-day or Divine-day, or concordism.* The gap theory was a concession to the geologists that the crust of the earth involved a great deal of time for its formation. For a while there was peace between Genesis and geology. But it soon became apparent that the problem of geology was not just the huge draft on the bank of time it demanded, but that the rocks presented a *sequence* among themselves, and that fossils were buried in these rocks and were a key to interpreting the *sequence* of the rocks. Now theologians had to wrestle with (i) time and (ii) *sequence*. The gap theory could provide time, but, as we have seen, it was mute on *sequence*.

What new theory could account for both time and sequence? Neither Cuvier, Agassiz, Smith nor Gosse could command too much of a following. The suggestion put forth and ably defended by such men as Hugh Miller, James Dana, and J. W. Dawson, was that the days of Genesis were periods of time representing in brief the geological and biological history of the earth.   This could then account for *time and sequence*.

This theory has been called the *age-day* theory because it considers the days of Genesis as being periods of time; it has been called *geologic-day* theory for similar reasons; it has been called the *Divine-day* theory after Augustine who said they were God-divided days, not sun-divided days. It is called *concordism* because it seeks a harmony of the geological record and the days of Genesis interpreted as long periods of time briefly summarizing geological history. The most scientific and thorough defence of it has been made by J. W. Dawson in his various works, and an excellent modern defence is made by Gedney in *Modern Science and Christian Faith* (second edition; 1950).

1. First of all, the theory affirms that the days of Genesis are to be interpreted metaphorically and not literally. A vast literature has grown up around the word *yom* (Hebrew for *day*). The flood geologists and the gap theorists vigorously defend the literal-day view and strongly attack the metaphorical interpretation.[53] Those defending the metaphorical use of the word *day* include such men as Guyot, Dana, Dawson, Hugh Miller, Michaelis, Reusch, Godet, Buswell, Sanden, and Magoun.[54]

Before beginning a serious exposition of this view it would be proper to be reminded that the two greatest geologists on the North American continent in the nineteenth century espoused this view. We refer to J. W. Dawson and to James Dana. Because we have quoted so much of Dawson we shall at this place mention only the view of Dana. In the second edition of Dana's very famous *Manual of Geology* he wrote:

> The record in the Bible is, therefore, profoundly philosophical in the scheme of creation it presents. It's both true and divine . . . There can be no real conflict between the two Books of the GREAT AUTHOR. Both are revelations made by Him to Man" (p. 770).

Writing on *Cosmogony,* he then proceeds to defend the age-day interpretation of Gen. 1, showing its concordism with the facts of Geology (pp. 765–770).

In view of the fact that such a great array of geologists and theologians accept the metaphorical interpretation of the word *day*, the case for the literal day cannot be conclusive nor the objections to the metaphorical interpretation too serious. In the first two chapters of Genesis the word day is used as follows: (i) in verse 5 it means daylight and (ii) a day marked out by an evening and morning; (iii) in verse 14 it means daylight in contrast to night, and (iv) in the expression "and for days" it means a twenty-four hour day; (v) in Gen. 2: 4 it refers to the entire period of creation.

We noted previously that even Rimmer believed it could possibly mean period. Scofield himself pens:

> The frequent parabolic use of natural phenomena may warrant the conclusion that each creative "day" was a period of time marked off by a beginning and ending.[55]

These periods of time are not necessarily equal. They are as long as was required to accomplish what should be accomplished. The steps in assembling a model aeroplane are listed in order, but there is no telling how long each step takes. The days of Genesis, further, need not fit any tight geological scheme. There are the *strict concordists* and the *moderate concordists* differing over the degree to which the Genesis account is to be harmonized with the geological record.

2. During each day the logical developments of the creative act were carried out. For example, whatever processes necessary to bring the light through to the earth or gather waters into one place or make the ocean teem with fish, were inaugurated and over a period of time realized. Thus the processes of Nature become the tool in the hand of the Divine Spirit to bring to pass the plan of God.

It must be kept in mind that there is an evident inverse correlation between time and level of existence. The basic physical and chemical processes may take thousands of times longer than the biological ones. Bettex writes:

> The crystal develops in millenniums, the tree in centuries, man by decades. It is perfectly natural that the earth should traverse cosmic epochs, whilst mankind exists for a much briefer, and, as it were, condensed interval of time.[56]

3. The expression "evening and morning" is capable of several interpretations. Some take it to mean a period of rest and a period of creation.[57] Others take it as a graphic means of describing a cosmic day. If one takes a metaphorical interpretation of the word *yom*, then *mutatis mutandis* the expression evening and morning, must be metaphorical. They do not mean that there is a day of a million years of light followed by a million years of darkness. The expression refers to something in the process of creation. No objection to the theory can be made on the basis of forcing a literal meaning into the expression "evening and morning."

4. The argument against the theory on the grounds of Ex. 20: 11 is not at all telling. It simply means that the *human* week of seven days takes its rise from the *divine* week of seven creative epochs.

5. Those who defend the theory constantly cite Augustine and Aquinas as men who anticipated the theory long before the days

of modern geology. Augustine does not call them geological days, and it has been argued that there is nothing in Augustine to justify any belief in a period of time for these days. The point Augustine actually makes is that the creation days are so great, so majestic, so profound that we cannot consider them as mere sun-divided days but as God-divided days. They are creative days, not solar days, and so he calls them *natures, growths, dies ineffabiles*.

6. This view has been inaccurately labelled as *disguised theistic evolution*. It is not theistic evolution, but as Gedney labels it, it is *progressive creationism*.[58] Theistic evolution teaches creation from within. In theistic evolution there is a continuous line from the original cells on the prehistoric waters to man. All divine working is immanental in Nature. But progressive creation teaches the transcendental activity of God. There is no continuum of life from amoeba to man, but the great phyla and families come into being only by the creative act of God. To equate this theory with theistic evolution is not proper.

7. Tayler Lewis has referred to other passages which indicate the vast antiquity of the earth. He cites such passages as Prov. 8: 22 ff., Mic. 5: 1, Psa. 104, Psa. 90, Psa. 49: 15 and a variety of passages in Job. The exegetical problem here is to determine what *antiquity* meant to the Jew. Since the advent of modern geology, a million years ago seems recent when compared to radio-activity dating of two to ten billion years for the age of the earth. Perhaps the Jewish mind looked at five hundred years in much the same way as we look at one million years. We must know more of what antiquity meant to the Jewish mind before we can know the full meaning of these verses cited by Lewis.

8. The great strength of the theory is the apparent harmony it creates between Genesis and the geological column. Many charts have been made showing the proposed harmony between Genesis and geology, of which Gedney's is typical.[59] Dawson many times in his writings draws a parallel between geology and Genesis, the fullest account being found in *The Origin of the World According to Revelation and Science* (pp. 343–357), in which he points out nine parallels:

1. Scripture and Science both testify to the great fact that there was a beginning—a time when none of all the parts of the fabric of the universe existed; when the Self-Existent was the sole occupant of space. 2. Both records exhibit the progressive character of creation, and in much the same aspect. 3. Both records agree in affirming that since the beginning there has been but one great system of nature. 4. The periods into which geology divides the history of the earth are different from those of Scripture, yet when properly understood there is a marked comparison. 5. In both records the ocean gives birth to

the first dry land, and it is the sea that is first inhabited, yet both lead at least to the suspicion that a state of igneous fluidity preceded the primitive universal ocean. 6. Both records concur in maintaining what is usually termed the doctrine of existing causes in geology. 7. Both records agree in assuring us that death prevailed in the world ever since animals were introduced.

At this point Dawson gives discussion to prove that animals died before the fall of man. Only in man's case is death the wages of sin.

8. In the department of "final causes," as they have been termed, Scripture and geology unite in affording large and interesting views. They illustrate the procedure of the All-wise Creator, during a long succession of ages, and thus enable us to see the effects of any of his laws, not only at one time, but in far distant periods. Lastly, both records represent man as the last of God's works, and the culminating point of the whole creation.

Gedney's procedure is to set before us the six facts of the geological record to which all must agree: (i) the earth was originally an astronomical body with an atmosphere and water and land masses on which the processes of erosion were already at work; (ii) the various geological strata contain fossils, some yet living, others extinct; (iii) that "all the invertebrate phyla appear contemporaneously with marked suddenness in the Cambrian, differentiated into phyla, classes, and orders, and with no clear indication as to how they developed into this condition if they did develop at all" (p. 31)[60]; (iv) since the Cambrian period new forms appear in the strata and their appearance is sudden and their form is increasingly advanced over previous life; (v) no transitional forms are found; and (vi) there is an upward progressive directionalism in the appearance of the forms.

Gedney affirms that no naturalistic explanation can account for these six facts of geology nor can fiat creationism nor the gap theory. The only theory which can explain them is the theory of progressive creationism linked with the metaphorical interpretation of the word *day* in the Genesis account.[61]

There are certain problems in connexion with this interpretation, the first being that of the order in geology and Genesis. Do the two orders concur? This will depend on how strongly we try to harmonize the two. The order in Genesis might be part chronological and part logical. Gruber believes that the order is part logical and part chronological. Leary has given us five criticisms he finds with the Genesis record as viewed by science.[62] (i) He says the word *day* is used in the ordinary sense, but even if not used in the ordinary sense it cannot be made to mean geological periods. In reply it is obvious that only a few of the most ardent concordists would try to press a given day of the Genesis record into the geological column in some close identification with a given epoch or period. (ii) His next objection is that the sun and the stars were created after the earth. If the record is logical as well as chronological this objection is invalid. If the word *made* means "cause to function as such" then again the objection is invalid. (iii) He objects again to the record on the basis that there is light and morning before the sun. First, what is said about the previous objection applies here. Second, if the word *day* is taken metaphorically then we must so take the expression "evening and morning" and therefore it would have nothing to do with the sun. (iv) His fourth objection is that plant life preceded sunlight. We reply: again, the order may be logical and not only chronological. Further, plants could have grown in diffused light. (v) His last objection is that birds preceded all land animals, and vegetation is complete in its highest forms before any animals appear. We reply: again, if the organization is logical or topical then again any specific chronological objection is invalid. Further, these descriptions of these days do not tell us *everything* created on each day. Obviously insects were necessary for plant life. But if God told us all that was done, Gen. 1 would be encyclopaedic in length. This is precisely the point made by Bettex.[63] Moses is not under obligation to tell us every speck of life created or not as yet created. He could speak of a vegetation period and not be guilty of error in not mentioning marine life. Further, there is nothing to prevent the creation of each day from overlapping in its development with the other successive days. Therefore the objection is invalid.

I. *Pictorial Day and Moderate Concordism.* The theory we shall defend has been defended in some one of its elements by such writers as J. Pohle, *God: The Author of Nature and the Supernatural* (1942); Hugh Miller, *Testimony of the Rocks* (1869); P. J. Wiseman, *Creation Revealed in Six Days* (1948); J. H. Kurtz, *Bible and Astronomy* (third German edition, 1857, in which Kurtz defends the gap theory in a most sane and reserved exposition, but also defends the pictorial method of revealing the acts of creation); Canon Dorlodot, *Darwinianism and Catholic Thought* (Vol. I, 1923); A. H. Strong, *Systematic Theology* (1907, II, 393, ff.); L. F. Gruber, *The Six Creative Days* (1941).[64] The elements of the theory are as follows:

1. The main purpose of Genesis is theological and religious. This has been said innumerable times already, but there is the temptation to get too involved in the details of science and to forget it. The theological purpose of the passage is negative and positive. *Negatively,* it is a prohibition of idolatry. The creature is created and not worthy of adoration. Creation makes idolatry an impossibility, when creation is rightly understood. *Positively,* the chapter

teaches that the universe has its origin in God and reveals in a magnificent way God's power, God's spirituality, God's wisdom, and God's goodness. This is more effectively brought out by an absence of reference to all secondary causes. *God speaks and it comes to pass!* Expositors have been mistaken in assuming that (i) this cannot involve time, and (ii) this cannot involve process. The religious consciousness is incurably metaphysical and wishes to know *what is ultimate.* The time element and the causal element are so completely the tool and instrument of the Divine Will that they are ignored in the *theological expressions* of creation. Finally, it is God who does, God who makes, God who forms, God who acts, God who creates. The *how* is so plastic to the divine that it loses its relevance to the divine. Only by the ponderous methods of science followed through centuries of time do we commence to unravel the *how* of the universe. From science we learn (i) any time element and (ii) any process involved. We agree with Kurtz when he wrote:

> The Mosaic history of the creation, as the Bible in general, was by no means designed to give instruction in regard to natural science. Nothing was more foreign to its object. The efforts of the human mind after secular culture, after art and science, were never designed to be mere tributaries to, and dependent upon, special Divine revelation. As man was to gain by the sweat of his brow, his daily bread, for the support of his *physical* life, from the earth he inhabits, so also must he acquire from nature *in, around, below* and *above* him, by wearisome effort and diligent research, science and knowledge for the support and culture of his *mental* being. In no case whatever has either mathematical, physical, or medical science, been communicated to him by Divine revelation.[65]

The religious intent of the creation narrative was: (i) to evoke from man the worship, adoration, obedience, and love which belong to God as faithful, powerful, good, and omnipotent Creator; (ii) to prohibit any and all superstitious views of the universe; (iii) to deny any view of Nature which denied the existence of God and a spiritual order. It thereby does not tell science what is right, but what science must not lead to. It sets limits and boundaries to science, but not highways and pathways.

2. With reference to the six days of creation, we reject the literal interpretation because by no means can the history of the earth be dated at 4000 B.C., or even 40,000 B.C. Our reasons for rejecting the gap theory have already been given in some detail. We also reject certain elements of the age-day theory, although we have much sympathy for it, and held it ourselves for many years.

Our criticisms of the age-day theory are as follows:

(*a*) We feel that if we are to make the record speak scientifically of the creation of God we discover that it does not speak in sufficient detail.   Not all types of life are included in the Genesis record. There is no mention of the crytograms and gymnosperms in the third day.   There is no mention of the amphibia among the animals. It is difficult to determine whether the word reptile is to denote what modern zoologists mean by the term or what it meant to the ancient world.

(*b*) It has been felt since patristic days that the Genesis account is not strictly chronological, but part topical and part logical.   The most obvious illustration is the creation of the astronomical bodies in the fourth day.   We have a botanical creation with no animals and a mammalian creation with no creation of plants, yet the science of biology tells us how intimately related plants, animals, and insects are in the order of Nature.   It is apparent that the six days are *topically* ordered or *logically* ordered, not only *chronologically* ordered.[66]

(*c*) It is not the intention of Genesis to describe modern science or even to write scientifically, hence it is improper to seek for scientific data in these verses.   The language is *phenomenal* and *popular,* not *scientific* and *causal.*   We are not to find modern scientific concepts smuggled into ancient Hebrew vocabulary.   We are not to make correlations between light (Gen. 1: 3) and modern knowledge of radiation, cosmic energy, stellar energy; nor are we to find Eucidean or Riemannian space in the word *firmament*; nor are we to find principles of zoological or botanical classification in the terminology of Gen. 1.   Notice the *phenomenal* and *popular* terminology in the first chapter of Genesis.   Using the ARV we note the following astronomical terms: heavens, earth, light, darkness, day, night, morning, firmament, lights, greater light, lesser light, and star.   Some of the botanical terms are: grass, herbs, fruit trees, green herb.   Zoologically we have: living creatures, birds, sea-monsters, cattle, creeping things, fish, beasts, man.   Geologically we have: waters, dry land, earth, seas.

(*d*) The problem of the meaning of *yom* is not fully decided as to whether it can mean period or not.   The word is one which has many uses, as we have already indicated.   We are not at present persuaded that it can be stretched so as to mean *period* or *epoch* or *age,* as such terms are used in geology.   Though not closing the door on the age-day interpretation of the word *yom,* we do not feel that lexicography of the Hebrew language will as yet permit it.

We believe, in agreement with the authorities which we have listed, that creation was *revealed* in six days, not *performed* in six days. We believe that the six days are *pictorial-revelatory* days, not literal days nor age-days.   The days are means of communicating to man the great fact that *God is Creator,* and that *He is Creator of all.*

Kurtz raised this problem as to how God would communicate the *unknown past* to a man.   His answer was that the *unknown past* is revealed pictorially, visually, optically, just as the *unknown future* is. Further, the past revealed by vision must be interpreted the same as the future revealed by vision.   Kurtz writes:

> Therefore, we come into possession of the very important hermeneutical rule that representations of *pre*-Adamite developments, founded upon revelations, must be viewed from the same standpoint, and interpreted according to the same laws, as prophecies and sketches of *future times* and developments, founded also upon revelation . . . [The Genesis record] consists of prophetico-historical tableaux, which are represented before the eye of the mind, scenes from the creative activity of God, each one of which represents some grand division of the great drama, some prominent phase of the development.   One scene unfolds itself after another before the vision of the *prophet*, until at length, with the seventh, the historical progress of creation is fully represented to him.[67]

If the order of this communication is partially a topical arrangement, then we must pledge ourselves only to a moderate concordism, *e.g.*, we believe man was the last creation of God so that the last creative act of God coincides with the geological record of the recency of man.   The theological importance of Genesis is that God is Creator, that God created all—not the specific order of creation.   A carpenter can tell his child that he made a house— the roof, walls, floors, and basement.   The child realizes that his father made the house even though the father gave a topical order, not a chronological order.   The creation record is part topical and part chronological to convey to man: (i) some sense of the order in creation; (ii) that God made everything, so nothing may be worshipped.   Man as the last in order is highest in importance, and for that truth the order is necessary.

3. Wiseman's interpretation is essentially that of Kurtz's, but with this difference.   Wiseman believes that God *told* man the story of creation, whereas Kurtz believes God communicated creation through *visions*.   The advantage of Wiseman's view is that it leaves us no problem as to when the vision leaves off and history begins.   However, if the days were given as visions, it is not the same as saying the record is mythological or allegorical.   The source of the information for the first eleven chapters of Genesis is not an easy problem to solve, and although a dogmatist may have a neat bit of *speculation* on the subject, any verifiable theory of the source of this information is not readily forthcoming.   We can presume faithful traditions from Abraham to Moses, but prior

to Moses it is very difficult to say where pure revelation ends and historical sources begin. If we date Adam back a few thousand extra years than Ussher did, and as many conservative scholars do, then we have the problem of the historical preservation of any data of the Fall. If we most surely ask the *Vedas* and the *Koran* and the *Book of Mormon* to come to some sort of responsible accounting of their origin and transmission, and to some accounting to historical fact and consistency of teaching, we cannot expect our doctrine of inspiration to *exempt* the Bible from such a similar calling to responsibility. We should be charitable toward all evangelical efforts which try to clear up the problems of the early chapters of Genesis.

Wiseman makes the Hebrew word *asah* (usually, *to make*) to mean *show* so that when the record says that "God made so-and-so" we should translate it "God shewed so-and-so." But Bruce has shown this is not possible from the standpoint of the Hebrew.[68]

Wiseman's basic theory is that God revealed creation in six days. The days of creation are not literal days nor age-days indicating the time of creation, but are literal days indicating the time of revelation. Creation accounts were customarily put on six tablets, as archaeological excavations around Babylonia show. Hence there was a day of revelation for each tablet, and the colophon (ending of the record, Gen. 2: 1-4) of the account is also in keeping with Babylonian methods. Wiseman then falls back on a mild form of concordism as we have discussed in this book. He will have nothing to do with the gap theory. Further, he argues that the Bible account mentions nothing about *speed* in creation. Milton, he informs us, presented the notion of *speed* in creation, and so prejudiced theology against geology from the very beginning of the modern period. But there is nothing necessary in the definition of a miracle demanding that it be instantaneous. Therefore, the geologist is to be given his vast period of time, with the realization that the world made in two billion years is no less a miracle than a world made in twenty-four hours.[69]

We agree—to return to our exposition—with such competent Christian geologists as Dana and Dawson that geological science is on the right track. There are atheistic geologists and evolutionary geologists. However, certain things must be said: First, our theological orthodoxy does not make us scientifically correct. We may have the truth of the gospel but that hardly gives us authority to write off all geology as of the devil. We certainly admit that there are atheistic scientists in all sciences and that their atheism does not prevent them from coming to much truth in their sciences. We may quarrel with these atheists over metaphysical problems, but their atheism does not necessarily interfere with their professional competence. Similarly, we cannot say that geology must be abandoned because it is developed by atheistis.   We have no part in the typical hyper-orthodox castigation of geology.

Secondly, geologists are a check on each other.   They argue, debate, criticize and quarrel among themselves.   Like other scientists they may be atheistic or anti-Christian, or modernistic or even conservative.   In their interactions with each other over their theories they tend to purge and purify their science so that it becomes increasingly objective.

If we believe in the divine inspiration of the Scriptures and in the pictorial-day interpretation of Genesis, and in the general truthfulness of modern geology, we are then driven to the theories of *moderate concordism* and *progressive creationism*.

4. By *moderate concordism* we mean that geology and Genesis tell in broad outline the same story.   Both agree that the earth was once in what may be called a chaotic condition.   Both agree that certain cosmical conditions had to be realized before life could begin, *e.g.* the need for light, dry land, separation of waters and atmosphere. Both agree that the simple is first and the complex later.   Both agree that the higher animals and man were the last to appear.   The *time* element is not stated in the Genesis record and must be learned from the geological record.   Both agree that man is the latest and highest of all forms of life.

Moderate concordism differs from strict concordism in (i) not affirming that the word *yom* means period, and (ii) in insisting that the days are not completely chronological in order but part topical or logical.

5. The truth about the geological record can only be settled with the combination of *geology* and *theology*.   If Genesis is completely silent about secondary causes, and if geology is ignorant about first causes, then it is only as we bring the first causes and secondary causes together that we will get the truth for the full understanding of the geologic record.   The theologian knows that God is Creator, but that fact does not tell him the *how* and *when*.   The geologist knows the *how* and *when*, but the *Who* is a mystery to him.   The Christian geologist, and the geologically minded theologian, alone can put together the *Who* of theology and the *what* of geology, and can show the connexion between primary causation and secondary causation.   For this reason we propound *progressive creationism*, which in turn drives us back to the earlier part of this book in which we discussed a Christian philosophy of Nature.

By way of recall: we indicated the strong theism of the Bible. God is Almighty Creator and all exists because He made it.   He is Nature's Preserver and Sustainer and Provider.   The laws of Nature are His laws, and the regularity of Nature is a reflection of God's faithfulness. This strong creationism and theism of the Bible must then be imported at this point into our considerations of the geological record. *All life, all forms, all geological changes, all geological laws* ARE OF GOD.

We also need to recall that in our philosophy of Nature we affirmed that God is world-ground. He is world-ground *to all geological phenomena* as well as to morality, ethics, and spirituality. God is in Nature, for God is *in* all things. *All* is according to His divine will and by His power. The Spirit of God is the Divine Entelechy seeing that the Divine will is accomplished in Nature.[70]

Progressive creation is the belief that Nature is permeated with the Divine activity but not in any pantheistic sense. The order is from blank and void to order and cosmos, from the seed to the full ear, from the cosmic to the organic, from the simple to the complex, from the sentient to the rational. The completed product is at the end of the process, not at the beginning.

Putting together our picture we have something like this: Almighty God is Creator, World-Ground, and Omnipotent Sustainer. In His mind the entire plan of creation was formed with man as the climax. Over the millions of years of geological history the earth is prepared for man's dwelling, or as it has been put by others, the cosmos was pregnant with man. The vast forests grew and decayed for his coal, that coal might appear a natural product and not an artificial insertion in Nature. The millions of sea life were born and perished for his oil. The surface of the earth was weathered for his forests and valleys. From time to time the great creative acts, *de novo,* took place. The complexity of animal forms increased. Finally, when every river had cut its intended course, when every mountain was in its purposed place, when every animal was on the earth according to blueprint, then he whom all creation anticipated is made, MAN, in whom alone is the breath of God.

This is not theistic evolution which calls for creation from within with no acts *de novo.* It is progressive creationism. We agree with Gedney that the geological record does not reveal a continuity, an evolution, but that it reveals great gaps. Animal forms appear suddenly. The geologist writes: "form X appears in the Devonian." The theologian informs him that from the theological vantage point the word *appeared* is to be rendered *created.* The geologist can record gaps and appearances and announce that he has no natural theory as to their origin. The theologian can inform the geologist of progressive creation. Progressive creationism follows neither the theory of Linnaeus, nor Cuvier, nor Agassiz, nor Bergson. It believes with all four that some form of creationism is alone the answer to the riddles of geology. It disagrees with Linnaeus and Cuvier because it believes additional forms have been created in the history of the earth.   It parts company with Agassiz in that it does not believe in sudden catastrophes, and that it believes in the progressive complexity of forms in the progress of creation. It parts company with Bergson in asserting that some creation is from without and *de novo* and, in place of Bergson's *elan vital,* suggests the Spirit of God.[71]

We believe then the harmony of Scripture with geology is achieved by uniting together (i) the pictorial-day theory of the days of Genesis, (ii) the moderate theory of concordism, and (iii) progressive creationism.

III. THE FLOOD

A. *The Ark.* Preliminary to discussing the flood it will be appropriate to discuss the ark described in Gen. 6.[72]   The word *ark* signifies a box (Hebrew, *tēbah;* Greek, *kibōtos*), not a boat-like structure of classical or modern times.   It was composed of gopher wood (Hebrew, *'atsē gopher;* Greek, *kuparissos*) which is usually taken to be cypress wood.   This is a light, durable wood.   Alexander built his fleet at Babylon of this wood, and the doors of the church of St. Peter at Rome were made of cypress wood and are a thousand years old.   It was also the wood used by the Phoenicians for their ships.   The ark had cabins (Hebrew *kinnim*) or nests of cells.   Their size is not indicated, but their function was (i) to separate the animals, and (ii) to supply the function of a modern bulkheading for bracing the ship.   The ark was pitched (Hebrew, *kopher;* Greek, *asphaltos*).   It has been suggested that this material was either the pitch of the cypress tree or bitumen, deposits of which have been found at Hit in the Euphrates valley above Babylon.   The function of the pitch was to supply a flexible waterproofing.   The ark was pitched inside and out and this served as modern caulking does.   Being of a flexible nature it would yield to pressure without cracking and would stretch without pulling away from the wood. The dimensions of the ark were 300 × 50 × 30 cubits.   Perhaps this was originally some Babylonian measurement of which the Hebrew cubit was the closest analogue.   The actual length of the cubit varies from 18 inches to 25 inches.   There were long cubits and short cubits and royal cubits and Egyptian cubits and Talmudic cubits; 22 inches was the legal cubit of the Talmudists.   We can know the actual size only within limits.   The dimensions of the ship are large and a vessel of such size was not built till modern times.   The ratio of the dimensions of the ark are also modern, and modern ships have been built approximating the dimensions and the ratios (*Celtic* of the White Star Line, 1901, 700 × 75 × 49$\frac{1}{3}$; *Great Eastern,* 1858, 629 × 83 × 58).

The most obscure reference is concerning the expression in verse 16. Does this refer to a ventilation system or to a lighting system, or just to a roof? The American Standard Version reads *light* and puts *roof* in the margin, whereas the Revised Standard Version reverses them and puts *roof* in the text and *light* in the margin. The interpretation about the cubit is just as uncertain. Does it mean that the light system or ventilation system was one cubit wide around the ark, or does it mean that the ark is so to slope as to come within a cubit of closing off the top? The text is too brief to allow us to come to any certain decision.[73]

The ark had a door and three stories. The stories functioned similarly to the cabins in providing a division of animals and a bracing of the structure. The shape of the ark was boxy or angular, and not streamlined nor curved. With this shape it increased its carrying capacity by one-third. It was a vessel designed for floating, not for sailing. A model was made by Peter Jansen of Holland, and Danish barges called *Fleuten* were modelled after the ark. These models proved that the ark had a greater capacity than curved or shaped vessels. They were very sea-worthy and almost impossible to capsize.

It has been suggested that the ark had sloping sides. If this were the case the waves would hit it and roll, as they do when hitting a sloping dyke. This would prevent the waves from shattering the ark with a direct impact upon it. Long experience with dykes has shown that sloping dykes parry the force of the waves. If the sides of the ark were slanted the waves would roll up the sides and not pound it. The covering of the ark is also a matter of conjecture. Some have thought that it was covered with a skin as the tabernacle was and that Noah had to roll back this skin when he came out of the ark.

The stability of such a barge is great and it increases as it sinks deeper into the water. The lower the centre of gravity the more difficult it is to capsize. If the centre of gravity were low enough the ark or barge could only be capsized if violently rolled over. Wherever the centre of gravity may have been in the ark, it certainly was a most stable vessel.[74]

Many other features are left untouched as to its construction. All opinions about the ark must be tempered with the realization as to how meagre are the details of its construction. We are not told of the water supply, sewage disposal, care of the animals, or if Noah had any help in constructing the ark. It was not the purpose of the writer to give anything but the most general details, and we should rest content within the boundaries of revelation at this point. Suffice it to say, the ark was a reasonable structure. For its specific purpose it was of credible shape, credible size, and credible proportions. It was made from a wood well adapted for such a barge and was divided into stories and state-rooms for proper bracing. It apparently had some system of lighting and ventilation. All in all, the record of the ark bears witness to the credibility of the construction of such a ship, and we believe its features were matters of revelation to Noah who, living in the plains of Babylon, was a "North Dakota" sailor.

Legends of finding the ark on Mt. Ararat have flourished for centuries. Only those unfamiliar with such matters were surprised by the recent expeditions to find the ark. These legends will be found in Baring-Gould, *The Legends of the Patriarchs* (n.d.) and should be consulted by those who seek further information of this nature. To date all such legends of finding the ark are fictions. As we shall subsequently indicate, the ark did not come down on the top of Mt. Ararat (some 17,000 feet high), but on the Ararat range. If that is the case the ark disappeared a long time ago through rot, or for firewood, or for building material.

B. *The Flood.* The flood is one of the most remarkable events in the story of the Bible, and Noah is one of its most remarkable men. Although the flood is mentioned but a few times in the Bible, it receives important attention in the New Testament. It has also been one of the sharpest centres of controversy in the history of the warfare of theology and science.

Heidel's work, which we have already cited, must be consulted in any serious study of the flood. Heidel shows the great contrasts between the Babylonian and the Hebrew accounts. The Hebrew account is sane, moral, theistic, whereas the Babylonian account is frequently silly or grotesque, and polytheistic. Heidel also tackles the lions of criticism and defends the unity of the flood account.[75] The so-called documentary features of the flood narrative have been one of the strongest illustrations of the documentary hypothesis of the Pentateuch.

1. *Pertinent facts about the flood today.*

(*a*) There is no question that the civilization that forms the setting of the account is the Mesopotamian. The ark was constructed there; we can trace Biblical traditions back to Mesopotamia; Abraham came from there; the tower of Babel was most likely a ziggurat; and the earliest civilization known to historians is Mesopotamian.

(*b*) The time of the flood is more difficult to determine. Ussher has Noah dated around 2300 B.C. The so-called flood deposits of Ur and Kish date earlier than 3000 B.C. The Babylonian tablets of the flood date around 2000 B.C. The early Babylonian and Egyptian civilizations date earlier than 4000 B.C. The end of the ice-age dates from about 10,000 B.C. according to carbon-14 method of dating.

This much is certain: (i) The flood deposits cannot be appealed to as proofs of Noah's flood because there are at least four such deposits and they are separated by 600 years.   This means that such a flood which could lay down several feet of pure clay was not unprecedented.   In that such floods happened at least four times and because the deposits are separated by about 600 years, we must be very cautious in using this material in support of Noah's flood.   If one insists upon appealing to the flood deposits of the Mesopotamian valley he must wrestle with all the problems which such an interpretation creates.   (ii) We concur with the judgment expressed by such a strong conservative writer as Unger:

> It is archeologically fantastic to place the Noahic flood so late as 2348 B.C. [Ussher's exact date], as would be the case if the Genesis genealogies are used for chronological purposes.   The deluge certainly took place long before 4000 B.C.[76]

(c) The causes of the flood according to the Bible are rain and water from the fountains of the deep.   This has generally been taken to mean rain from a steady downpour and the coming up of some other source of water from wells, springs, or the ocean. Water from the rain would hardly be sufficient to cause a flood of such proportions, although even this has been maintained on the basis of how much water could come down in one cloud-burst of a few minutes duration.   Other writers have associated the ice-age with the flood, either as a result of the flood or as the agency of the flood.   If climatic conditions were suddenly changed, it is argued, the waters of the flood would freeze at the poles and make the ice-age.   Or, a sudden warming of the atmosphere would cause the existing ice of the ice-age to melt and form the huge body of water necessary for the flood.   It is no longer possible to maintain that the ice of the ice-age came from the flood unless one believes in several floods and of their commencing about a million years ago. That the tilting of the earth caused the great ice fields to melt suddenly is a theory, but that is about all it is.[77]

Another theory is that the earth from at least the time of man's creation till the flood was surrounded by a canopy.[78] We have had difficulty getting back to the original sources of this theory even though we have been after it for years.   Whether broached for the first time by Vail or not, we are not sure, but the trail usually leads to him.   He has written *The Earth's Annular System* (date ?), and *The Deluge and its Cause* (date ?).   Available is H. W. Kellogg, *The Coming Kingdom and the Re-Canopied Earth* (1936) which apparently follows Vail closely.   Kellogg has also published *The Canopied Earth* (n.d.).   Another version of it will be found in C. T. Schwarze, *The Harmony of Science and the Bible* (1947).   Schwarze accepts the gap theory and believes that God exploded the surface of the earth. The first thing to go up was the water and it formed an ice-lens miles thick.   Schwarze writes:

> It [the canopy theory] claims that water on the earth was the first to feel the effect of that prehistory explosion and was shot out into or beyond the stratosphere where it solidified into hard ice, miles in thickness, forming an oblate spherical canopy around the earth.[79]

Following the water the other layers of the earth came up.   When God said "Let there be light" these layers of dust and debris drifted down and formed the so-called onionskin layers of uniformitarian geology, but the ice-lens remained.   At the time of the flood this lens was melted and that is what supplied the water for the flood in such a great amount and so suddenly.

The proposed basis for such a theory is that the ice-lens would have the effect of making the entire world a hothouse.   Uniform temperature would prevail everywhere.   This would account for tropical plants and animals found in present-day polar regions.   It is also claimed that it would account for man's longevity, and for Noah's new and startling experience with fermented grape juice, and for man's vegetarian diet.

Its belief nowadays must be considered an oddity.[80]   Certainly with the ice-age lasting till 10,000 B.C. the lens must have been of recent origin and, at least, such a lens is not known to geology. Fossil tropical plants found in present-day polar regions date long before 4000 B.C. or 6000 B.C.   Kitchen-middens of ancient man prove that he was a meat-eater from the most ancient antiquity. Observations about man's longevity and fermenting grape juice are surmises and nothing more.

The most popular theory as to the origin of the waters is that the breaking up of the fountains of the deep involved some sort of geological change in the crust of the earth, either in the ocean or in the Mesopotamian valley, which sent ocean water pouring inland, and a reverse of the event to drain it off.   This appears to be the most satisfactory explanation to date as to the origin of the flood waters in such great abundance.

2. *Belief in a universal flood*.   Except for a rare scholar here and there the church has accepted a universal flood—by which we mean a flood which covered the entire globe and rose higher than the mountains.   The arguments proposed as a defence of such a universal flood are:

(*a*) The language of Gen. 6 through 9 is universal.   Gen. 7: 19–23 speaks of *all* the high hills under the *whole* heaven as being under water, and that *all* flesh which moved on the earth died—*all* creatures with breath in their nostrils, of *all* the dry land; *every* living sub-stance was destroyed. It is argued that the plain intent of such universal language is that all the world was covered with water and all men and animals died.

(*b*) It is argued that the traditions of the flood are universal with respect to man. If all races came from Noah they would carry with them a common body of traditions. The universality of the flood legends is due to the origin of all peoples from the sons of Noah who carried with them everywhere the essential facts of a universal flood, although later these facts were distorted and twisted and supplemented.

(*c*) The presence of world-wide distribution of *diluvia* or pheno-mena (rubble drift, loess, former inland lakes) attributed to the washing of water is urged as a proof of a universal flood.

(*d*) It is also argued that the sudden death of animals, especially the mammoths of Siberia frozen in ice, proves a universal flood.[81] According to Davies, land conditions in Siberia had to be different from what they are now to support the flora necessary for the mam-moths to feed on. Further, the ground must have been soft in contrast to its present frozen condition. All these considerations indicate a sudden change of climate, which could be accounted for only by something like a flood. Further, these mammoths died from choking or drowning, not from the frost.

(*e*) Flood geologists especially argue that the so-called depletion of species can be accounted for only by the flood. They argue that there are so few living species compared to the number recorded in the rocks that the flood must have greatly cut down the number of species.

Rimmer's account of the flood is not internally coherent.[82] He appeals to (i) universal traditions of the flood among various peoples, (ii) archaeological discovery of flood deposits by Woolley, (iii) the geology text of Price which he calls "the most up-to-date book of geology extant today . . . a masterpiece of real science,"[83] and (iv) Vail's ice-lens theory. He states that the flood was not necessarily universal, but was as wide as the human race.

First, Rimmer has no right to appeal to Price. Price denies the gap theory which Rimmer defends. Some fundamentalists have not realized that one cannot hold to both Price and the gap theory. Either geological phenomena are due to the long ages in the gap theory (which Price most enthusiastically rejects) or to a universal flood. Further, if Price is right the flood *must* be universal. If you appeal to Price you cannot stop short of a universal deluge.

Second, there are severe problems in identifying the flood de-posits of Woolley with the Noachian flood. If you have Price then a few feet of clay in Mesopotamia is insignificant. An appeal to

Woolley could be only on the basis of a local flood. Then you have to realize that there are four different flood deposits—at Warka (Erech), at Kish (1½ feet), at Ur (8 feet), and one at Shuruppak. Then you have to fit all this in with the date of the flood which Unger says is beyond 4000 B.C., which would disqualify all four of these flood deposits.

Third, the appeal to the ice-lens theory is quite unreliable. There is no real evidence of the existence of such an ice-lens. Rimmer also says that ice-age phenomena are proof of the ice-lens collapsing. Here again problems mount. If you appeal to the ice-age you appeal to just a small part of geological phenomena, whereas if you accept Price *all* geological phenomena is caused by the flood. Glaciation is but a mere ripple of evidence. Again, the ice-ages end around 10,000 B.C., and lasted a million years.

3. *Arguments for a local flood.* Although many Christians still believe in the universal flood, most of the recent conservative scholarship of the church defends a local flood.[84] Those who defend a local flood believe that the *time* of the flood was some time prior to 4000 B.C. The waters were supplied by the rains from above and the ocean waters beneath. Some sort of geological phenomenon is indicated by the expression "and the fountains of the deep were broken up." This caused the ocean waters to creep up the Mesopotamian valley. The waters carried the ark up to the Ararat range. The Hebrew text does not mean that the ark was deposited on the 17,000 foot summit of the peak, but that the ark rested somewhere on the Ararat range. It would have taken a special miracle to get Noah and his family down from such dizzy mountain heights where the cold would have been extreme. By the reversal of the geological phenomenon, the water is drained back from the valley. The reader must keep in mind, as stated in a leading conservative commentary:

> There is in Western Asia a remarkably depressed area, extending from the Sea of Aral to the Steppes of the Caucasus on the north, and sweeping round the southern shores of the Caspian, comprehending Ararat and the Great Salt Desert, which, as Ansted has remarked "forms no inconsiderable portion of the great recognized centre of the human family. The Caspian Sea (83½ feet below the level of the sea, and in some parts of it 600 feet deep) and the Sea of Aral occupy the lowest part of a vast space, whose whole extent is not less than 100,000 square miles, hollowed out, as it were, in the central region of the great continent, and no doubt formerly the bed of the ocean" [and into this natural *saucer* the ocean waters poured].[85]

From this natural saucer the waters were drained. The purpose of the flood was to blot out the wicked civilization of Mesopotamia, and being a local flood of a short duration we would not expect to find any specific evidence for it, especially after the minmum of another six thousand years of weathering.

There are three views of the local flood: (i) Some assert that man never spread beyond the Mesopotamian valley. This is impossible to defend in that it is so well proven that men were to be found outside the Mesopotamian area long before the flood.[86] (ii) G. F. Wright believes that the ice-age drove man into the Mesopotamian valley. (iii) A third view, and the one which we hold, is that the *entire record* must be interpreted phenomenally. If the flood is local though spoken of in universal terms, so the destruction of man is local though spoken of in universal terms. The record neither affirms nor denies that man existed beyond the Mesopotamian valley. Noah certainly was not a preacher of righteousness to the peoples of Africa, of India, of China or of America—places where there is evidence for the existence of man many thousands of years before the flood (10,000 to 15,000 years in America). The emphasis in Genesis is upon that group of cultures from which Abraham eventually came.

We pause here to call in an authority such as Dawson. He discusses various opinions on the flood and sternly rejects a universal flood.

> Such universality could not have been in the mind of the writer [the covering of the entire globe with a sheet of water], and probably has been claimed knowingly by no writer in modern times.[87]

He also rejects the interpretation that the flood was universal as far as man and his special animals are concerned. Rather, he adopts the view we have expounded that the deluge was universal *in so far as the area and observation and information of the narrator extended*.[88] Whatever existed beyond the scope of the narrator's knowledge the record is silent about.

4. *Criticisms of the universal flood interpretation.* Much of the weight of evidence for the local flood consists in showing the imponderable difficulties of a universal flood. Before we critically examine the universal flood interpretation two things must be said: (i) It is not a question as to what God can or cannot do. Those who believe in a local flood believe in the omnipotence and power of God as much as any other Christian does. The question is not: "What *can* God do?" but, "What *did* God do?" (ii) The problem is one of interpretation, not inspiration. Those who believe in the local flood believe in the divine inspiration of the Bible; otherwise they would believe in no flood. It is improper to affirm that only those who believe in a universal flood really believe in the inspiration of Scripture and the omnipotence of God. It is also

improper to imply that those who believe in a local flood do not believe in the omnipotence of God and believe in the peccability of Scripture.[89]

(*a*) First of all, in criticism of the universal flood interpretation, this theory cannot demonstrate three of its most necessary propositions.

(i) *It cannot demonstrate that totality of language necessitates a universal flood.* Fifteen minutes with a Bible concordance will reveal many instances in which universality of language is used but only a partial quantity is meant. *All* does not mean *every last one* in all of its usages. Psa. 22: 17 reads: "I may tell all my bones," and hardly means that every single bone of the skeleton stood out prominently. John 4: 39 cannot mean that Jesus *completely* recited the woman's biography. Matt. 3: 5 cannot mean that every single individual from Judea and Jordan came to John the Baptist. There are cases where all means all, and every means every, but the context tells us where this is intended. Thus, special reference may be made to Paul's statement in Romans about the universality of sin, *yet even that "all" excludes Jesus Christ.*

The universality of the flood simply means the universality of the experience of the man who reported it. When God tells the Israelites He will put the fear of them upon the people *under the whole heaven,* it refers to all the peoples known to the Israelites (Deut. 2: 25). When Gen. 41: 57 states that *all countries* came to Egypt to buy grain, it can only mean all peoples known to the Egyptians. Ahab certainly did not look for Elijah in every country of the earth even though the text says he looked for Elijah so thoroughly that he skipped *no nation or kingdom* (I Kings 18: 10). From the vantage point of the observer of the flood all mountains were covered, and all flesh died. We must concur that:

> The language of the sacred historian by no means necessarily implies that the flood overspread the whole earth. Universal terms are frequently used in a partial and restricted sense in Scripture.[90]

The ark had a draught of about 15 cubits (Gen. 7: 20) and so the writer inferred that the water rose that high above the mountains because the ark did not ground on any of them. The highest mountain in the region was Ararat at about 17,000 feet; the Himalayan range rises to 29,000 feet. Do those who defend a universal flood wish to assert that the waters mounted to a depth of six miles?

(ii) *The universality of flood traditions cannot be uncritically appealed to.* Flood stories are to be found widely distributed throughout the world, with such notable exceptions as none in Japan or Egypt and few in Africa.[91] We must carefully distinguish between what is certainly related to the Biblical accounts; what is probably related;

what is conscious or unconscious assimilation of flood data as related by missionaries and merged into local flood stories; and what are purely local affairs having no connexion at all with the Bible. Simply to list flood stories and identify them all as versions or perversions of the Biblical flood is not a valid procedure.[92] It is a difficult task for a scholar to untangle all of these stories to see how dependent or independent they are.   Woods concludes:

> Though the common derivation of Deluge stories from the Bible deluge can no longer be maintained, the Bible story and those related to it have had in various ways a wide and important influence upon a large number of them.[93]

The data are not such that from a wide spread of flood legends a *universal* flood may be properly inferred.

(iii) *There is no known geological data to support those who defend a universal flood*.   A local flood could come and go and leave no trace after a few thousand years, but could a universal flood be a traceless flood?   Price's view we cannot but emphatically reject.   The appeal to the so-called *diluvia* of washes, loess, and gravel deposits, can no longer be made.   They are the results of the ice-age which cannot be identified with the flood of Noah, if for no other reasons than that there were really a series of ice-ages lasting over a million years. There remains no distinctive geological proof of a universal flood. Any good book on the history of geology will indicate how theory after theory of identification of the flood with some geological phenomenon had to be given up, till today there is no remaining evidence for a universal flood.[94]

(*b*) The problems in connexion with a universal flood are enormous.   We can but summarize here the lengthy refutations found in commentaries and Bible dictionaries and encyclopædias.   One point must be clearly understood before we commence these criticisms: *the flood is recorded as a natural-supernatural occurrence*.   It does not appear *as a pure and stupendous miracle*.   The natural and the supernatural work side by side and hand in hand.   If one wishes to retain a universal flood, it must be understood that a series of stupendous miracles is required.   Further, one cannot beg off with pious statements that God can do anything.   We concur enthusiastically with Smith when he wrote:

> "That the Omnipotent could effect such a work [a universal flood], none can doubt; *but we are not at liberty thus to invent miracles, and the narrative in the Book of Genesis plainly assigns two natural causes for the production of the diluvial waters*."[95]

(i) There is the problem of the amount of water required by a universal flood.   All the waters of the heavens, poured all over the earth, would amount to a sheath seven inches thick. If the earth were a perfect sphere so that all the waters of the ocean covered it, the depth of the ocean would be two and one-half to three miles.[96] To cover the highest mountains would require eight times more water than we now have. It would have involved a great creation of water to have covered the entire globe, but no such creative act is hinted at in the Scriptures.

(ii) The mixing of the waters and the pressure of the waters would have been devastating. Many of the salt-water fish and marine life would die in fresh water; and many of the fresh-water fish and marine life would die in salt water. An entire marine creation would have been necessary if the waters of the earth were mixed, yet no such hint is given in the account. Furthermore, the pressure of the water six miles high (to cover the Himalayas) would crush to death the vast bulk of marine life. Ninety per cent of marine life is within the first fifty fathoms. The enormous pressure of six miles of water on top of these forms (most of which cannot migrate, or migrate any distance) would have mashed them.

The result on plant life would have been equally devastating. Practically the entire world of plants would have perished under the enormous pressure, the presence of salt water, and a year's soaking. Innumerable life cycles of plants and insects would have been interrupted and would have required a creative work almost as extensive as the original creation to restore the earth. No such destruction and no such re-creation is hinted at in the Scriptures.

(iii) Getting rid of such a vast amount of water would have been as miraculous as providing it. If the entire world were under six miles of water, there would be no place for the water to drain off. Yet the record states that the water drained off with the help of the wind (Gen. 8: 1). A local flood would readily account for this, but there is no answer if the entire world were under water.

(iv) Two other matters with reference to the water demand our attention. The astronomical disturbances caused by the increase of the mass of the earth, if there was at one time a sheath of water six miles thick (from sea level), would have been significant, and could be detected by astronomers.[97]

Again, in Auvergne (France) there are cones of loose scoria and ashes from long-extinct volcanoes.[98] They are many thousands of years older than the flood could possibly be, yet they show no sign of having been washed or disturbed by flood waters. One theory is that the universal flood was so gentle that it lifted these cones up and dropped them back again, and that other heaps of scoriae are not of the loose variety. A universal flood could hardly have been that gentle, especially not if Price's view of tidal waves of a thousand miles an hour is accepted.

(v) The final problem with the universal flood belief is the multitude of improbabilities connected with the animals. Again, it is not what God could do, but what seems most consistent with the record. How did the animals get from distant lands to the ark? We have already indicated that an older theory had them transported to and fro by angels. Rehwinkel believes that at the time of the flood there were no high mountains, no deserts, no arctic regions, and that there was a uniform world temperature.[99] The animals were not distributed as they are now, but representatives of each species were near the ark. Others have suggested that the North American and South American continents were conjoined to Europe before the flood, and then "floated" apart after the flood (Gen. 10: 25, "the name of one was Peleg, for in his days the earth was divided" RSV). There would be no need for the animals to cross oceans.

As far as the science of geology can determine—and how else can we determine it?—no such major shift in the geological formation of the earth has taken place in the past several thousand years. If the world was then as it is now, it would take a series of remarkable miracles to get all the animals of the world, two of each species, to the ark and back again—over oceans, over deserts, over strange terrain, over difficult terrain.

Once in the ark the problem of feeding and caring for them would be enormous. The task of carrying away manure and bringing food would completely overtax the few people in the ark. Writes Woods:

> In a word, four men and four women were able to do [if the universal flood version is true] under such conditions, without, it would seem, the slightest difficulty, what taxes the utmost skill and ingenuity of zoologists with such space and under such conditions as are possible in our Zoological Gardens.[100]

Bede long ago suggested that the animals needed only one day's feed as they were all put to sleep.[101] To this day defenders of the universal flood teach that all the animals hibernated so that they needed no attention.

There is the problem of the special diets required for the animals, and the problem of special conditions for the animals. Some animals need a moist environment, and others a very dry one; some need it very cold and others very warm. Again, there is no question what Omnipotence can do, but the simplicity of the flood record prohibits the endless supplying of miracles to make a universal flood feasible.

B. C. Nelson (*The Deluge Story in Stone,* 1931) and A. M. Rehwinkel (*The Flood in the Light of the Bible, Geology, and Archaeology,* 1951) are modern scholars defending the universal flood. Rehwinkel's volume is a very ambitious work. Both depend on the geology of Price and are therefore, to our thinking, invalid.[102]

5. *The Babylonian Flood account.* This account is another factor to be reckoned with. The most detailed analysis of the parallelism between the Biblical account and the Babylonian account written from an evangelical viewpoint is that of G. F. Wright's essay, "The Deluge of Noah" (ISBE, II, 821–826). George Smith in 1872 discovered the twelve tablets of the Gilgamesh Epic, the eleventh tablet of which describes a Babylonian flood. The original copies of the tablets date back to 2000 B.C. Other versions of the flood are found in the Nippur Tablet (2100 B.C.) and tablets found at Nineveh and Kish.

In comparing and contrasting the two accounts, Wright notes that: (i) the Babylonian account is polytheistic and the Biblical account is monotheistic. (ii) Both agree that the flood came as a divine punishment for man's sins. (iii) The dimensions of the Babylonian ark are unreasonable (140 × 140 × 140 cubits), whereas the proportions and size of the Biblical ark are about the same as those of modern ocean vessels. (iv) The moral tone of the Babylonian epic is substandard. (v) There is no mention of geological phenomena in the Babylonian account, but the breaking up of the fountains of the deep means a rising ocean bed to bring waters in, and a falling one to drain them off. (vi) Both agree in the general details for the collecting of the animals, but the Babylonian account omits any reference to clean animals, and also includes other people in the ark. (vii) In the Babylonian account the structure had a mast and a pilot. (viii) The Babylonian flood lasted fourteen days and the Biblical flood one year and seventeen days. (ix) The Babylonian account has a dove and a raven in reverse order and adds a swallow. (x) The Babylonian account has the altar after the flood but in a polytheistic context. (xi) Both agree that the human race will not be destroyed after the flood. Wright concludes:

> It is in the highest degree improbable that correct statements of such unobvious facts should be due to the accident of legendary guesswork. At the same time, the duration of the Deluge, according to Genesis, affords opportunity for a gradual progress of events which best accord with scientific conceptions of geological movements.[103]

The general relationship of all Babylonian and Hebrew parallels is that of *cognateness,* which means *common source without any necessary mutuality,* and has been ably defended by J. McKee Adams (*Ancient Records and the Bible,* 1946). Both came out of the same common ancient tradition and so both possess similarities. The Babylonian account represents the tradition freely corrupted by human imagination; the Hebrew account is that which was kept chaste and pure through divine providence and then recorded through divine inspiration.

The flood was local to the Mesopotamian valley. The animals that came, prompted by divine instinct, were the animals of that region; they were preserved for the good of man after the flood. Man was destroyed within the boundaries of the flood; the record is mute about man in America or Africa or China. The types of vegetation destroyed quickly grew again over the wasted area, and other animals migrated back into the area, so that after a period of time the damaging effects of the flood were obliterated. An examination of the references of the New Testament to the flood are not conclusive, one way or the other, but permit either a local or universal flood interpretation.

We judge, then, that within Christian and supernaturalistic premises, there is nothing in the Scriptures about geological matters which should cause offence to anyone; on the contrary, we may believe the Biblical records with full assurance of being in agreement with geological science according to the principles developed in this chapter.

NOTES

1. Cf. J. W. Dawson, *The Origin of the World According to Revelation and Science* (1877), p. 229.

2. J. Pohle, *God: The Author of Nature and the Supernatural* (1942), p. 111. It would be well to keep in mind in the following discussion the advice of Melvin G. Kyle: "Whatever theory of the 'days' may be held, excepting the symbolical [modernist] view, *it does not become any one to call into question the faith of any one who accepts an alternative view.*" BS, 86: 307, 1929. Italics are ours.

3. W. F. Albright, "The Old Testament and Archaeology," *Old Testament Commentary* (edited by Alleman and Flack), p. 135.

4. E. T. Brewster, *Creation: A History of Non-Evolutionary Theories* (1927), p. 109.

5. A. D. White, I, 242–243, cites Anton Westermeyer, *The Old Testament Vindicated from Modern Infidel Objections* as a vigorous defender of the notion that fossil monsters were created by the Devil to frustrate God.

6. *Ibid.,* I, 214.

7. *Ibid.,* p. 216.

8. W. M. Smart, *The Origin of the Earth* (1951), Table V, p. 105, gives the dates of the geological eras and epochs as determined by radio-active methods.

9. Cordelia Erdman, "Stratigraphy and Paleontology," JASA, 5: 3–6, March, 1953, demolishes the idea that the dating of strata is circular. She is able to do this without any reference to radio-active dating of the rocks. The convergence of conclusions of the older and newer methods in geology is impressive.

10. Unfortunately orthodoxy has been too unsympathetic with geological science. From the early days of geology till now it has been a story of the vilification of scientists by the hyper-orthodox. Cf. "The favourite weapon of the orthodox party was the charge that the geologists were 'attacking the truth of God.' They declared geology 'not a subject of lawful inquiry,' denouncing it as 'a dark art,' as 'dangerous and disreputable,' as 'a forbidden province,' as 'infernal artillery,' and as 'an awful evasion of the testimony of revelation,'" White, I, 223.

11. Quoted by White, I, 19.

12. Fervent disciples of Price claim that he has never been refuted by competent geologists. In an informal discussion on geology, in which the author participated, the geologists present were put on the spot in this regard. One geologist said in substance that no reputable geologist feels it worth his time to refute something so preposterously false. Another remarked that his geology professor would not let anybody pass sophomore geology till he had refuted Price.

The professional geologists have said something, however. Cf. Schuchert, "The New Geology," *Science*, 59: 486–487 (1924); an address by Linton referring to Price *in passim*, *Science*, 63: 195–201 (1926); and Miller, "The New Catastrophism and its Defender," *Science*, 55: 702–703 (1922). Schuchert notes that Price requested from Wiley and Sons, publisher and copyright owner of Pirsson-Schuchert, *Text-book of Geology*, permission to use thirty-two photographs in *The New Geology*. Wiley and Sons thought this excessive and gave permission for three. Yet when Price published he used fourteen pictures from Pirsson, *Physical Geology* and eighteen from Schuchert, *Historical Geology*.

Miller notes the rather inadequate training in geology Price has had, the variety of subjects he taught, and the wide range of geological writers Price has read. He accused him of not being able to follow an argument which would be "understood by any high school student of physiography" (p. 702). He concludes his article by stating that: "This then is the man *who while a member of no scientific body and absolutely unknown in scientific circles* has in at least one of his contributions to the religious press . . . had the effrontery to style himself 'geologist' in the expression he there used, 'we geologists'; and this is the man who in his support of a literal Genesis is hailed by the fundamentalist as their great champion" (pp. 702–703. Italics are ours).

13. J. Laurence Kulp, "Deluge Geology," JASA, 2: 1–15, January, 1950. Price's own exposition will be found in his *The New Geology* (1923), Part V: Theoretical Geology.

14. *Ibid.*, p. 2.

15. *Ibid.*, p. 10.

16. The American Scientific Affiliation has put in mimeographed form a series of essays on the age of the earth entitled *A Symposium on the Age of the Earth* (1948). It was edited by Dr. Kulp, who also contributed an article on "Present Status of Age Determination in Geology," and Dr. Kulp also supplied excellent bibliographical references for the entire symposium.

A person who entitled himself only as "An A.S.A. Member" sharply criticized Kulp's criticism of Price (JASA, II, 2, June, 1950). His grounds are (i) that Kulp gives too much weight to uniformitarian geology, and that (ii) Kulp did not scientifically evaluate Price's position but tore it up in terms of his preconceived opinions. As for objection (i) it is puerile. It is condemnation on the grounds that "the enemy believes it; it must be wrong." But that has been the most discouraging thing about the hyper-orthodox in science, namely, that a theory is judged wrong on the sole grounds that the wrong people believe it. If uniformitarianism makes a scientific case for itself to a Christian scholar, that Christian scholar has every right to believe it, and if he is a man and not a coward he will believe it in spite of the intimidation that he is supposedly gone over into the camp of the enemy. After reading Kulp's article many times, I utterly fail to see how objection (ii) has any merit at all. Kulp has seriously and honestly gone after the facts and carefully presented them. I personally can find no point where Kulp has been unfair, or shoddy, or careless, or unscientific.

R. M. Allen's, "The Evaluation of Radio-active Evidence on the Age of the Earth" (JASA, 4: 11–20, December, 1952) is an effort to upset much of the certainty in radio-active dating, but Kulp has an able reply to it. Again, to destroy the testimony of radio-active dating you have to prove it well over 99 per cent wrong.

17. Cf. Brewster, *op. cit.,* p. 196 ff.

18. *Ibid.,* p. 222.

19. p. 231.

20. p. 233.

21. *Ibid.,* p. 176.

22. W. N. Rice concurs in our judgment. Speaking of Smith's theory he wrote: "To save the supposed inerrancy of the first chapter of Genesis, at the cost of stripping it of all its dignity and significance, is a very poor service to Christian faith." *Christian Faith in an Age of Science* (1903), p. 95. It is also possible to do geological research in this restricted territory of Smith's and show that no such renovation has occurred in recent times; and this geological research can be supplemented by the work of anthropologists, and the same conclusion is reached.

23. p. 126.

24. p. 123. Italics are his.

25. Gosse admits he was influenced by (i) a tract which he chanced upon, the author of which he never discovered; and (ii) by Granville Penn's, *The Mineral and Mosaical Geologies* (1822). Gosse's view is also discussed in Brewster, *op. cit.,* p. 112 ff.; and in White, I, Chapter V,

"From Genesis to Geology." This chapter of White's is to be consulted for many of the men and problems discussed in this chapter.

26. Thomas Chalmers, *Works,* I, 228; XII, 369. Dr. Anton Pearson sets forth the history of the gap interpretation as follows: It was first broached in modern times by Episcopius (1583–1643), and received its first scientific treatment by J. G. Rosenmuller (1736–1815) in his *Antiquissima Telluris Historia* (1776). It was also used by theosophic writers in connexion with notions suggested by Böhme, *e.g.* F. von Meyer and Baumgarten. It was picked up by such theologians as Buckland, Chalmers, J. P. Smith, and Murphy. ("An Exegetical Study of Gen 1: 1–3", *Bethel Seminary Quarterly,* II: 14–33, November, 1953).

This theory was also defended by J. H. Kurtz, *Bible and Astronomy* (third German edition, 1857) and in the footnote of p. 236 it is traced from Edgar, king of England in the tenth century, to modern scholars as Reichel, Stier, G. H. von Schubert, Knieivel, Dreschler, Rudelbach, Guericke, Baumgartner, Lebeau, and Wagner.

Buckland's sane and sober defence will be found in Treatise VI of the *Bridgewater Treatises* entitled *Geology and Mineralogy Considered with Reference to Natural Theology* (second edition; 2 vols. 1837), Chapter II, "Consistency of Geological Discoveries with Sacred History." He has no doctrine of the fall of angels or Satan which many commentators brand as more theosophical than Scriptural.

27. Biographical details of Rimmer will be found in *Who's Who* (vol. 28) and in Kathryn Rimmer Braswell, "Harry Rimmer—Defender of the Faith," *The Sunday School Times,* 95: 263–264, March 28, 1953. Rimmer audited medical college for one year, and attended one year each: San Francisco Bible College, The Bible Institute of Los Angeles, and Whittier College. Mrs. Braswell states that "Dr. Rimmer was largely self-educated" (p. 264). His son has a novel-biography of his father (*In the Fullness of Time*). Some biographical details and account of the Scientific Research Bureau of Rimmer will be found in Norman F. Furniss, *The Fundamentalist Controversy,* 1918–1931, Yale University Press, 1954.

28. *Reference Bible,* p. 4, note 3.

29. *Earth's Earliest Ages,* p. 22.

30. *Ibid.,* p. 25.

31. *Ibid.,* p. 27.

32. *Ibid.,* p. 28.

33. *Ibid.,* p. 35.

34. *Ibid.,* p. 74.

35. O. T. Allis, *God Spake by Moses* (1951), p. 153.

36. See Allis' point by point refutation of this exegesis. *Op. cit.,* p. 155 ff. He calls the exegetical arguments "very weak," p. 155.

37. 78: 13–37, 1946.

38. E. K. Gedney, "Geology and the Bible," *Modern Science and Christian Faith* (second edition; 1950), p. 49, fn. 30.

39. All of the Hebrew scholarship of the King James, Revised Version,

and Revised Standard Version agree with the traditional interpretation of these verses.   The latter two, which use marginal notations, do not give *became* as an alternate to *was*.

40. F. Godet, *Studies in the Old Testament* (1874), pp. 104–105.

41. Elmer E. Flack, "God is not the Author of Confusion," *Christian Faith and Life*, 39: 190, April, 1933.   Italics are his.

42. *Reference Bible,* p. 776, note 1.

43. *Op. cit.,* p. 153.

44. J. S. Baxter, *Studies in Problem Texts* (1949), pp. 83–84.   Italics are ours.

45. *Ibid.,* p. 191.   Italics and caps are ours.   Baxter is a literalistic dispensationalist at Isa. 9: 5 and a very good spiritualizing amillennialist at Ezek. 28 and Isa. 14.   Allis rejects the Satanic fall interpretation of these passages and remarks: "When the attempt is made to treat poetic and figurative language as matter-of-fact prose, the result is often very wide of the mark, if not positively grotesque."   *Op. cit.,* p. 156.

46. J. W. Dawson, *Nature and the Bible* (1875), p. 85 fn.   Dawson repeatedly and in strong language repudiates the gap theory and his judgment ought to be seriously weighed.   See his further strong condemnations of it in *The Origin of the World According to Revelation and Science* (1877), pp. 103, 106.

47. Allis correctly observes that if the gap theorists smuggle in great periods of time in Gen. 1: 2 they are hardly in a position to oppose those who smuggle it in under the word *yom*.   *Op. cit.,* pp. 153–154.

48. R. A. Torrey, *Difficulties in the Bible* (1907), pp. 27–32, has the same undigested gap theory.   He accepts the gap theory and also the possibility that the days were long periods of time.   He then *inconsistently* appeals to the proposed harmony of the days of Genesis with the epochs of geology.   You cannot appeal to *both* the gap of Gen. 1: 2 *and* the age-day interpretation of the days without throwing the whole process of reconciliation of Genesis and geology into confusion.   Who could ever tell which belonged to the ages of the gap, and the ages of the six age-days?

49. J. Pohle, *God: The Author of Nature and the Supernatural* (1942), p. 113.   He says that A. Westermeyer attributed this catastrophe to angels in his *Erschaffung der Welt und der Menschen und deren Geschichte bis nach der Sündflut* (1861).

50.   Tayler Lewis, "Genesis," LANGE, pp. 167–168.

51. Hugh Miller, *Testimony of the Rocks* (1869), p. 121.   It must be pointed out that Miller was a capable field geologist as far as the development of the science in his time was concerned, and that he is one of the greatest harmonizers of Genesis and geology the evangelicals have ever had.

52.   Gedney, *op. cit.,* pp. 48–49.   J. O. Buswell, Jr., rejects the gap theory rather strongly.   Cf. "The Length of the Creative Days," *Christian Faith and Life,* 14: 123 ff., April, 1935.   Rice criticizes it on the grounds that all it gives the geologist is time.   But just as soon as

uniformitarianism became an issue in geology, especially as coupled with evolution, the gap theory no longer could hold the line.   It was replaced by the age-day theory.   Rice, *op. cit.*, p. 92 ff.   However Rice did not anticipate the tremendous revival of the gap theory in the twentieth century.

53. Cf. A. Higley, *Science and Truth* (1940), p. 86, J. P. Smith, *op. cit.*, p. 171 ff.   J. H. Pratt, *op. cit.*, p. 44 ff.   K. L. Brooks, *Don't Kid Yourself about the Days of Genesis* (pamphlet, 1947).

54. H. W. Magoun has defended the age-day interpretation with great ability.   He quotes Naville as saying that the Egyptians had no word for period so they used *day* to indicate a span of time.   Cf. "The Creative Days," *The Bible Champion*, 36: 537–541, October, 1930; and, "Are Geological Ages Irreconcilable with Genesis?" BS, 88: 347–357 (1931). J. O. Buswell writes: "We hold that the word 'day' used here as elsewhere, figuratively, and represents a period of time of undesignated length." *Op. cit.*, p. 117.   C. B. Warring, "The Hebrew Cosmogony," BS, 63: 50–65 (1896) believes that Genesis is remarkably true to science. The Babylonian account is mythical and where true is platitudinous. Warring makes a strong defence of the cosmogony of Genesis from the age-day position.   See also his article, "Professor Huxley versus Genesis 1," BS, 49: 638–649, 1892.   On the word "day" the learned S. R. Driver wrote: "In spite of the phrases *evening* and *morning*, which seem to imply literal days, the supposition that the narrator meant his 'day' as the figurative representation of periods, should not, as the present writer ventures to think, be ruled as inadmissible."   "The Cosmology of Genesis," *The Expositor*, third series, III, 27, 1886.

55. *Reference Bible*, p. 4, footnote No. 2.   We cannot insist too strongly the inconsistency of this position.   It presents us with the geologic hodge-podge of geologic periods accounted for by the gap concept, and then by the age-day concept.   Who can ever unscramble the geologic record if this is the case?   The gap theory for accounting for geologic ages must be given up or else the age-day theory consistently denied, not flirted with.

56. F. Bettex, *op. cit.*, p. 27 fn., quoting his *Das Lied der Schöpfung*, p. 274.

57. See Tayler Lewis's fine remarks about this phrase.   *Op. cit.*, p. 132.   In agreement is Bettex, *op. cit.*, p. 190.

58. Gedney, *op. cit.*, p. 49.

59. *Ibid.*, p. 52–53.   Dawson's will be found in *The Origin of the World According to Revelation and Science* (1877), p. 353.

60. There are more than 5,000 species in the Cambrian strata.   All phyla are represented but vertebrates.   The phyla, classes, families, genera, and species are all clearly marked.   Cf. D. Dewar, "The Earliest Known Animals," JTVI, 80: 22–29, 1948.

61. We must call attention to L. F. Gruber, *The Six Creative Days* (1941) which we believe to be the simplest, grandest, clearest exposition of the harmony of Genesis and geology we have read.   It is in the tradition of Dawson.

62. Gaston Lewis Leary, "Cosmogony," *A New Standard Bible Dictionary*, pp. 152–154.

63. Bettex, *op. cit.*, p. 191.

64. In other words, we are in exact agreement with Melvin G. Kyle when he wrote: "A combination of the revelatory view with the geologic view is thus probably the true explanation of the 'days' of creation in the Genesis account." "The Bible in its Setting," BS, 86: 307, 1929.

65. Kurtz, *op. cit.*, p. 22. Italics are his. There is evidence that Moses was given certain medical knowledge for the *miraculous* preservation of the Israelites in the wilderness.

66. "The order observed [in Genesis] is logical rather than chronological." H. J. T. Johnson, *The Bible and Early Man* (1948), p. 63. S. R. Driver, after reviewing the various theories of harmonization and indicating their weaknesses, believes that only a very general correlation between Genesis and geology can be made with the arrangement more topical than chronological, Driver, *op. cit.* Driver also rejects the interpretation that the astronomical bodies were "caused to function" in the fourth day. He examines the Hebrew word so used and says it will not bear this meaning.

67. Kurtz, *op. cit.*, pp. 107, 110–111. Italics are his. Those accepting Kurt's hypothesis as to the means of revealing the creation of the world are: Godet, *Studies in the Old Testament* (1874), p. 80. C. W. Shields, *The Scientific Evidences of Revealed Religion* (1900), p. 29. J. W. Dawson, *The Origin of the World According to Revelation and Science* (1877), pp. 49 and 65.

68. See F. F. Bruce's review of Wiseman's book in *The Evangelical Quarterly,* 20: 302, October, 1948.

69. P. J. Wiseman, *Creation Revealed in Six Days* (1949), p. 76 ff. Two ideas have prejudiced orthodoxy against geology. First, orthodoxy has believed that unless creation were *speedy* we detracted from the glory or omnipotence of God. Hence orthodoxy has had to fight all science which demanded long periods of time as in geology or biology. But nowhere in Sacred Writ is speed made an *essential* criterion of the supernatural. Because a sudden cure is certainly supernatural we cannot argue that all things supernatural must be speedy. Because natural processes may take periods of time we cannot argue that a supernatural work thereby cannot consume a period of time in its realization. No more can we argue that a natural event is really supernatural because it is practically instantaneous as is the case in the atomic world. Second, orthodoxy has put a premium on the catastrophic, and thereby has had to fight all uniformitarianism in science. Because the divine at times appears as catastrophic does not mean that the divine is never uniformitarian. In fact, as we saw in our discussion of the Biblical view of Nature, the orderly, the uniform, the stable, is one of the very marks of the divine. Orthodoxy will be at odds with natural science till it relinquishes its unjustifiable beliefs that the divine is *always* (i) instantaneous, and (ii) catastrophic.

70. See our discussion of this in Chapter III.

71. However, with the safeguards we put on this interpretation in the third chapter. God is in the *innermost* of things by the Spirit; not as essence or accidence. So if you cut off a leaf you would not have cut off a piece of the Spirit. Nor will the scientist ever find the Spirit at the other end of the microscope.

72. For a comparison of the sane Biblical account of the ark with the rather fantastic Babylonian ideas see A. Heidel, *The Gilgamesh Epic and Old Testament Parallels* (1946), p. 232 ff. Heidel does a serious job in trying to interpret the Genesis account, giving special reference to etymology and cognate languages.

73. Heidel, *op. cit.,* p. 234, takes it to be a window system one cubit high running around the ark.

74. Considerable details about the ark and its stability will be found in JFB, I, 92 ff.

75. Heidel, *op. cit.,* pp. 245 f.

76. M. F. Unger, *Introductory Guide to the Old Testament* (1951), p. 194. Discussion of carbon-14 method of dating will be found in Zeuner, *op. cit.,* and a popular explanation in Ruth Moore, *Man, Time, and Fossils* (1953), Chapter XVIII. Any number of materials of human association have been dated prior to 4000 B.C.

77. The thesis that the ice-age provided the water and a tilt of the earth on its axis the necessary change to melt it, is defended by T. C. Skinner, "The Ice-Age: Its Astronomical Cause, and the Bearing of Drayson's Discovery on the Bible Account of the Deluge," JTVI, 61: 118–139, 1929; and M. G. Kyle, "The Deluge and the World Before and After," BS, 87: 452–464, 1930.

78. Supposedly first advocated by Jerome who got it from Ezekiel ("the crystal stretched above the Cherubim," reference?). Cf. A. D. White, I, 324.

79. p. 71.

80. Treated sympathetically by A. M. Rehwinkel, *The Flood* (1951), p.p 12–13. He suggests also that (i) titling of earth's axis would have brought a change in climate; or (ii) warm ocean currents could have kept the climate idyllic.

81. Cf. L. M. Davies, "Scientific Discoveries and Their Bearing on the Biblical Account of the Noachian Deluge," JTVI, 62: 62–95, 1930. Davies defends an extensive but not necessarily a universal flood. However, these mammoths are found in several strata covering perhaps hundreds of thousands of years, and the *latest* is more than 30,000 years ago.

82. H. Rimmer, *The Harmony of Science and Scripture* (third edition, 1936), Chapter VII, "Modern Science and the Deluge."

83. *Ibid.,* p. 238.

84. We consider the best discussion on the flood to be George Frederick Wright, "The Deluge of Noah," ISBE, II, 821–26. The

local flood was first advocated in modern times by Bishop Stillingfleet, *Origines Sacrae,* Book III, Chapter IV. However in recent times H. C. Leupold, *Exposition of Genesis* (1950, Vol. I), defends a universal flood.

85. JFB, I, p. 100.

86. R. M. Rehwinkel admits this. *Op. cit.,* pp. 32–40.

87. J. W. Dawson, *The Meeting-Place of Geology and History* (1894), p. 151.

88. *Ibid.,* p. 152.

89. Rehwinkel, *op. cit.,* p. 90, very unfairly identifies his view with inspiration, so that to disagree with him is to deny the inspiration of the Bible. There is also a trace of this in KD, I, 146–147.

90. JFB, I, 98.

91. For a critical discussion of flood legends see F. H. Woods, "Deluge," ERE, IV, 545–557.

92. R. Andrée, *Die Flutsagen* (1891) is considered by scholars as the most thorough collection of these flood legends. The most complete record of them in English is to be found in James Frazer, *Folk-lore in the Old Testament* (Vol. I, 1918).

93. *Ibid.,* IV, 550.

94. Cf. to the contrary Prestwich's view that some watery catastrophe had to occur as the only possible explanation of the disappearance of late-glacial and post-glacial man about 10,000–12,000 B.C. Prestwich was a great and honoured British geologist. G. F. Wright, "Professor Prestwich on Some Supposed New Evidence of the Deluge," BS, 72: 724–740, October, 1895.

95. John Pye Smith, *op. cit.,* p. 132. Italics are ours. For example, it was formerly believed that angels picked up the animals and brought them to the ark, and then redistributed them after the flood was over. Cf. White, I, 45. Rehwinkel constantly solves his difficulties by recourse to the miraculous or to the sheer omnipotence of God. With this type of argumentation any theory, no matter how feeble, can be *ad hoc* patched up.

96. So state both K. Kinns, *Harmony of Science and the Bible* (1881), p. 398; and L. J. Henderson, *The Fitness of the Environment* (1913), p. 78.

97. "Deluge," MS, II, 737.

98. *Smith's Bible Dictionary,* III, 2183.

99. Rehwinkel, *op. cit.,* p. 47. *But where in the simple record of the flood is the basis of such a profound geological, geographical, and meteorological change?* Where is the sanction from the science of geology? What is the *control* put upon such assertions?

100. Woods, *op. cit.,* IV, 545.

101. Bede, *Hexaemeron,* i and ii.

102. In the preface Rehwinkel says that he wishes "to acknowledge particularly his debt to Dr. George McCready Price, a noted geologist ... Dr. Price is a brilliant champion of Biblical truth." *Op. cit.*, pp. vii and viii.   Later he calls Price "an able geologist and a brilliant writer," p. 102.   He also notes that J. W. Dawson is a great defender of Genesis. Let us keep the facts straight.   Price will have nothing to do with Dawson's Lyellian geology, and Dawson will have little to do with diluvialism.

103. Wright, *loc. cit.*, p. 824.

CHAPTER VII

BIOLOGY

I. Toward a Philosophy of Biology

THE author has read much in the field of the philosophy of biology, looking especially for a Christian vantage point. It is our conviction that the fundamental problem of Christianity in biology is not really evolution but a philosophy of biology. If we have a philosophy of biology we will have the proper setting and orientation for all our thinking in biology. To show that a philosophy of biology is more fundamental an issue than evolution, let us propose imaginatively, and we trust accurately, the reactions to evolution of a Roman Catholic, an idealist philosopher (who believes in the reality and primacy of a spiritual order), and an extreme hyper-orthodox.

The idealist would say something like this: "All reality is spirit or mind or *Geist*. No material substance in the sense of a non-mental or non-spiritual reality exists. What we call *matter* or *scientific law* are established patterns of the succession of representations in the spiritual world. The evolution of life is part of the vast over-all pattern of the succession of representations as ordered by God. Evolution is no more materialistic or atheistic than anything else in our experience, for *all experience is mental or spiritual.* If evolution be true it makes no difference to me, for all reality is spiritual; so evolution must be part of that spiritual reality, and evolution is but the orderly succession of ideas as ordained by God."

The Roman Catholic biologist would say: "I adopt the fundamental thesis of Aquinas, namely, that all things are moved toward their goal by God. Whether it be the growth of an egg into a chicken, or the growth of sensations into truth, or the development of the crust of the earth, it is God moving all things. *Without God, motion—spiritual, intellectual, material—is impossible.* The problem of direct creation or mediate creation through evolution is immaterial to me. Neither could happen without God. Therefore, because we have established on other grounds that no motion can happen without God, it is immaterial whether life was suddenly created or slowly evolved. In either case it is God who does it and therefore evolution is neither here nor there as far as Catholic faith is concerned."

[1] For notes see page 208.

The extreme hyper-orthodox would perhaps reply: "Men, these philosophical subtleties are the workings of your own mind and not God's Word.   God said what He meant, and meant what He said.   God said He *made* life, the animals and man.   I take this as a literal, direct fact, and seek no evasion from it.   Therefore, I must believe in fiat creation or none at all.   If evolution is true, the Bible is wrong; and I must give up Christ, salvation, and all the truth of the New Testament.   Because so much is at stake I must fight evolution at every turn."[1]

The very obvious mistake of the extreme hyper-orthodox is that he equates *divine causation* with *sudden creation* and his thinking is brittle right at this point.   He makes his entire theological system— the Deity of Christ, original sin, atonement, resurrection—hang on *sudden creation,* and one bone from a fossil pit can *potentially* bring the whole edifice down.   Surely, Christianity cannot live in constant dread as to what some palaeontologist or archaeologist is going to bring to light—so that one fossil can spell the doom of orthodoxy. There is only one sure approach to evolution and biology and that is through a well-defined Christian philosophy of biology.[2]

Plato and Aristotle had a system of idealistic biology, although Aristotle's was developed in far greater detail than Plato's.   Plato's thought suffers from a certain artificiality because he never solved the problem in his philosophy as to how ideas participate in objects (*methexis*).   How does birdness and sparrowness participate in one object to make a sparrow?   Aristotle's more empirical approach and more profound analysis of causation led him to a more tolerable system of biology.   With his concepts of form and matter, potentiality and actuality, and four-fold causation, he worked out an impressive metaphysics and philosophy of biology.   Aquinas adopted the basic features of this system and created a "Christian" philosophy and indirectly a "Christian" philosophy of science and a philosophy of biology.

Modern philosophy of biology has stalemated into either some form of vitalism or mechanism.   Mechanism in biology is not easy to define, as a reading of Woodger's *Biological Principles* will prove, but in broad it refers to the effort to interpret biological phenomena as special cases of chemistry or physics.   Negatively defined it is the conviction that there is nothing more to biological data than chemical and physical events.   Vitalism, again difficult of simple definition, believes that there is something more to organisms than chemical or physical properties, but the "something more" has always been elusive of definition, especially of *operational* definition.

In the earlier part of this volume we developed our own effort to set forth a philosophy of Nature, and that our philosophy of Nature is directly related to our philosophy of biology.   In summary, we accept progressive creationism, which teaches that over the millions of years of geological history God has been directly creating higher and higher forms of life.   Progressive creation tries to free itself from loaded *a priori* assumptions, and tries seriously to be inductive and empirical.   It accepts the *a priori* of Divine Creation and the inspired account, but it turns over the million odd empirical details to science and does not try to pre-empt too much for theology. Further, we believe that creation is the *realization* of certain forms or ideas, and it is this realization in Nature which admits a teleological ordering and understanding of Nature.   As we previously wrote, we believe that the Divine Entelechy in Nature, realizing the forms and ideas of God, is the Holy Spirit.   This basic pattern of thought we apply directly to a Christian philosophy of biology, and by so doing we endeavour to escape so much of the brittle thinking of extreme fundamentalism on biological matters.

II.   The Origin of Life

The origin of life on naturalistic premises is that life emerged through some fortunate situation in some primeval pool of water. It was not a sudden passage from the inorganic to the organic, but it was through a series of ever-increasing complex combinations, with many borderline combinations that would be half chemical and half living.   Finally, true protoplasm emerged, possessing the required properties to be defined as living.   O. A. Oparin, *The Origin of Life* (1938), is one of the better modern attempts to explain the origin of life on a chemical basis.[3]   He surveys the condition of the earth from its proposed origin till the time when life could emerge.   He tries to find the series of chemical bridges from the inorganic to life.   It is refreshing that Oparin does not dogmatize, but labels his effort as speculatory, with many gaps in the evidence. It is a treatise on how it might have occurred, not on how it actually did occur.

S. L. Miller, working under the direction of Harold Urey, performed an experiment in which he was able to synthesize amino acids with elements and conditions which supposedly represent the original conditions on the earth.[4]   In a closed system, water, methane, ammonia and hydrogen were heated so that they were vaporous and passed through a small electric corona discharge whose purpose was to simulate the radiation of the sun and the electrical phenomena of the primitive atmosphere.   After a week the liquid was red and contained three amino acids which are the basic stuff of protein, and a number of unidentifiable, more complex compounds.   Miller and Urey do not believe they have created life, but they feel they have made a significant start in the laboratory to unravel the problem of the origin of life.

Harris has surveyed all the contemporary theories of the origin of life from non-living materials and finds them all defective.[5] The six theories examined and rejected are that life originated by (i) spontaneous generation; (ii) from cosmic panspermia; (iii) from cell models; (iv) from colloids; (v) from enzymes; and (vi) from viruses.   Approaching the problem from a different perspective, Clark arrives at a similar negative judgment to Harris.[6] He asserts that no definition of life or scientific explanation of its origin can stand up to criticism. The usual procedure is to explain one mystery by means of another. The fundamental criticism is that modern science works on the basis of a *scientific monism* by which he means that all there is is matter or substance or Nature. But, Clark continues, in that Nature operates on the grounds of *random activity* and the human intelligence on the principle of *organization and control*, we have a *final dualism*. A theistic explanation of the origin of life is the only possible explanation.

It is du Noüy's contention that chance cannot account for life. The simplest protein molecules are so complex that there is no possibility that they could have their atoms lined up in the correct order and number. Taking a protein molecule of two thousand atoms and presuming that there are only two elements necessary, the calculus of probability is such that the possibility of such a molecule forming by chance is for all practical purposes impossible. Even if 500 trillion shakings per second were employed the possibility of a chance variation occurring which would be a protein molecule is one in 10^{243} billion years.[7] Since du Noüy is such a controversial figure we refer also to Butler, who says much the same thing:

> In fact, we can hardly imagine how these complex structures came to exist on the earth. We find it difficult to conceive of any natural process by which any structure even as comparatively simple as a protein molecule could be formed. It is hardly conceivable that the atoms of a protein molecule spontaneously could come together in the right order to form a protein. Calculations have been made of the probability or chance of this happening fortuitously. The result is a "chance" which is so small as to have no real meaning.[8]

Butler gives the figures as one chance in 100^{160} or once in 10^{243} billion years. The identical figures are given by McCrady, who attributes them to Professor Charles-Eugene Guye.[9]

But supposing that life could originate in the laboratory, as already hinted in the Miller-Urey experiment? What should be our judgment if some day a scientist actually makes a living cell or something akin to an amoeba? Men used to believe that man could change or duplicate only the inorganic, for only God could make living creatures and their products. But since the synthesis of urea a good number of organic compounds have been created and the entire debate ceased. Even the staunchest hyper-orthodox would hardly reopen this debate. If man can think God's thoughts after Him, why is it incredible that man can do some of God's works after Him? Further, because man with a vast chemical equipment and an equally vast body of chemical data at his disposal can synthesize complex chemicals, it does not mean that Nature with only chance as its guide and creator can make life and foster it into complex creatures over the millions of years.

At our present state of knowledge two things may be stated. (i) Man has not produced life chemically. That he may produce protoplasmic specks is a possibility, but the production of even the smallest organism is as yet a long time away. In view of our inability to produce life with our vast chemical knowledge and our ability to reproduce almost any condition we wish of pressure, temperature or motion, we must still view a chance origin of life as a faith and not as a verified hypothesis. (ii) Unless a person is very anti-Christian it cannot be denied that the most satisfactory explanation to date is that life is the creation of the Living God. There is certainly nothing scientifically disrespectable in this connexion, even though a person is not a believer. Those who do believe it, may do so without fear of contravening scientific fact and without prejudicing the character of their judgment. Or, in the words of Short:

> We conclude, then, that science is still unable to put forward any satisfactory explanation as to how life arose in the first place. We must either accept the Bible doctrine that God created life, or go on making improbable speculations.[10]

III. Evolution

Perhaps the strongest clash between theologians and scientists has been over evolution, at least in modern times. The sordid history, from Bishop Wilberforce's disgraceful attack in his debate with Huxley to Bryan's miseries at the Scopes' trial in America, and the extreme remarks of the contemporary hyper-orthodox, we will not trace. Matching such extreme remarks have been the equally dogmatic utterances of irreligious biologists, and dishonesty among biologists, e.g. Haeckel and Kammerer. The less said of this disgraceful chapter in the progress of both religion and science, the better. Nor shall we review all there is to say about evolution. To keep our task within limits of space we shall discuss principally the philosophical and theological aspects of evolution.

A. *Improper spirit of controversy.*   In that the evolution issue has become so emotionally charged it is difficult to discuss it with calm. A biology professor harassed by hyper-orthodox students over a number of years might become bitter and sarcastic.   Or he might judge all such by a few outspoken and cantankerous representatives. Or the teacher of biology might have a very limited knowledge of philosophy of biology, or epistemology, or logic, or theology, or Scripture, and accordingly make statements that are far more narrow or dogmatic than the facts in the case allow.   Engrossed in biological matters year after year, he might become incompetent to make dependable judgments in the larger areas of philosophy and theology It is unfortunate when such an individual makes dogmatic statements about evolution and theology.

The hyper-orthodox who insist that all evolutionists are Satan-inspired or dishonest, or too stupid to see supposedly obvious and grotesque flaws in evolutionary theory, is equally to blame.

Certainly—and we say it with tears—the *finer spirits* in both science and theology will repudiate both gentlemen.   The hyper-orthodox need a new calm, a new reserve, a new reverence for *all* truth so that they may sympathetically, intelligently, and honestly reconsider the relationships between orthodoxy and biological science.   Biologists are to be under an equal moral and intellectual responsibility to weigh carefully the nature of biological science, and mark out its limitations and boundaries, and keep their generalizations within these bounds.

Our own spirit in this matter is neither that of the religious dogmatist who refutes evolution by the simple recourse of damning it, nor the scientific idolator who thinks it impious to criticize anything in science and who looks upon evolution as a sacred cow.

B. *Types of evolutionary theory.*   The overwhelming number of hyper-orthodox articles, booklets, and books on evolution which we have read set the scene for discussion of biology as follows: (i) a man believes in fiat, immediate creation; (ii) or he subscribes to atheistic, ungodly evolution; or (iii), in a condition of mental weakness and intellectual confusion, he believes in theistic evolution. The facts of the case are not so simple.   There are many types of evolution.   We do not refer to such theories as orthogenesis or nomogenesis, nor to macromutations or micromutations,[11] but to the larger interpretations of the philosophy of biology.

1. There is without question an anti-Christian version of the theory of evolution.   Evolution has been used by atheists and naturalists and materialists to bolster their metaphysics and to club the orthodox.   Dialectical materialism, the official philosophy of Russia, glories in evolution as the scientific doctrine of creation which frees man from faith in God.   Evolution has been used to

support atheism, ethical nihilism, and much anti-God, anti-Bible, and anti-Christian thought.   Strauss, in his *Der Alte und Der Neue Glaube*, greatly rejoices over evolution in that Darwin releases us from creationism.   Miracles, he claims, are gone forever![12] Romanes in his *Thoughts on Religion*, avers:

> All, taken together as Christian dogmas, are undoubtedly hard hit by the scientific proof of evolution . . . and, as constituting the logical basis of the whole plan, they certainly do appear at first sight necessarily to involve in their destruction the entire superstructure.[13]

With this form of the theory of evolution, or with this use of the theory of evolution, evangelical Christianity will always be at war.   In discussing the *expanded* theory of Darwin, namely, the conversion of evolution into a naturalistic or materialistic philosophy, and thereby ruling out anything spiritual or ethical, Rudolph Otto correctly wrote:

> To this *expanded* Darwinism not an inch of ground can be yielded from the side of religion; nor from the side of any idealistic conviction, nor from the side of spiritual knowledge in general.[14]

2. However, evolution is not always set in a materialistic or atheistic or naturalistic or positivistic setting.   That evolution has aided anti-Christian systems of thought no informed person can doubt; but that it has also been turned to other purposes, no informed person can doubt either.   *There are several forms of a spiritualistic interpretation of evolution.*   The mistake of Straton is that he bases his entire attack on the anti-Christian and anti-spiritual interpretation of evolution, or else tries to force all spiritual interpretations into the anti-spiritual mould.[15]   This greatly detracts from the cogency of his position.   Even more distracting is his high regard for Price's geology and the adoption of the universal flood as the cause of all geological phenomena.

(*a*) There is the *modern Thomistic interpretation* of evolution constructed on the philosophy of Aristotle as formulated by Aquinas. Evolution is but the *modus operandi* by which the ideas or forms or universals are realized in the animal and plant world.   God as the cause of all motion is the spiritual and intelligent force behind evolution, and evolution occurs solely because there is a God, and because Nature is constituted in the terms described by Aquinas. Hence, evolution is fitted into a theistic scheme of things and is completely deprived of its so-called anti-spiritual force.

(*b*) Augustine suggested that God sowed *seminal principles* in Nature or matter and they taking root, as it were, developed the world of animals and plants.[16]   God, Augustine so argued, did not create things directly, but created them in seminal form.   From seminal form, *under the guidance of God*, the final creatures were realized. Modern Catholic writers teach that evolution was the *modus operandi* whereby these seeds became forms. Again the result is a theory of evolution which is spiritualistic and teleological.

(*c*) The theory of *emergent evolution* has been developed by men who reject the crass materialistic interpretation of evolution. These men believe that life arose miraculously and that mind appeared miraculously, and that from original life to mind, life kept emerging on higher and higher levels. By recombination due to the God-imparted *nisus* within Nature, life passed upward into more complex forms. The new levels were not reached by chance evolution but were sudden and novel appearances. In that the whole is more than the sum of its parts the new form with a certain rearrangement of old parts is a very *new* creature. This again is a spiritualistic form of the theory of evolution.

(*d*) Henri Bergson in his theory of *creative evolution* endeavours to re-think evolution in a spiritual context. His works contain a powerful dissection of materialistic evolution, and a strong appeal for a spiritualistic interpretation of biology. He pictures evolution as a creative process driven on by a spiritual force. He argues that life-forms would not develop unless there were something urging life on and directing it. Forms expanding and radiating over the ages of geology cannot be accounted for in terms of a mechanistic and deterministic biology. Evolution can only be understood when pictured as a dynamic movement of spiritual life.

(*e*) L. du Noüy's theory of biology is very similar to Bergson's. He too was a French biologist, and he too saw the bankruptcy of evolution mechanistically and atheistically interpreted. He named his system *telefinalism*. The Divine Spirit has led the path of evolution up to man. Biological evolution reaches its climax in man. Man is now to carry on moral evolution. Again, we have the theory of evolution set within a spiritualistic system.

(*f*) Finally, just to mention them, for we shall say more about them later, there are evangelical Christians who have espoused theistic evolution, and see no incompatibility between this acceptance and their Christian faith. Asa Gray, James McCosh, James Orr and A. H. Strong were all evangelical believers who accepted theistic evolution. Benjamin Warfield in a carefully guarded statement seemed to teach that if evolution were properly defined, he would not be adverse to it. It must also be kept in mind that orthodox Catholic theologians with just as high a view of inspiration as evangelical Protestants, and with just as much at stake in theology, also believe in theistic evolution, not to mention orthodox Jewish believers. Religious modernists and neo-orthodox thinkers almost to a man have accepted theistic evolution and see no incompatibility in accepting evolution with their theistic metaphysics.

These various interpretations indicate that the dilemma of fiat creationism *versus* atheistic evolution, into which the hyper-orthodox try to force the issue, is not possible. It is not fiat creationism *or* atheistic evolution (with theistic evolution as a sterile hybrid), but there is also progressive creationism, and evolution interpreted in the larger framework of a theistic or spiritualistic or idealistic metaphysics.

C. *Evolution as a scientific theory.* Both the dogmatic evolutionist who calls evolution a theory proved beyond any doubt, and the dogmatic fundamentalist who brands it as a mere theory, are wrong. Scientific epistemology knows no absolutes in scientific theory. Cohen and Nagel write:

> A hypothesis becomes verified, *but of course not proved beyond every doubt,* through successful predictions it makes.[17]

We cannot speak of the theory of evolution as possessing a certainty which belongs only to formal logic.

The most characteristic feature of science is its process of generalization. These generalizations may be very limited in what they include or they may be very comprehensive. Statements about the properties of lead are not nearly as comprehensive as those about the nature of gravitation. These generalizations are otherwise called laws, and it must be kept in mind we never *see* a law; we only see instances which exhibit the law. Nature posits the problem and the mind posits the hypothesis; and experimentation and logic tell us if the hypothesis is true or not. Every generalization or law or theory or hypothesis must face both *logical* and *material* entailment. If we find that our hypothesis jars with other hypotheses we must do something about it. We may discover that our hypothesis is wrong and the general body of established hypotheses is correct; or, we may feel that our hypothesis is correct and the whole body of theory must be overhauled. It was the genius of Einstein to see that it was all of physics which needed basic reconstruction, and not new solutions within the old physics of certain particular difficulties.

On the other hand the law or generalization must be put to some experimental or material test. Rigorous experimentation may show that our generalization is premature or false. Or, it may indicate that we are on the correct track but we should refine our hypothesis. Or, we may have remarkable experimental confirmation of our hypothesis. If a hypothesis meets with such confirmatory results it passes from the state of mere theory or hypothesis to the status of scientific law.

The simple laws or generalizations are the easiest to establish. The factors are few and the experimental procedures clear and decisive. As our generalizations widen and include more data the problem of verification becomes more difficult and complex. The specific heat of iron or the life cycle of some garden plant or insect may be rather easy to determine. Universal generalizations about physics, chemistry or psychology are not capable of such neat verification unless the theory has been blessed with an *experimentum crucis* as, for example, the confirmation of relativity theory by Eddington's pictures of the bent light from the stars in the eclipse of 1919. Therefore, whereas there might be unanimous agreement over the atomic weight of carbon, or the life cycle of the fruit fly, or the cause of malaria fever, there can still be much disagreement over basic psychological theory, or the mechanism of heredity, or the origin of the solar system. The credibility of broad generalizations is more in terms of the trend of evidence or even the aesthetic feeling of a pattern of evidence, than it is simple experimental confirmation.

1. Applying these principles of the nature of scientific law to evolution, the first observation is *that evolution is not a perfectly nor infallibly verified law*. No theory of science enjoys such status. Scientists who might speak as if evolution were established beyond all possibility of doubt, or beyond all possibility of supplantation, are speaking from ignorance of the nature of scientific generalizations. If we are to thank the logical positivists for nothing else, we can at least thank them for the hard work they have put into showing the probability status of scientific law, and for working effectively on the notion of degree of confirmation.[18] Although it would be rather difficult to put down the degree of confirmation of the theory of evolution, we at least know its limits, and in view of the shifting around in evolutionary theory since its proposal by Darwin, we know that the confirmation is not as high as it is usually made out to be.

2. The theory of evolution in terms of the philosophy of science *is a probability statement*. It is based on a great number of observations—geological, biological, embryological, psychological. From these observations certain limited generalizations are made about individual species or families. Increasingly larger generalizations are made as to the broader laws of heredity, embryology, tissue structure, or reproduction. Finally, the great bulk of the data of life is summarized by the most universal generalization possible, which is some form of the theory of evolution. This generalization is substantiated with a variety of arguments which are usually collected in some text on evolutionary theory.

No one has seen evolution at work over the hundreds of thousands of years of geological time. What we have is a vast collection of data of almost every conceivable sort. All this data is organized by the theory of evolution, a generalization of the broadest possible type. *It is, therefore, a probability statement and not anything like absolute or eternal truth.* Such a generalization is not as yet capable of clear, univocal verification.

As a hypothesis it can survive only if no serious logical inconsistencies develop within it. At the present time it is working with two contradictory assertions: (i) life comes only from life, and (ii) life originally arose from the inorganic. Perhaps a hundred years of biological experimentation will prove this to be a fatal contradiction. Or we may assert that (i) offspring keep within a well-defined range of variability, and (ii) offspring occasionally jump well outside the usual range of variability. Perhaps in years to come this too will prove to be fatal to evolution.

If evolution runs into serious material trouble it will have to be modified or discarded. Perhaps it will be shown that genes and chromosomes are too complex ever to have evolved but had to be created. Perhaps after two hundred years of intensive experimentation all proposed mechanisms of evolution will have to be discarded. Typical of many evolutionists is Howells, who admits that there is no known mechanism for evolution yet accepts the theory without facing the implications of a theory without a mechanism. He writes:

> And there is also the mystery of how and why evolution takes place at all . . . Evolution is a fact, like digestion . . . Nor is it known just why evolution occurs, or exactly what guides its steps.[19]

The geological record might be troublesome to evolution. One hundred more years of palaeontology might show the invalidity of many present assumptions.

Although Standen writes popularly he nonetheless has put his finger on two of the sorest points of evolutionary theory, showing its possible ultimate embarrassment with facts. (i) He correctly observes that there is the *vague theory* and the *precise theory*. The vague theory is the belief of scientists that evolution has occurred. The precise theory is the hypothesis as to how evolution actually works. There is no known satisfactory and clearly demonstrated precise theory of evolution. If evolution is to "stick" as a scientific theory it must establish *precise theory*. In spite of the fact that as yet no precise theory is forthcoming, the evolutionists have unbounded faith in the *vague theory*. This is not science at its best. (ii) He correctly observes that the so-called evolutionary trees are all leaves or twigs with no branches or trunk. Theoretically we should be able to trace an entire series of forms from some primeval creature to a present day creature.   It is not a matter of a missing link, but of countless missing links.   The wood which should support all these branches and twigs is, as Standen says, "hypothetical wood."[20] The geologist or evolutionist might claim that the geological record is imperfect.   Even so, the careful scientist is expected to keep his theories close to the evidence.   Creating vast genealogical trees out of hypothetical wood is not keeping close to the actual data of palaeontology.

All we are trying to assert at this point is a call for a clear recognition that the theory of evolution is a probability statement.   Its life must not depend on dogmatism of biologists, but on the actually forthcoming evidence and data.   This data may increase the status of the theory, or weaken it or even destroy it.   It is not true to scientific epistemology to give it the benediction of finality or even to treat it as a scientific sacred cow.[21]

3. The broad generalizations are *usually the most difficult statements to verify*, because they are at the end of a long series of probability statements and because the verification of such statements is fraught with so many problems—the possible bias of the scientist; the welter of the data; the number of possibilities of interpretation at several points of the evidence; trying to weigh the significance of certain phenomena or experiments.

The history of science is the history of ruined and wrecked generalizations.   This is a sign of health, exhibiting the power of science to correct itself.   It is also a sign of the tentativeness of all scientific theory, evolution included.   Two great generalizations have been accepted by western culture only to be subsequently discredited by later developments.   The first was Ptolemaic astronomy, which seemed so obvious to the medieval astronomers.   Today it is outmoded, though once universally believed in the western world. The second is Newtonian physics, which had acquired more prestige than the Ptolemaic system.   Scientists boasted that Newton had discovered the very laws of God, and for over two hundred years his system reigned supreme.   Newton's system is now a special condition within the more comprehensive system of Albert Einstein, and the atomic physicists have told us that Newtonian physics has little applicability to the microcosm.   Hundreds of other generalizations in all the sciences have suffered the same fate.   Evolutionists must seriously face the significance of the history of science before evolutionary theory becomes knighted as the everlasting law of biology.

If the theory of evolution be a generalization of a host of lesser and greater generalizations, then it is not possible to show with our present state of knowledge *that all possibilities are exhausted*.   Evolutionary theory in theory could suffer the same fate as the Ptolemaic and Newtonian theories. It is an effort to reconstruct the past history of biology, and understand the present phenomena. It is the best guess the biologists have made at the present to harmonize all the biological phenomena.

As developed in Chapter III, the theory of *progressive creationism* is that interpretation of life which the author advocates and which he thinks is a more comprehensive theory than the theory of evolution. Progressive creationism endeavours to explain much that the theory of evolution tries to explain, and many of the things that the theory of evolution leaves unexplained. Gen. 1 records the broad outline of the successive creative acts of God in bringing the universe through the various stages from chaos to man. Being a very general sketch it leaves considerable room for the empirical determination of various facts. A multitude of biological facts now generally accepted by the biologists would remain unchanged.

In progressive creationism there may be much horizontal radiation. The amount is to be determined by the geological record and biological experimentation. But there is no vertical radiation. Vertical radiation is only by fiat creation. A *root-species* may give rise to several species by horizontal radiation, through the process of the unraveling of gene potentialities or recombination. Horizontal radiation could account for much which now passes as evidence for the theory of evolution. The gaps in the geological record are gaps because vertical progress takes place only by creation.

Creation and development are both indispensable categories in the understanding of geology and biology. The fiat creationist can be embarrassed by a thousand examples of development. Progression cannot be denied geology and biology. The chasms in the order of life can only be bridged by creation. Biology cannot be rendered totally meaningful solely in terms of progression. Both Genesis and biology start with the null and void, both proceed from the simple to the complex, and both climax with man.

A series of guerilla fights with evolution showing its weaknesses and inconsistencies will not win the day. Convictions are surrendered only when a more unifying, a more integrating hypothesis is suggested and demonstrated. The Christian approach to evolution cannot consist of snipings at the theory; but it must supply an interpretative theory of biology which will do all the evolutionary theory does for modern biologists, and something more besides. Until then we may sting the theory of evolution with some factual embarrassments here and there but we will never force a retreat. It is our hope that a theory like progressive creationism will form the basis of a new biological synthesis which will be to biology like relativity theory was to physical theory.

D. *Necessary restrictions on the theory of evolution.* The author does not have the necessary learning in biology to attempt a refutation of the evidence of evolution. However, there appear to be problems in the evolutionary theory which are obvious to those who are not trained biologists. There as yet remains the proof of the inorganic origin of life. It may be assumed, but it is not yet verified. There is the problem of the rugged species which have endured without change for millions of years. There is the problem of the sudden appearance of new forms in the geological record. There are as yet multitudes of missing links among the species. As yet biologists are not agreed as to the mechanism of evolution, and those mechanisms advocated do not as yet possess a high degree of verification. Our particular problem is this: *what are the necessary limitations of evolutionary theory?* There are limits beyond which the theory of evolution may not be pushed, and we wish to examine those limits.

1. *Evolution can never become the self-creation of Nature.* By an *actual cause* we mean that which is the ultimate and final cause of a thing. By a *mediate cause* we mean that which is the tool of the actual cause. The carpenter is the *actual* cause of a house; the hammer, nails, etc., are the *mediate* causes, or *secondary* causes. It is the firm teaching of Sacred Scripture, Christian theology, and Christian theism that the sole *actual* cause of the universe is Almighty God. God is the First Cause, the Actual Cause, and the *world-ground* of all things. Without God matter could not be, laws could not be, processes could not be. The universe in every dimension and at every point depends upon God. Therefore, evolution cannot be conceived as *actual cause*. Nature cannot create itself. To give evolution the status of *actual causation* is the terrible mistake —from the perspective of theism—of naturalism, pragmatism, materialism, and positivism. The only possible status which evolution could have is that of any other scientific law, *viz*. that of *mediate* or *secondary* causation.

2. *Evolution can never be the rationale of the universe.* Evolution has been taken (*e.g.* Spencer) as the key interpretative concept of the universe. The universal law of evolution has been invoked to explain the development of the cosmos, the solar system, the elements, the crust of the earth, the flora and fauna of the earth, man, and all social institutions—marriage, family, agriculture, legal systems, political systems, economic systems and religion. This is hardly a defensible use of the word *evolution*. It could only be so applied if it were to mean simply change, but if that is all it means it becomes a rather empty term, a truism of not too great sophistication. Evolution applied to inorganic things can mean only a series of states, or a succession of processes, but always with a

balanced equation. There are other serious problems when the term is applied to social institutions. Evolution in biology must fear the significance of *epigenesis*. By *epigenesis* we mean the constant increase of the complexity of forms over a period of time. We mean that *something new* is constantly added; that there is something additive to evolution, something quasi-creative. It must be something more than mere change or re-arrangement.

Evolution, if it be true, is a law of biology. It is not a law of the elements, nor of social institutions, nor of man's higher powers. It may be a powerful interpretative principle in biology, but it cannot serve as the rationale of the universe any more than Newton's concept of gravitation could. Nature, man, and society are richer in content than can be accounted for by the biological concept of *epigenesis* or *transformation*. Evolution as a biological theory cannot be artlessly transmuted into metaphysics, epistemology, and *religion*. No matter how thoroughly a man of biology may believe in evolution he must not be an idolator and worship his theory. He must have the humility to realize that there are other windows on reality.

3. *Evolution must reckon with energy and design in Nature*. The second law of thermodynamics cannot be ignored in the construction of evolutionary theory.[22] Evolution and entropy are headed in opposite directions. Clark's fundamental thesis is that entropy represents a random and degenerative process, whereas life represents an ordered and generative process. Entropy is the gradual equalization of molecular velocities through random collisions, and it is degenerative in the sense that the physical state of energy levels is decreased. Life is possible only if miraculously these two features of entropy are reversed, and certainly entropy is the more basic and universal law than evolution.

Betts agrees with Clark that entropy is a downhill process, and although while not an outright refutation of evolution, it poses serious problems to evolution. The fundamental energy process of Nature is disintegrative, not integrative. In radio-activity the process is from the complex to the simple. As Betts writes:

> Indeed, modern astronomical evidence is showing that there is unidirectional "evolution" of matter from the state of high atomic complexity to one of atomic simplicity and a breakdown of matter farther into radiation.[23]

It is at this point that clear metaphysical positions come forth. Even the most positivistic scientist must say something. We are faced clearly with the two theories of (i) the recoverability of energy and (ii) the irrecoverability of energy. If energy is irre-coverable we are faced with the doctrine of creation. If energy is recoverable we are not forced into creationism. If we believe in irrecoverability we believe in an omnipotent God; if not we believe in the Epicurean god of Chance. Energy confronts us with the problem of choosing between Epicurean Chance and the Eternal Deity. To this hour no known process of recoverability is proven. The Christian is convinced that of the two possibilities creation is more intellectually respectable.[24]

Modern scientific thought has been insistently against any interpretation of Nature by design or final causes. Evolutionary thought must take account of at least two matters in this regard. (i) There are a large number of cosmic and inorganic features necessary for life on this planet. The earth must fulfil certain cosmic relations or life would be frozen out or burnt out, or there would be wrong proportions of gases or incorrect proportions of land to water. Such a list becomes encyclopedic in length and I am sure we have not begun to determine all the necessary cosmic and chemical features of the earth *absolutely* necessary for life. The facts of the case are that these facts do exist so as to make life pos-sible. *Life is a cosmic function*, not just a mould on the crust of this earth. Not a bit of protoplasm could appear on this earth unless the entire cosmic structure gave its assent. NOT ONE CELL OF LIFE COULD EMERGE IN SOME PRIMEVAL POOL OF WATER UNLESS THE ENTIRE STAGE OF THE COSMOS WERE SET FOR IT. *On what grounds can such facts be ignored?* To assume all is chance, with not even the flutter of the eyelash, is not becoming the genuine openmindedness that characterizes science at its best. Which is the greater strain on our credulity: (i) that these countless of thousands of facts of cosmic, chemical, and physical properties—all of which are absolutely necessary to life—occurred by chance on this one planet; or (ii) that a God of omnipotence raised his Son from the dead?

(ii) Evolution must reckon with the multitude of facts now known about sensory perception. It takes considerable experi-mental work and scientific erudition to discover how the eye, ear and nose function. Psychophysicists have discovered that these organs are highly engineered products. There must be sensitivity to the right ranges of energy in sound and light. There must be energy transformations and even, as in the case of the ears, reduction of gears! The eye must have a reasonably clear, workable lens, a photographic plate, and a chemical reagent to develop the picture. When we consider how much technical construction goes into the construction of a television set, and what a big mechanism it is, and then contrast it with the human eye which receives pictures in colour with automatic adjustment features built in, yet all contained in about one cubic inch, we cannot but marvel at the intelligence of the man who still insists upon chance factors alone in Nature. Our thesis at this point is this: *If Darwin's evolution broke the back of Paley's organic teleology,*[25] *modern psychophysics is in turn breaking the back of chance creation. Only in the twentieth century has science begun to unravel in detail the intricate engineering technicalities of human sensory organs.* And this is but a token of the evidence available, for there is the inexhaustible study of the sensory powers and "instincts" of animals. It is further conceivable that when the biochemists tell us the fairly complete story of the chemistry of the human body we will bow our heads in holy reverence and admit the only feasible accounting of this is the work of an Omnipotent Wisdom.

If evolution is the law of biology, it cannot be developed in independence of these matters we have here presented, and *therefore evolution cannot expect to account for all biological phenomena by chance or random.*

4. Evolution must face *the transcendental nature of man.* In the nineteenth and twentieth century man had ganged up against himself. Taxinomically he put himself with the brutes. Biologically and physically he made himself only a physical object with no mind or soul. The central nervous system is now his soul or mind. Everything in traditional philosophy and religion based on the presupposition of a soul, and thus yielding a normative discipline must now be rejected, *e.g.* a true religion, normative ethics, eternal laws of the true, the beautiful, and the good, and in their places has been put a positivistic, anti-metaphysical, and relativistic scientism. It is our contention that this is a gross misconstruction of the facts. Man has four types of experiences which prove that although he is part of Nature in that he possesses a physical body, he yet transcends his own physical nature, *proving that he also has a mental or spiritual nature which must come from above and not from below.*

(*a*) Man has the power of *rational thought.* Anti-metaphysical positivism can only be propounded and defended by a man with the powers of rational thought. All science is based on man's power of conceptualization. *Rational thought is only possible because man can step out of the circle of necessity.* Correct answers are not discovered by following through a series of physical states, but by following through a series of steps dictated by logic and inference. To convert ice to steam is to subject the ice to a series of states. The same is true of the conversion of crude oil to gasoline. But an entirely different sequence is followed in finding the cube root of 27. These thought processes have to step out of the circle of determined physical states—of the brain itself—and they thereby testify that there is something in man that is more than body, nerves, and chemicals.

(*b*) Man has the ability to have *moral experience*. In moral experience there is a definite structure. There are always two or more possibilities of moral choice, and these possibilities create a tension. The most ardent convert to materialism must decide many times a day which alternative he shall choose in a moral situation. Annually he must self-test his honesty with his income tax return. This moral structure is in all of us, and even if we get so hardened as to ignore it, we greatly resent those who ignore it in their injustices upon us. After all the psychologists have had their say about social conditioning, and after all the anthropologists have had their say about cultural conditioning, *the moral structure* is still part of the fundamental psychic equipment of all normal people. Such a structure escapes physical determinism. There is no way of accounting for moral experience from below; *it is a part of man which comes from above*.

(*c*) Man has an *aesthetic structure* within him. The sense of the beautiful is not *in* the sense organ but *through* the sense organ. Dogs may hear better than humans but they hardly enjoy a concert as a trained musician does. Birds have magnificent eyes, but they are hardly the world's great art critics. We believe that animals have the incipient structures of personality and so experience certain things which humans do, but only at a greatly reduced level. Animals exhibit certain emotions and certain powers of thought, and perhaps even have rude aesthetic experiences. Such powers are necessary for their survival and existence. But the full range of these powers is found only in man. The power to detach an object of sense from all else but its aesthetic quality is a power that is from above, not from below. Only by taking a stand outside the state of physical determination can man enjoy the beautiful.

(*d*) Man's belief in God, his sense of the transcendental as seen in worship, and his experience of the spiritual order, are all matters of daily experience of Christians and are not accountable on naturalistic premises. As far as can be determined nothing corresponding to religious experience or worship or adoration is detectable among animals. Erratic as metaphysical beliefs of some thinkers may be, they at least testify to man's power to think above transitory experience, and to try to peer over his narrow cell of space and time and try to catch a vision of an eternal order. Even though a man may reject the proofs for the existence of God, there is something to weigh and measure in these proofs in that man has (i) the power to construct such elaborate chains of argumentation, and that (ii) he has a sense of something eternal, transcendent, the ground of all being. Man's power to create a world other than the sensory world, and his power to worship and venerate that world, is a testimony to the fact that there is more in man than physical states, and this *power is from above and not from below.*

The conclusion at this point is this: evolution may be entertained as a possible *secondary* cause or *mediate* cause in biological science. *But to raise it to a metaphysical principle or as the all-embracing key or category or scheme of Reality and to cancel out the metaphysical worth of all other possible clues is improper science and doggerel philosophy.* If evolution be used so as to relativize all ethics, logic, beauty, and religion, and completely to animalize man, we can judge only that it must be severely condemned by evangelical Christianity, and by *all* philosophies and *world views* which seek genuine significance for human personality, worth, and value, and which believe in purpose in human history. Evolutionary theory must be developed within the confines of what we have here endeavoured to set forth.

IV. Theistic Evolution

Can evolution be accepted in Christian faith as theistic evolution? So much bitterness has entered this controversy that it is difficult to discuss it with any sort of sympathetic hearing from a hyper-orthodox audience. The author has been told that many evangelicals in Britain and Germany have accepted evolution into Christianity as theistic evolution and have left the controversy alone and gone on to other things. In America we have had such bitter debates that the word *evolution* is a loaded word, and with many implies something evil, sinister, satanic, and atheistic. The anti-evolutionary literature is staggering in its bulk. Is there a case for theistic evolution?

A. One group of writers insists that evolution itself is anti-Christian and therefore *theistic evolution is an impossible theory for a Christian to believe.* Straton certainly believes this. He writes:

> Those who try to reconcile these theories [of evolution] with the Christian system of truth assert that such is not the case . . . yet the definitions given . . . prove that God *is of necessity ruled out,* and that in favour of chance.[26]

Higley's opinion is:

> Theistic evolution, then, is a contradiction in terms. To maintain that evolution can be theistic is as inconsistent as to claim that falsehood can be true.[27]

Whitney asks if evolution can be theistic and he answers with a dogmatic negation.[28] In a prize-winning essay read before the Victoria Institute in Great Britain, G. M. Price debates this very question. Price states his position in these very clear words:

It is thus very evident that there is no similarity between the idea of Evolution and that of Creation; it is all contrast.   The two terms are antonyms; they are mutually exclusive; no mind can entertain a belief in both at the same time; when one notion is believed, the other is thereby denied and repudiated.[29]

B. There are on the other hand a number of orthodox thinkers who believe that this is not the case.   They believe that theistic evolution is a Christian option.   It is true, they admit, that evolution has been used for atheistic and materialistic purposes, but that is an abuse of the theory.   Contrary to what some thinkers have said, evolution may be incorporated into Christian faith, they assert. Evolution is not in essence anti-Christian; it is only anti-Christian when put to service by anti-Christians.

1. We find a group of theistic evolutionists among the Roman Catholics.   None can doubt the orthodox rigidity and dogmatism of Roman Catholic theology.   If theistic evolution is so anti-Christian and so incompatible with Christian faith, we have the strange situation that the most dogmatic version of the Christian faith is the most tolerant Church in all Christendom toward theistic evolution.   Zahm, a very learned Catholic scholar, has defended theistic evolution very stoutly.   He writes:

> From the foregoing pages, then, it is clear that far from being opposed to faith, theistic Evolution is, on the contrary, supported both by the declarations of Genesis and by the most venerable philosophical and theological authorities of the Church.[30]

The Roman Catholic Church, he affirms, is not pledged to any theory as to the secondary causations for the origin of life.   It tolerates either evolution or special creation and *awaits the verdict of science* as to which was the *modus operandi of God*.[31]

> [Rather than let evolution be the sole property of the materialistic and pantheistic and atheistic philosophies] it should be converted into a power which makes for righteousness and the exaltation of holy faith and undying truth.[32]

St. George Mivart, the great Catholic biologist of the last century, affirms:

> It appears plain, then, that Christian thinkers are perfectly free to accept the general evolution theory.[33]

Canon Dorlodot, an outstanding French Catholic geologist, has argued that Christianity is not opposed even to a naturalistic theory of evolution, for he says:

I maintain, then, that one cannot find in Holy Scripture, interpreted according to the rules of Catholic exegesis, any convincing
argument against the theory of natural evolution—even that of
absolute evolution.[34]

E. C. Messenger has written a work which has been heralded as
one of the most significant works in the entire history of the Bible
and science within Roman Catholic circles. It is his treatise,
Evolution and Theology (1931; the American edition published in
1932.) The plates of this book were destroyed in the London
blitz of World War II, and to preserve the theory of the work he
published *Theology and Evolution* (1951) which consists principally of
book reviews from the Catholic journals of the world of his first
work. He is in much agreement with Dorlodot. It is surprising
(i) to find how many of the great Catholic theologians accept his
rather strong evolutionism, and (ii) to find how many Catholic
scholars are strong fiat creationists. But to date Messenger has not
been rebuked by his Church and neither had Dorlodot.[35]

2. When we turn to Protestant evangelicals we find a sure but
slender thread of theistic evolutionists, and some of these names
which compose this thread are very imposing. However, Rice's
judgment in 1893 was too optimistic:

> Now and then some theological Rip Van Winkle attempts the old
> Sinaitic thunders in denunciation of the essential atheism of Evolution;
> but his utterances are regarded by his brethren in the church not with
> sympathy, but with amusement or mortification. The curriculum of
> an orthodox theological seminary is hardly regarded as complete
> today without a course of lectures in the consistency of Evolution with
> theistic philosophy.[36]

When the theory of evolution first reached American soil Asa
Gray, one of America's great botanists, accepted it immediately and
asserted firmly that it was not contrary to orthodox Christianity.
He labels himself as one " who is scientifically and in his own fashion,
a Darwinian, philosophically a convinced theist, and religiously an
acceptor of the 'creed commonly called the Nicene' as the exponent
of the Christian faith."[37] Charles Hodge, the great Presbyterian
theologian, had vigorously attacked evolution as being atheistic.
Gray takes Hodge to task for misrepresenting or at least misunderstanding evolution.

> The stain of atheism, which, in Dr. Hodge's view, leavens the
> whole lump, is not inherent in the original grain of Darwinism—in
> the principles posited—but has somehow been introduced in the
> subsequent treatment.[38]

In 1874 Dana, the greatest American geologist of the nineteenth century, and an evangelical believer, endorsed natural selection in the final edition of his famous *Manual of Geology*.[39]   In 1871 President McCosh of Princeton accepted evolution in his *Christianity and Positivism*.   In an essay on evolution he affirmed that the Bible taught a doctrine of evolution.   For proof he cited the developmental progress in the six days of creation and Psa. 139: 15-16; and proceeded to defend a spiritual, theistic, Biblical evolutionism.[40]

In 1882, J. W. Dawson, the great Canadian geologist and evangelical believer, wrote:

> It may be asked, Is there, then, no place in the geological record even for theistic evolution? *This it would be rash to affirm.* We can only say that up to this time there is no proof of it.[41]

James Orr in the Kerr Lectures of 1890-91 stated:

> On the general hypothesis of evolution, as applied to the organic world, I have nothing to say, except that, within certain limits, *it seems to me extremely probable, and supported by a large body of evidence.*[42]

Most amazing is that in *The Fundamentals* (IV, 91-104) Orr defends theistic evolution as interpreted by R. Otto's *Naturalism and Religion*. Orr calls it *creation from within*, and accepts a sudden mutation as in the case of the origin of man.   Shields, in 1900, affirms that there is no discrepancy at all between the picture science paints of man evolving up through anthropoid species, and the Biblical picture of the early chapters of Genesis.[43]

In 1897 J. C. Jones in a work of solid orthodoxy and complete loyalty to Scripture (*Primeval Revelation*) admits that he does not think evolution is proved, but as a theory it can be held by Christians, if held in the *super-naturalistic version*.   This he refers directly to the origin of man, *e.g.*:

> Man may, if the phrase be allowed, be a *supernatural* development from a prior animal; he cannot be the product of *natural* evolution.[44]

With reference to evolution in general he wrote:

> *A modified form, however, of the doctrine of evolution is possible—that which I have named supernaturalistic.   This admits of immediate Divine intervention at certain critical moments in the creation and development of life, by which God introduces new staple into the loom, new material into the machine. But these interventions should not be viewed as so numerous as to crowd the universe with miracles.   The laws of nature are allowed to work out their own results for millions of years—results seen in innumerable varieties and improvements of species.*[45]

In 1907 Strong wrote in the preface of his *Systematic Theology* that he had accepted evolution into his thinking. He believes that the world had an evolutionary origin and progress.

Neither evolution nor the higher criticism has any terrors to one who regards them as part of Christ's educating process.[46]

In 1898 Torrey hinted that evolution might be true of animals but not of man:

Whatever truth there may be in the doctrine of evolution as applied within limits to the animal world, it breaks down when applied to man.[47]

In 1911 Warfield makes a very similar statement. If evolution be carefully guarded theologically it could pass as a tenable theory of the "divine procedure in creating man." Evolution cannot be a substitute for creation but "at best can supply only a theory of the method of divine providence."[48]

Gruber, an orthodox Lutheran, wrote in 1941 that the evolutionary origin of man would be permissible in Christianity if evolution be conceived as God's method of creation.

God as the Great Personal First Cause would be the Author or Creator at every point throughout the whole life-history.[49]

As yet Gruber does not believe theistic evolution has made its case. Short, an outstanding British surgeon and evangelical Christian, wrote in 1942 that men before Adam might not have been men in the full sense of the term *man*.

What sort of material the Creator used to make man, whether the dust of the earth directly, or the pre-existing body of a beast, we leave an open question.[50]

In 1943 Albertus Pieters in his *Notes on Genesis* admitted that one could believe in cosmic evolution or organic evolution and not compromise his Christianity.[51] He himself does not accept evolution, but he is not willing to brand those who do as non-Christian. He also says:

If a Christian believer is inclined to yield as far as possible to the theory of organic evolution, he can hold that man's body was prepared by God through such a natural process, and that, when this process had reached a certain stage, God took one of the man-like brutes so produced, and made him the first human being, by endowing him with a human soul and a morally responsible nature . . . In such a conception there is nothing contrary to the Bible.[52]

This admission is all the more important realizing that it comes from a strong Reformed Church source.

Very recently other evangelicals have said that we must give up the fixity of species and admit derivation of species from species. They assert that we cannot identify the Biblical world *min* (kind) with *species*. Mixter in a series of articles bound together as *Creation and Evolution* cites such evangelicals as Hamilton, Dewar, and Short as believing in development within restricted areas. Mixter commits himself when he writes:

> As a creationist I am willing to accept the origin of species from other species called micro-evolution.[53]

However, Mixter is careful to reject macro-evolution. Carnell defends threshold evolution, which is much the same as Mixter's position. He asserts that there is a wide possibility of change within the *kinds* originally created by God, but these variations cannot step over prescribed boundaries. He concludes:

> Observe therefore that the conservative may scrap the doctrine of the "fixity of species" also without jeopardizing this major premise in the least.[54]

After a discussion of the vexing problem of the definition of a species, Bullock, assistant professor of zoology at the University of New Hampshire, writes:

> Meanwhile, it is ill advised to champion the cause of fixity of species under the banner of Christianity.[55]

To this point we have shown that evolution with all necessary qualifications has been adopted into both the Catholic and Protestant evangelical theology and has not meant the disruption of either. The charge that evolution is anti-Christian, and that theistic evolution is not a respectable position, is very difficult to make good in view of the evidence we have here given.

C. What is the real issue in evolution? It is this: *is it in its essence anti-Christian?* But this question is based upon a prior one of greater importance: *when is any scientific theory anti-Christian?* We cannot answer the former till we have worked out the details of the second. We must not so concentrate on evolution as to miss the essential structure of the relationship between any theory of science and Christianity. Evolution is contrary to Christianity only when it can be shown to be anti-Christian in essence, and that can be shown only when we set forth the pattern by which any theory conflicts with Christianity. In order to do this intelligently we must pay some attention to the historical features of this problem.

1. *Many theories of science, once declared anti-Christian, are now held by millions of Christians with no evil effects on Christianity.* It would be a very enlightening experience for many a hyper-fundamentalist to read White's history of the conflict of theology with science, and note how many heretical beliefs of the past he now holds! Copernican astronomy was assailed with all the venom the Church theologians had. It was declared that if this astronomy is true, all the Bible is false and all its glorious doctrines! Today, the author has yet to meet an evangelical believer who crosses Copernicus. *All the dire predictions about what would happen if Christianity admitted the truthfulness of Copernican astronomy failed to materialize!*

Another one of the violent debates was over the existence of the antipodes, the distant ends of the earth. That heresy of former centuries is now believed by all Christians! We now have missionaries at the antipodes! Yet to believe in the antipodes at one time was to fly in the face of God's Holy Word, so we were told. It was not too long ago that surgical operations were considered as mutilations of the human body or wicked schemes to evade the curse of the Fall. Today there are hundreds of Christian surgeons, numerous medical missionaries, and thousands of evangelical Christians who yearly submit to operations. Vaccination was considered the work of the devil and a blasphemy against God, yet the arms of millions of Christians bear the tell-tale pattern of the needle. Pain-killers and anaesthesia were considered man's sinful devices for avoiding the curse of the Fall, yet morphine, aspirin, ether, etc., are administered daily to Christians and by Christian doctors. Open sewers were not closed up because that would be preventing plagues, and plagues were God's judgments upon man. Lightning rods were considered insults to God—holy bells in the towers were to keep lightning away. In all these cases dire predictions were made as to how Christianity would be dead or impossible of belief or that great apostasy would set in, yet these consequences have not followed. Millions of evangelicals believe today the terrible heresies of yesterday. *Evidently there was a complete misunderstanding as to what was fatal to Christianity.*

2. *Further, many scientific theories of every kind are held today by evangelicals and that without controversy.* Where is the anti-Einsteinian literature? the anti-Newtonian society? the anti-de Broglie booklets? The mass of evangelicals accept the mass of data in the mass of books of modern science. Why? Because nobody can find any point of friction between, say, the law of chemical valence, and Christianity. Most evangelicals accept modern dental and medical theory, and the same holds for atomic theory, chemical

theory, and astrophysics. If there is danger in these theories it is not apparent as yet. Therefore, we acquiesce and permitt these theories within the Christian fold.

3. The data of history drive us to the conclusion that a theory *is anti-Christian when it denies something in Christian metaphysics, i.e.* when it attacks the very roots of the Christian faith. The evolutionary theory of the origin of the religion of Israel is anti-Christian because it clearly clashes with the Biblical doctrine of divine revelation in Israel. Behaviouristic psychology (after Watson) is anti-Christian because it denies a soul to man. Positivistic sociology is contrary to Christianity because it denies human guilt. A chemist or physicist may be anti-Christian if he asserts the eternity of matter, for that conflicts with divine creation.

The reason all these dire predictions of previous centuries about scientific theories did not materialize is that these theories in reality *said nothing against the Christian metaphysical system.* It was thought that they did, but they really did not. We accept them today with no evil consequences whatsoever.

4. *Theistic evolution.* To which class does theistic evolution belong? Is it a theory that is violently anti-Christian because contrary to the metaphysics of Christianity? Or, have we just made a monster out of a balloon? Should we deflate the monster and go our way?

(*a*) If it can be demonstrated to the satisfaction of all that evolution is contrary to Christian metaphysics then we must brand theistic evolution as an impossible position. We shall either be Christians or evolutionists. If men make evolution a basic system of philosophy or use it to discredit Christianity, then evangelicals have no recourse but to rebut that interpretation of evolution.

(*b*) If evolution is purely a *secondary law,* if it is *derivative* creation, then it has no profound metaphysical status, and can be tolerated in Christianity. If it is a secondary law of biology, and not the metaphysics of creation, but viewed as part of the divine creation, an element in providence, then evolution is as harmless as, say, the relativity theory.

(*c*) The decision as to which classification fits evolution is to be made by *competent Christian scholarship.* We have noted that already orthodox thinkers (Protestants and Catholics) have affirmed that evolution, properly defined, can be assimilated into Christianity. *This is strong evidence that evolution is not metaphysically incompatible with Christianity.* The final answer, however, must come from the one with responsible scholarship. It must come from the best of evangelical scholarship which is *fair, competent,* and *learned.* It must come from our better thinkers in biology, geology, and theology, not from more vocal but less able men. It must not come by the cheap anti-evolutionary tract nor from pulpiteering, but from that evangelical scholarship which is loyal to the best of academic scholarship and to the sound teachings of Holy Scripture.

(d) The writer is not a theistic evolutionist. He is a progressive creationist for he feels th t in progressive creationism there is the best accounting for all the facts—biological, geological, and Biblical. He has friends who are fiat creationists and theistic evolutionists. Their respect for the Bible and their loyalty to Christ he admires. But progressive creationism is that theory of the relationship of God's works and God's Holy Word which makes the most sense to the author—and upon what other basis can he make up his mind?

V. THE VIRGIN BIRTH

The virgin birth of Jesus Christ is a biological miracle.[56] Being a miracle it is not capable of biological proof, analogies of parthenogenesis in the biological world being irrelevant. Its justification must be documentary, historical, and theological. We can offer no *biological* proof of the virgin birth, and yet we can offer justification of this biological miracle.

A. *The virgin birth is possible on Christian presuppositions.* A virgin birth could be the result of (i) artificial insemination; (ii) chemical activation of an ovum (results in a female)—eggs of sea urchins can be chemically activated to reproduce; or (iii) by the act of God. Cows are being artificially inseminated, but artificial insemination is not a proper analogy and may be dropped from the discussion. Certainly at the time of Christ there was no known means of chemically activating a human ovum. We are shut up to a normal birth or a miracle.

Granted an omnipotent God, original creator of the human body, the *possibility* or *conceivability* of a virgin birth is established. God could do it. The Christian has the sufficient presupposition for it in his doctrine of God.

B. *The virgin birth fits into the Christian scheme.* A man may believe in an omnipotent God and deny the miraculous birth of Christ. A religious modernist believes in God but hardly the virgin birth. Evangelicals insist that *the virgin birth is part of the Christian system.* The virgin birth focuses on the *incarnation of* GOD. The Scriptures tell us of two Adams, the First and the Last. One came into existence by creation, and the other by the creation of the virgin birth. The virgin birth finds its rationale in the incarnation and the incarnation finds its rationale in the drama of Divine Love and Redemption. The virgin birth is part of the great love-story of divine redemption and human salvation, and to drop it out is to spoil one of the most critical scenes of the entire drama—*the incarnation*. It is, therefore, logical, reasonable, and a necessary part of the Christian faith. The virgin birth was the doorway by which the Son of God stepped into humanity as part of humanity, yet free from original sin, and to free man from sin.

C. The *factuality* of the virgin birth is a matter of seeing the testimony of history through the perspective of Christian theology. We could know that the virgin birth took place by being told so by God or by the personal testimony of the virgin. *We have both* in the New Testament. We have the supernatural disclosure to Joseph that through the Holy Spirit his betrothed had become pregnant. Mary is told what is to take place in her, *and her permission is given*: "And Mary said, 'Behold I am the handmaid of the Lord; let it be to me according to your word'," (Luke 1: 38 RSV). Without these special disclosures the virgin birth would hardly have been ethical or understood by her. The plain record of the New Testament is that by divine revelation, through angels, both Joseph and Mary were informed of the virgin birth, *and of the modus operandi*.

Do we have the testimony of Mary? Naturally, this would be a delicate subject for discussion while Mary was alive. The resurrection was the miracle of Jesus Christ which gripped the disciples. It would be the reflection of later theology which would see the connexion of the virgin birth and the incarnation. Certainly, the virgin birth was no second century accretion to the gospel—the uniform testimony of the church shows its acceptance in the earliest of Christian times. There is no variation in the Apostles' Creed at this doctrine. The problem narrows down to the reliability of the gospel accounts of the virgin birth. Since this is not properly a matter of Bible and science we refer to Machen's famous *The Virgin Birth of Christ* (1932) for a defence on documentary grounds.

Taking the traditional dates of the Gospels we cannot doubt that Matthew and John were personal friends of Mary, and this cannot be doubted if we take Acts 1 as reliable history. Peter too was a friend of Mary, and Peter is behind Mark's Gospel. Is it not possible that Luke had personal conversations with Mary? There is the interesting statement which Luke makes of Mary: "But Mary kept all these things, pondering them in her heart", (2: 19, RSV). Could not all of the apostolic company have heard the Christmas story from Mary? Could not Luke have heard it in tender but holy counsel with Mary as he collected the materials of his gospel?

There is no biological evidence for the virgin birth. The evidence is *theistic*: we believe in an omnipotent God who could do it; and *theological*: we see its place in the incarnation and we see the place of incarnation in redemption; and *historical*: we have the records of trustworthy men before us in the writings of the Gospels and in the earliest documents of Church history. Let no man feel that he is compromising intelligence or critical spirit if he believes in the virgin birth of Jesus Christ.

VI. JONAH

Commentators on Jonah remark that it is tragic that the powerful message of Jonah is lost in the bickerings over a fish incident. Rationalists insist that this is one Biblical story which must be rejected.

1. The first proposition to establish is the historicity and authenticity of the book of Jonah. This has been done recently by G. C. Aalders, an outstanding evangelical Old Testament scholar of Holland, in his Tyndale Lecture, *The Problem of the Book of Jonah* (1949). Aalders examines the critical evidence against the book of Jonah and finds it inconclusive. It is not our purpose to enter Biblical criticism to any extent in this treatise, so we must leave these details to conservative Old Testament introductions.

2. The next proposition is to establish the literal interpretation of Jonah. Aalders examines the allegorical interpretation of Jonah at great length and shows that Jonah does not have the usual typical allegorical pattern. However, if it be proved that Jonah is allegorical then immediately there is no scientific problem with Jonah.

3. That creatures exist that could swallow Jonah cannot be denied, nor can the occasional story be denied wherein other men have had a similar experience of being swallowed by a fish and rescued alive. If we take the Hebrew word *fish* as meaning exactly a fish, then a whale of any type is ruled out. However, we can hardly impose our rules of taxinomy on the author of Jonah. There is a shark (*Rhinodon Typicus*) which could swallow a man. The Greek word, *kētos*, although translated *whale* in KJ, means any large sea creature. Rimmer gives a popular but interesting discussion of the various possible whales which could swallow Jonah,[57] and Aalders mentions other possibilities. Both Rimmer and Aalders mention a whale which could hold a man alive in its air tract. The story of Jonah cannot be rejected on the grounds that (i) no such creature exists that could swallow a man; and that (ii) such an incident is out of bounds of all human experience. Such creatures are known to exist; and men have had a Jonah experience.

4. The record clearly calls the creature a *prepared fish* and if this means a special creature for a special purpose we need not search our books on sea creatures to find out the most likely possibility. It would be a creature created of God especially for this purpose, and that is where our investigation ends.

The evangelical accepts a supernatural theism, and the centrality of redemption and moral values. The necessity of getting the message of redemption to Nineveh is the sufficient rationale for God to have made such a creature.

There is another possible feature which would add to the rationale of the book. We know that fish-gods were worshipped in that ancient world. The evidence is not completely certain if Dagon was actually a fish-god or not.[58] However, half-men and half-fish bas-reliefs have been discovered in that ancient world, especially at Nineveh. As Layard observes, if Jonah appeared as having had this experience with the fish he could have been received as a messenger of the gods.[59] The king would have done anything he said, and the people in complete fealty to the king would have imitated him in all he did. The story of one man causing an entire city to repent, including the king, now appears as a strong historical probability, and adds to the rationale of the miracle of the fish in the book of Jonah.[60]

NOTES

1. These are practically the words of J. R. Straton, "Evolution," ISBE, II, 1048A–1049. For a magnificent interpretation of evolution within the bounds of religious liberalism (and a penetrating critique of evolution mechanistically interpreted) see John Oman, *The Natural and the Supernatural* (1931), Chapters XV and XVI.

2. A classic treatise on philosophy of biology is J. H. Woodger, *Biological Principles* (1929). J. von Uexküll's *Theoretical Biology* (1926) is too one-sided and lacks the comprehensiveness of Woodger. Cf. also J. S. Haldane, *The Philosophical Basis of Biology* (1930); L. Hogben, *The Nature of Living Matter* (1931); E. S. Russell, *The Interpretation and Development of Heredity* (1930); Edward McCrady, "Religious Perspectives in Biology," *Theology Today*, 9: 319–332, October, 1952; E. S. Russell, *The Directiveness of Organic Activities* (1945); D'Arcy Thompson, *On Growth and Form* (new edition, 1948).

3. E. O. Dodson, *A Textbook of Evolution* (1952) discusses the various theories of the origin of life and sympathetically treats Oparin's view as the best present option. P. 106 ff.

4. S. L. Miller, "A Production of Amino Acids Under Possible Primitive Earth Conditions," *Science*, 117: 528–529, May 15, 1953. Miller states that the work of Urey and Bernal is an extension of ideas suggested by Oparin, p. 528.

5. R. J. C. Harris, "The Origin of Life," JTVI, 81: 58–84, 1949.

6. R. E. D. Clark, "Modern Science and the Nature of Life," JTVI, 77: 60–69, 1943.

7. L. du N^cüy, *Human Destiny*, (1947), p. 34.

8. J. A. V. Butler, *Man is a Microcosm* (1951), p. 112.

9. McCrady, *op. cit.*, p. 322. Biologists demur at such a mathematical representation of the situation. The number of atoms available plus the number of possible *workable* combinations would appreciably reduce these figures.

10. A. R. Short, *Modern Discovery and the Bible* (1942), p. 33.

11. For a rather complete history of theories of the mechanism of evolution see the epochal work of Philip G. Fothergill, *Historical Aspects of Organic Evolution* (1952).

12. Quoted by F. H. Reusch, *Nature and the Bible* (1886), II, 47 fn.

13. Quoted by James Orr, *Sin as a Problem Today* (19??), p. 129 fn.

14. Rudolph Otto, "Darwinism and Religion," *The Crozer Quarterly*, 8: 150, April, 1931. Italics are his.

15. Straton, *op. cit.*, pp. 1043–1048A.

16. Cf. W. A. Christian, "Augustine on the Creation of the World," *The Harvard Theological Review*, 46: 1–26, January, 1953. Cf. "Thus the world came into existence in the beginning. But not all things were created 'visibly and actually.' The living things which inhabited the earth were created 'potentially or causally' in the form of 'hidden seeds' or 'seminal causes' (*rationes seminales*). From these seminal causes, or 'reasons,' they were to be brought forth later, in the providence of God and in due time, in the visible forms in which they are now known to us," p. 16.

17. Cohen and Nagel, *An Introduction to Logic and Scientific Method* (1934), p. 208. Italics are ours. Cf. also: W. McDougall, *Religion and the Science of Life* (1934), p. 1–2; "Equally conducive to caution and humility is the mutability of scientific theories. I have seen many theories come and go. I have seen the answers of science which seemed satisfying and final to one generation thrown by the next to the scrap-heap of exploded fallacies."

18. Cf. R. Carnap, "Testability and Meaning," *Philosophy of Science*, 3: 419–71, 1946; and, 4: 2–40, 1947. H. Reichenbach, *Experience and Prediction* (1938), Chapter I.

19. W. Howells, *Mankind so Far* (1944), p. 5. Le Conte may assert the following for a while, but evolution cannot continue indefinitely as a theory without a mechanism: "In conclusion, let me again impress upon the reader that all the doubt and discussion . . . as to the factors in evolution, is entirely aside from the truth of evolution itself, concerning which there is no difference of opinion among thinkers." *Evolution* (1901), p. 80. Are other scientific theories accorded the status of facts or truths if they are theories without verified mechanisms?

20. A. Standen, *Science is a Sacred Cow* (1950), p. 104.

21. F. E. Zeuner (*Dating the Past,* third edition, 1952) has an interesting chapter on "Biological Evolution and Time" (Chapter XII). The conclusion he comes to is that evolution works too slowly to be experimentally verified in the lifetime of an experimenter or even of humanity.

It is almost an admission that evolution can never be strictly demonstrated, for its mechanism works too slowly to be a matter of experimentation. If this is the case then the probability status of the theory of evolution is greatly lowered, and biologists must accordingly moderate their spirit of certainty in speaking of its confirmation.   It is the conclusion of Tinkle and Lammerts in the chapter on biology in *Modern Science and Christian Faith* that all experimental evidence in the field of mechanisms of evolution show that such proposed mechanisms work too slowly to account for evolution within the time-limits set by physicists and geologists for the age of the earth.   However, in this field an enormous amount of experimental work is being done, producing an extensive literature.   It was started with G. G. Simpson's *Tempo and Mode in Evolution* (1944), and by 1951 so much new material had arisen on the subject that Simpson had to write another book to summarize it all, *The Major Features of Evolution* (1953).   Typically enough, Simpson says the only extensive criticism of his *Tempo and Mode in Evolution* was in a British Sunday school paper (p. xii).   The bulk of anti-evolutionary literature is now out of date, in view of the rapid developments in biological theory.

22. That thermodynamics may be fatal to evolution has been argued by R. E. D. Clark, "Evolution and Entropy," JTVI 75: 49–71, 1943; and E. H. Betts, "Evolution and Entropy," JTVI, 76: 1–18, 1944. J. A. V. Butler, *op. cit.,* admits that evolution runs contrary to entropy but see no significance in it, p. 110 ff.

23. Betts, *op. cit.,* p. 6.   It must be granted however that there can be a local reversal of the disintegrative process, *e.g.* the heat from the sun constantly supplies the earth with new energy.   This weakens somewhat the argument of Clark and Betts, but it still leaves the larger question of why this peculiar reversal of life and evolution in a cosmos which is headed toward maximum entropy.

24. A. S. Eddington, *The Nature of the Physical World* (1929), contains the most sustained defence of the metaphysical significance of entropy in recent literature.   Philipp Frank, "Foundations of Physics," *International Encyclopædia of Unified Science*, Vol. I, No. 7, adopts Epicurean chance. E. A. Milne, "Some Points in Philosophy of Physics," *Philosophy*, 9: 35, January, 1934, adopts continuous creation as the solution to entropy.

25. Not all biologists believe that Darwin negated teleology.   If Darwin's observations be taken as restricted to phenomenological observations, then we have yet to seek the *source* of variations, and that which gives them their obvious *directional* and *adaptational* characteristics.

26. Straton, *loc. cit.,* 1048B.   Italics are ours.

27. A. A. Higley, *Science and Truth* (1940), p. 31.

28. D. J. Whitney, "Can Evolution be Theistic?"   *Christian Faith and Life,* 37: 131–132, March, 1931.   The evidence need not be extended. American fundamentalism almost to a man has been sturdily opposed to theistic evolution, calling it a fatal compromise.

29. G. M. Price, "Revelation and Evolution: Can they be Harmonized?" JTVI, 57: 169 (1925).   Note in the very title of his paper that Price equates his *interpretation* with revelation.   The issue is between fiat

creation and theistic evolutionary creation.   Revelation is not the point at all with, for example, a Catholic theistic evolutionist who *must* believe in revelation.   The Victoria Institute Journal has the custom of recording the comments of those who participate in the discussion after the paper is read.   What extremes are met!   One writer hesitates to open his mouth as he is so disgusted with Price's view, and claims it will only drive a deeper rift between science and Christianity and that such a paper does more harm than good.   Others very piously acclaimed the paper as a masterpiece.   J. Lever's analysis of the problem is the same brittle pattern of atheistic evolution or fiat creationism.   Pull the rug of progressionism out from under the geologist and biologist and he has little to work with.   Cf. J. Lever, "Evolutionism and Creationism in Biology," *Free University Quarterly*, 2: 141-155, May, 1953.

30. J. A. Zahm, *Evolution and Dogma* (1896), p. 312.

31. *Ibid.,* p. ix.

32. *Loc. cit.*

33. St. George Mivart, *On the Genesis of Species* (1871), p. 279.

34. Canon Dorlodot, *Darwinism and Catholic Thought* (1923), I, 6.

35. Jewish scholars divide over evolution, just as Catholic and evangelical Protestants.   In an essay entitled "Creation and the Theory of Evolution" in M. M. Kasher's *Encyclopædia of Biblical Interpretation* (Vol. I, 1953), the writer defends creation as against evolution and argues much like a conservative Protestant or a Catholic.   But he is fair enough to cite in some detail the opinions of Rabbi J. H. Hertz who believes that there is nothing "un-Jewish" in the idea of evolution nor in the idea of the evolution of man, pp. 234–235 fn.   It is of interest to note that this Jewish author of this article cites Price from time to time in a German translation of his works!

36. W. N. Rice, "Twenty-five Years of Scientific Progress," BS, 50: 27 (1893).   Theistic evolution had become so popular by the end of the nineteenth century that some writers voiced their opinion that the controversy was over.   They did not reckon with the fundamentalist movement in the twentieth century and its dynamic, militant attacks upon evolution and theistic evolution.

37. Asa Gray, *Darwiniana. Essays and Reviews pertaining to Darwinism* (1876), p. vi.

38. *Ibid.,* p. 271.   Gray is insistent that you cannot deduce the *method* of creation from the fiats of Gen. 1, p. 131.

39. Cf. R. Hofstadter, *Social Darwinism in American Social Thought* (1945), p. 5.

40. James McCosh, "On Evolution" in J. G. Wood, *Bible Animals* (1877), pp. 726–755.   In *Christianity and Posivtiism* (1871) in speaking of evolution he writes: "There is nothing irreligious in the idea of development," p. 37.

41. J. W. Dawson, *Facts and Fancies in Modern Science* (1882), p. 134 Italcs are ours.   In another work he tells us that the term evolution.

"need not in itself be a bugbear on theological grounds. The Bible writers . . . have no objection to it if understood to mean the development of the plans of the Creator in nature." It is the atheistic interpretation of evolution that is anti-Christian. *The Origin of the World According to Revelation and Science* (1877), p. 363.

42. James Orr, *The Christian View of God and the World* (1891), p. 99. Italics are ours. He too objects to evolution conceived materialistically. See also his *Sin as a Problem Today* (n.d.), Chapter V, "Sin and Evolutionary Theories."

43. C. W. Shields, *The Scientific Evidence of Revealed Religion* (1900), p. 133.

44. *Op. cit.,* p. 126. Italics are Jones'.

45. *Ibid.,* p. 143. Italics are mine.

46. *Op. cit.,* p. vii.

47. R. A. Torrey, *What the Bible Teaches* (1898), p. 249.

48. B. B. Warfield, *Biblical and Theological Studies* (1911), p. 238. It is interesting to note that in the same volume ("Benjamin B. Warfield," by Samuel G. Craig, pp. xi–xlviii) it is pointed out that in his youth Warfield was a convinced Darwinian. Cf. p. xii.

49. L. F. Gruber, *The Six Creative Days* (1941), p. 68.

50. A. R. Short, *Modern Discovery and the Bible* (1942), p. 81.

51. *Op. cit.,* p. 45.

52. *Ibid.,* pp. 51, 52.

53. R. Mixter, "The Science of Heredity and the Source of Species," *Creation and Evolution* (1948), p. 2.

54. E. J. Carnell, *An Introduction to Christian Apologetics* (1948), p. 238.

55. W. L. Bullock, "The Kinds of Genesis and the Species of Geology," JASA, 4: 6, June, 1952. As a purely historical observation we indicate that Catholic thinkers gave up the fixity of species in the nineteenth century. F. H. Reusch, in his great treatise, *Nature and the Bible* (2 vols.; 1886), asserts that we do not know the basic animals forms created by God. It is up to the scientist to try to discover them but to the theologian the problem is academic. The Bible, he continues, does not teach what Linnaeus thought it taught, namely, that all present species descended from their original ancestors. Neither science nor Scripture states how many species were created. He concludes: "No objection, theologically speaking, can be made to the idea that the more nearly related types of the vegetable and animal world are descended from a common ancestry." II, 60. Of equal interest is the opinion of the great evangelical geologist of the nineteenth century, J. W. Dawson. He wrote: "Still, with reference to this last idea, it is plain that revelation gives us no definition of species as distinguished from varieties or races, so that there is nothing to prevent the supposition that, within certain limits indicated by the expression 'after its kind,' animals or plants may have been so constituted as to vary greatly in the progress of geological time." *The Origin of the World According to Revelation and Science* (1877),

p. 225. Cf. also, A. C. Rehwaldt, "Some Phases of 'After His Kind' in the Light of Modern Science," *Concordia Theological Monthly*, 24: 330–349, May, 1953.

56. See a splendid article on science and the virgin birth in: B. T. Stafford, "The Science of the Virgin Birth," BS, 84: 167–176, 1927. Matthew reports the virgin birth from Jewish and theological considerations; Luke reports it from the perspective of a Greek interested in the factuality of the case. Both perspectives converge and make the virgin birth worthy of belief.

57. H. Rimmer, *The Harmony of Science and Scripture* (3rd edition; 1936), Chapter V, "Modern Science, Jonah, and the Whale."

58. Although accepted by some as meaning fish-god others think it means corn-god. Cf. Paton, "Dagon, Dagan," ERE, II, 386–388.

59. A. H. Layard, *Discoveries Among the Ruins of Nineveh and Babylon* (1853), p. 540. Cf. also p. 295.

60. F. W. Mozley argues that it is the rationale of the spiritual character of the book which justifies belief in the miraculous element. This is an exceptionally fine essay. "Proof of the Historical Truth of the Book of Jonah," BS, 81: 170–200, 1924. For a strong defence of the authenticity and historicity of the book of Jonah see F. J. Lamb, "The Book of Jonah," BS, 81: 152–169, 1924.

CHAPTER VIII

ANTHROPOLOGY

I. Introduction

ANTHROPOLOGY is the broadest possible study of man. Imitating the physicist, anthropologists define anthropology as the study of man in time and space. This means anthropology claims as its field *the study of man from his first appearance till now*, thus differentiating itself from history, which studies the *recorded* past; *and in all space*, thus including primitive man and differentiating itself from sociology. In that it studies man's culture in great detail, especially descriptively, it differentiates itself from psychology. Physical anthropology studies the body of man primarily to determine matters of race, but also to trace pre-history and the influence of culture or climate on man's body. Cultural anthropology studies the social structures of humanity; material anthropology studies the tools, weapons, houses, clothing, etc., of cultures.

The Bible and anthropology have a great deal of relevance to each other. The Bible has a doctrine of the origin of man, the nature of man, and claims to have much history of the infancy of the race. The problems of anthropology are far more pressing to evangelical Christianity than those of geology or astronomy, and even a theologian like Brunner, who rejects the plenary inspiration of Scripture, finds himself concerned with the problems which anthropology presents to Christian theology.[1]

II. The Unity of the Human Race

The unity of the human race is one of the most important matters in Christian theology. The Genesis record implies the unity of the race, and Paul's affirmations in Romans 5: 12–17 and I Cor. 15: 21–58 clearly teach it. Warfield writes:

> So far from being of no concern to theology . . . it would be truer to say that the whole doctrinal structure of the Bible account of redemption is founded on its assumption that the race of man is one organic whole, and may be dealt with as such. It is because all are one in Adam that in the matter of sin there is no difference, but all have fallen short of the glory of God (Rom. 3: 12 f.), and as well that

[1] For notes see page 238.

in the new man there cannot be Greek and Jew, circumcision and uncircumcision, barbarian, Scythian, bondman, freeman; but Christ is all and in all (Col. 3: 11). The unity of the old man in Adam is the postulate of the unity of the new man in Christ.[2]

It is part of the investigations of anthropology, especially physical anthropology, to decide if the human race is one or not. Warfield has clearly set before us the theological issues at stake. Gates has made a stout defence of the *polygenetic* origin of man. He rejects "divergent [races] from a single stock," and accepts "much independent evolution (partly parallel and partly divergent) on the different continents from diverse ancestral stocks."[3] But the problems of a polygenetic view of the origin of man are great. The calculus of probability is such that the chances of several sub-human ancestors evolving the same human races so that they are inter-fertile are so small as to make the entire phenomenon miraculous. Moody takes Gates to task and avers:

If one race arose from one group of lower primates and another race arose from another group of them, how could the descendants possibly become so intricately alike in generic constitution and in all aspects of physiology as to develop the interfertility observable between races today? . . . But it stretches credulity to believe that, starting with two distinctly separate ancestral species . . . convergence could be so perfect in detail as to lead to the breakdown of previously existing reproductive isolation (so that the descendants of the two species of apes could breed together with entire fertility even though the ancestors could not do so). At least until we have a proved case of such breaking down of reproductive isolation between two groups of animals formerly distinctly isolated in this manner, we need not take very seriously the application of this theory to man.[4]

The unity of the human race is capable of real defence. *Anatomically* the human body is the same form from pygmies to the giant Wattusies and from the fairest Scandinavian to the darkest negroid. Racial differences are superficial and are certainly of little survival value. *Physiologically* the race is one. Tests on pulse rate and breathing, show some variations which are not significant. *Psychologically* speaking, the powers of perception, the patterns of reaction, and the function of the central nervous system are similar in all the races. *Physically* the unity of the race is proven by racial interfertility. As far as we understand, the modern scientific anthropologists agree that mentally and physically the human race is one. Letting Weidenreich speak for all, we note his saying:

The members of present mankind, whatever their physical appearance and geographical distribution may be, reveal the irresistible trend and faculty to inter-breed. In no cases have sexual aversions been

216 THE CHRISTIAN VIEW OF SCIENCE AND SCRIPTURE

manifested unless enforced by the interference of man himself. This fact proves that mankind in its entirety represents one species in the morphological or physiological sense of the term. Differences among even the most diverging subgroups are not greater than those found between the manifold races of domesticated animals. On the contrary, as far as size, proportions, and special features of the body or nuances of complexion or texture of the hair are concerned, the overwhelming majority of those differing features are much smaller in man than those encountered in animals which have been submitted to domestication.[5]

III. The Antiquity of the Human Race

Warfield asserts:

> [The antiquity of the human race] has of itself no theological significance. It is to theology, as such, a matter of entire indifference how long man has existed on earth.[6]

The reason for this assertion is obvious. The sin of Adam imputed to humanity depends on the unity of humanity, not on the antiquity of humanity. Theology is more concerned with the proof that man is one, rather than the near or far antiquity of man. Polygeneticism is far more damaging to theology than any teaching of the vast antiquity of man. In order to clear the atmosphere about the antiquity of man certain notions very widespread among evangelicals must be corrected.

A. *Incorrect notions about the study of fossil man.*

1. It has been incorrectly asserted that the *fossil remains of man are few and fragmentary.* It is argued that from a small basketful of enigmatical bones an entire evolutionary history of humanity is constructed. This might have been the case a half-century ago but it is no longer a valid objection. There are fifteen skulls or fragments of Sinanthropus Pekinensis, and of other prehistoric men there are as many as forty skeletons. For one Piltdown skull which must be given up there are one or two dozen to take its place. Dr. Broom has scurried around South Africa with great zeal, turning up numerous skulls. If a hundred Dr. Brooms were to work as diligently in all the world we might well fill a museum up with prehistoric human fossils. *Evangelicals must seriously reckon with this as a real possibility and be prepared for it.* The anthropologist cannot be discounted any longer on the ground that all he has to work with is a basketful of controversial bones.[7]

2. It has been incorrectly asserted that the fossils are found *in washes or other superficial places so that any vast antiquity cannot be deduced from where the fossils are found.* Competent geologists now examine all fossil finds and such finds are held suspect until geologists have examined the site. We are now sure that there are fossils of

man in places where they were not washed up nor covered up in some superficial drift *but are part of a datable geological sequence.* Smalley and Fetzer in their essay in *Modern Science and Christian Faith* present a considerable portion of this material; and the total amount of material available is quite impressive.

3. It is incorrectly asserted that all these fossils *are within distribution spreads of modern man.* This cannot be maintained, as some skulls are smaller than modern man and some are larger and some are more peculiarly shaped.   Miss Fetzer's judgment is:

> A careful study of comparative morphology shows that there are large differences between the structure of man today and the structure of many of the fossil men.[8]

She observes that there is no evolutionary sequence demonstrable in these fossil finds of man.   This observation coincides with the best scholarship today among the physical anthropologists.

4. It is incorrectly asserted that geologists and anthropologists cannot be trusted *in view of some of their stupid mistakes in the past.* There is a collection of such mistakes that anti-evolutionary literature has been passing on from decade to decade.   A scientist would say: "Yes, we made those mistakes.   So what?   All the sciences have such a record.   It is to be expected from the very nature of the scientific quest."   The logic of the hyper-orthodox is that if anthropologists have made some grave mistakes in the past we cannot trust them in anything they say of fossil men.   The hyper-orthodox create the impression that the study of fossil man is filled with guesses, surmises, and fanciful reconstructions to the degree that the entire procedure is very unscientific though carried on by scientists in the name of science.

But it was the scientist who discovered his error and willingly rectified it.   Science does have the self-corrective principle and over a period of time corrects itself.   If science made the error, science also made the correction.

Since the above paragraph was originally penned, the Piltdown hoax has come to light, and the facts of this case are a perfect illustration of the self-corrective principle in science.   *All* the dozen or so reports of the Piltdown hoax which we read in typical hyper-orthodox journals missed the point of the entire affair.   These editorials read for the most part as follows: (i) scientists admit the hoax of the Piltdown man; (ii) it shows how untrustworthy the entire evolutionary approach to anthropology is; and (iii) it proves that we must be suspicious of all finds.   *But what are the facts of the case?*

(*a*) This *hoax* was discovered by scientists, not by the hyper-orthodox.   When the facts of the case were presented, no scientist tried to cover up the facts, but they were freely admitted by all. To put it another way, if the scientists were hoaxed into the Piltdown affair by a scientist, they were corrected by scientists, and not by the hyper-orthodox.

(*b*) The Piltdown I find (there was also a Piltdown II find) was controversial from the first announcement of it, and there were two schools of interpretation. William Strauss says that the Piltdown man "evoked a controversy without equal in the history of paleontological sciences" ("The Great Piltdown Hoax," *Science*, 119: 265, February, 26, 1954). Strauss gives a list of the scientists who said that the skull was human but the jawbone anthropoid.[9] This find was not universally accepted by anthropologists as a genuine addition to paleontological knowledge. To cite Strauss again:

> Certainly, those best qualified to have an opinion, especially those possessing a sound knowledge of human and primate anatomy have held largely . . . either to a dualistic [that the cranium and jawbone come from different creatures] or to a neutral interpretation of the remains.[10]

The clearing up of the hoax was due principally to two things: (i) the use of fluorine-dating of the bones; and (ii) a discovering of the fact that the teeth of the jawbone had been artificially abrased and stained to give a human rather than a simian appearance. According to reliable anthropological and paleontological knowledge it seemed incredible that an anthropoid ape could be found in England in the Lower Pleistocene period. The history of fluorine-dating of bones commences with Morichini in 1802. More information was added by Middleton (1844) and Carnot (1892). Dr. Oakley, in studying fluorine in connexion with the last war, decided that bones could be sorted by their fluorine content. Unnoticed by hyper-orthodox journals, the Galley Hill skull was tested by Oakley's fluorine method in 1948 and redated from Middle Pleistocene to modern times. Oakley was able to solve other conundrums by the fluorine method. Finally the method was tested on the Piltdown I. It proved to be a skull not more than 50,000 years old —still a sizeable age, mind you—rather than a million. But there still was the problem of the teeth. Dr. Weiner suggested they might be faked. By means of microscope and X-ray the artificial abrasion and staining were demonstrated. The skull is (upper) Pleistocene, but the jawbone is of a modern age.

(*c*) Hardly any change occurs one way or the other in evolutionary theory because anthropologists never heartily accepted the Piltdown skull into their system. Strauss says this find has never been "universally accepted into polite anthropological society."[11] Dr. Harry Shapiro, head of the department of anthropology of the

American Museum of Natural History, says that the Piltdown find "never was consistent with other data. He was out of line chronologically. His removal, instead of weakening, in effect strengthens our knowledge of the evolutionary process," and Hooton of Yale says the hoax "doesn't disturb our ideas of human evolution at all. If it is right that the head is a fake, it loses all its significance and removes a very puzzling link" (both men quoted in *Minneapolis Star,* December 5, 1953).

(*d*) The real issue is this: *are the sciences of anthropology and geology working with reliable methods?* Because the first two efforts of immunization against polio failed, is all medical science discredited? To what extent does one or a dozen mistakes discredit any science? The point is this: (i) we do not discredit other sciences wholesale because of even sizeable blunders, and (ii) the Piltdown hoax was discovered by the use of scientific methods. *The hyper-orthodox are enjoying the exposure of the hoax only because of the reliability of the scientific methods employed and the honesty of the scientists.* The real meaning of the Piltdown hoax is not that a prop has been pulled out from under the evolutionary theory, but that the methodology of the sciences is trustworthy. The exposure was possible only because of the methodology employed.

To put it very plainly: if the anthropologists and geologists cannot be trusted, *we cannot even trust the exposure of the hoax*! If the methodology is trustworthy at the point of the hoax, it must be trustworthy elsewhere. We cannot enjoy the honey from this flower without realizing that we are giving quite a recommendation to the methodology employed. I know it is not popular for a conservative Christian to be the *advocatus diaboli,* but we are not interested in being popular, but in being fair and factual.

Still further, unless a person has read in physical anthropology he has no idea of the amount of knowledge scientists have of bones, human and primate, and how much they can tell from a bone. Hundreds of facts are known about the dentition of man and monkeys, and the amount of information deducible from a jawbone is nothing short of fantastic. True, even now competent anthropologists might differ radically over the interpretation of some fossil, but these differences, and the past errors, must not cloud out the great body of evidence all concur upon.

With these incorrect notions about the study of fossil man cleared up, it is now necessary to clear up other notions about what Holy Scripture says, and what it does not say, about the origin and antiquity of man.

B. *Other notions about the origin and antiquity of man.*

1. It is admitted by practically all conservatives that *Ussher's system of dating the age of man is not tenable.* It was William Henry

220 THE CHRISTIAN VIEW OF SCIENCE AND SCRIPTURE

Green of Princeton Theological Seminary who demonstrated for certainty to Biblical scholars that the genealogies of Genesis were not strict father-son relationships. He has been followed by such men as Orr, Warfield, and Allis. How much time we can wedge into the genealogies is another matter. But it is now conceded that we cannot determine the precise age of man from the genealogies of Genesis.[12]

2. *The Bible itself offers no date for the creation of man.* We mean by this that there is no such statement in the text of the Bible at any place. We may feel that 4000 B.C. or 15,000 B.C. is more consonant with the Bible than a date of 500,000 B.C. But we must admit that any date of the antiquity of man is an inference from Scripture, not a plain declaration of Scripture.

If the anthropologists are generally correct in their dating of man (and we believe they are), *and if the Bible contains no specific date as to the origin of man, we are then free to try to work out a theory of the relationship between the two, respecting both the inspiration of Scripture and the facts of science.*

Frank Cramer, after an analysis of just how much information the early chapters of Genesis contain of a very concrete nature, concludes:

> The Bible furnishes neither information for reliable theories concerning the age of the human race, the method of man's creation, or the place where he first appeared.[13]

We are therefore driven from the problem of the antiquity of man to the more fundamental one: *the origin of man.*

IV. THE ORIGIN OF MAN

We believe that modern science has demonstrated a great antiquity of man, relatively speaking. His antiquity of somewhere near 500,000 years is large compared to Ussher's 4004 B.C., but recent compared to the 500 million years ago when life is abundantly detected in the rocks. Evangelicals will applaud the almost universal testimony of modern anthropology to the unity of the human race, but are apt to be very chary over an antiquity of about 500,000 years for man. The answer to man's antiquity must hinge in large part on our presuppositions as to the origin of man.

A. *Presuppositions as to the origin of man.*

1. We may assert that *the geologists are completely wrong and that man was created a few thousand years before Christ.* We may affirm that geologists and anthropologists are so dedicated to evolutionary biology and uniformitarian geology that they are completely blind to the facts of the case. Or we may have recourse to Price and hold

that all geological phenomena are accounted for by the universal flood.

An evangelical must make a fundamental decision at this point. He has to decide which geology makes the most sense. We have already repudiated Price, and we have accepted the findings of geology about the age of the earth, and the anthropologists about the age of man. We realize all the possibilities of atheism, evolution, and an anti-Christian spirit in influencing geologists and evolutionists, but we believe that the facts are so demonstrated as to be independent of these biases. We cannot write off all modern geology and anthropology in defence of the origin of man about 4000 B.C.

2. We may assert that *there is a difference between fossil man and Biblical man.* Different alternatives are possible here. We may believe that fossil man was part of the original creation of Gen. 1: 1, if we are adherents of the gap theory. We may teach that fossil man is sub-human or pre-human. Or, we may resort to some theory of pre-Adamism. If we reject the gap theory there is no source of help in that direction. Pre-Adamism was systematically defended by Isaac Peyrere in his *Systema Theologicum ex Praeadamitarum Hypothesi* (1655). It was also defended by Winchel (*Preadamites, or a Demonstration of the Existence of Man Before Adam,* 1890), and by Fabre d'Envieu (*Les Origines de la Terre et de l'homme,* 1878) who argued that these men before Adam had died before Adam was created.[14] Short thinks that these fossil men might have been pre-humans, and that Adam was a *de novo* creation possessing spiritual qualities these pre-Adamites lacked.[15] Torrey accepts the pre-Adamite theory, but believes some of them were alive at Biblical times.[16]

There are problems with this theory before it can be a good option. It seems too much like having our cake and eating it. We can admit all that the anthropologists say; and then announce that it has nothing at all to do with the Biblical account of man. We can have the antiquity of man, and the recency of Adam! But who is to tell where one leaves off and the other begins? Certainly, if pre-Adamism leads to the breakdown of the unity of the race we have theological problems with the imputation of sin through the fall of one man. The American Indian has been here for about 20,000 years according to some estimates.[17] Is he pre-Adamite or Adamite? Indians reveal typical signs of a fallen nature, and Christian Indians manifest the fruits of the new birth. Adam must be as old as the migrations of the Indians. This makes it very difficult to tell which are pre-Adamite men and which are Adamite men in archaeological research in human palaeontology.

According to Torrey pre-Adamites were alive during Biblical

222   THE CHRISTIAN VIEW OF SCIENCE AND SCRIPTURE

times. How do they fit into the doctrines of redemption and sin?
We judge that the pre-Adamite theory, as nicely as it gives us both
ancient and recent man, also has its vexing problems.

3. We may believe that *the Biblical account is metaphorical and we
must look to science for the actual data of man's origin.* We may accept
the Genesis account as *theologically* true, but believe that this *inspired
truth* is set forth in allegorical or figurative or metaphorical or symbolical or mythical literary structure. According to this interpretation we would have the following elements: (i) the theological
content of the document is true—man is a creature of God, who
sinned, and is in need of redemption; (iii) the account is pre-scientific
and adapted for the understanding of the millions of peoples who
would have little education or training, and therefore we must look
to science for the *scientific* account which will be the divine *modus
operandi*; and (iii) our knowledge of the theological truthfulness of
the Genesis account stems from our experience of Jesus Christ in
which we learn that God is not only Lord and Saviour but also
Creator, and that we are not only sinner but also creature.

This last point is the view of Emil Brunner and requires some
extra comment in that he really wrestles with the problems. Liberalism shrugged off any serious talk at this point, as its own theology
needed no historical anthropology. The brute evolved till he
became a man and was then capable of religious experience and
that is all religious liberalism needed. It taunted the orthodox by
saying that man fell *upward.* When man discovered conscience he
did feel guilty, but the very fact he could now feel guilty meant he
had crawled up another step in spiritual and moral development,
and so it was an upward fall. But in that neo-orthodoxy takes
creation, original sin, the Fall, and redemption seriously it must
say something where liberalism had no need to speak.

Brunner believes that the Old Testament is approached correctly
Christologically and existentially.[18] The witness of Christ is not
only that God is Father but also that God is Lord. Involved in the
Lordship of God is his Creatorship. If Lord, then Creator. Thus
through Christ I find that God is Creator. But in my own existential response to God I truly discover myself as creature. If I am
creature, God is Creator. Therefore, when I come to Genesis I do
not come to find how God made the heavens and the earth. It is
not a cosmology nor a cosmogony. It is a purified ancient world
myth. But through it shines the truth that God as Lord is God as
Creator. It is not a scientific truth but an existential one.

In this background and pattern of thought he sets his discussion
about Adam. There was no historical Adam nor historical Fall,
at least not as stated in Scripture. The Bible contains the Jewish
version of the origin of man and sin, and is at variance with science,

and it is to Brunner stupid to attempt any sort of reconciliation with science. Further, Brunner takes evolution as an established fact. Man became truly man at that point in his evolution when he became *self-reflective*.[19] Brunner has a great admiration for Bergson's *Creative Evolution,* which gives evolution a spiritual interpretation. Further, there must have been an act of God in making some pre-human a human. Who that pre-human was, and when man fell into sin, is all lost in the vast stretches of prehistory and are irrecoverable to the theologian. But none of this alters the Biblical essentials about man and sin. To Christian theology Adam represents the unity of the human race, and in another place Brunner says Adam means man in the age of childhood. The record of the Fall means that sin and imperfection are universal in humanity. Brunner rejects the Augustinian doctrine of original sin, and the usual interpretation given of Rom. 5: 12. All these matters, he holds, are not historical incidents but characteristics of all human beings as religious personalities.

Certainly, this sort of theology is new in non-evangelical circles, and one hopes that it might be the harbinger of a great revival of evangelical theology. On the debit side of the ledger is a certain disquietude with Brunner's exegesis, and especially the loose ends he leaves us with. We pass from the concrete statements of Scripture to the belief that sometime a pre-human became a human, and sometime such a being fell into sin. Brunner hopes to save a doctrine of man in the image of God, and a Fall, by paying respect to Scripture and science. Once again we wonder if he has not paid too great an attention to criticism, and forced the Bible into an unnatural position. There is still the third view that the Genesis account is neither literal science nor ancient mythology, but a purified, non-postulational literary vehicle for conveying the revelation of God.

It is argued that the picture of God working like a potter with wet earth, anthropomorphically breathing life into man, constructing a woman from a rib, with an idyllic garden, trees with theological significance, and a talking serpent, *is the language of theological symbolism* and not of literal prose. The theological truth is there, and this symbolism is the *instrument of inspiration.* We are not to think in terms of scientific and *anti*-scientific, but in terms of scientific and *pre*-scientific. The account is then pre-scientific and in theological symbolism which is the garment divine inspiration chose to reveal these truths for their more ready comprehension by the masses of untutored Christians.[20]

This is the view of James Orr who wrote:

> I do not enter into the question of how we are to interpret the third chapter of Genesis—whether as history of allegory or myth, *or most*

probably of all, as old tradition clothed in oriental allegorical dress—but the truth embodied in that narrative, *viz*. the fall of man from an original state of purity, I take to be vital to the Christian view.[21]

Mivart follows with a similar view.   He believes the theological truth is *pictorically represented*.   Making man from the dust of the earth is a pictorial way of saying man's body was by *derivative creation,* and the breathing of a soul into him is a pictorial way of representing man's soul as from God *directly*.[22]

A variant of this view is that of Shields who believes that there were men before Adam (co-Adamite and pre-Adamite), and that these men survived down to our very day.   The Genesis record deals with the Adamite-Caucasian race *as typical of* or *as representing* the entire human race, although the human race is wider than the scope of the Caucasians and much earlier than the Adamites.   It is through this strand that God shall ultimately save the world, and therein lies its great importance.   In that this is the divinely ordained strand which typically represents all men, the unity of the race—so necessary in view of Rom. 5: 12 ff.—is maintained.   It is also literally true that all men are physically and psychologically the same.   He concludes:

> Nor is it necessarily hostile to the doctrine of the First Adam, since Caucasian Man would still represent all mankind in the old economy and become a figure of Christ as the second Adam in the new economy, while the mystery of original sin remains the same inscrutable fact as on the other hypotheses.[23]

Many evangelical scholars would feel apprehensive over taking too many liberties with the interpretation of the text, but it must also be kept in mind that a crass, literalistic interpretation with its literal anthropomorphisms is also objectionable to good exegetical taste.   There is nothing *a priori* in the exegesis of the passage which enables the literalists (at this point) to pre-empt the position of orthodoxy to themselves.   The account is graphic and it is somewhat anthropomorphic and it is somewhat pictorial.   The true interpretation will be somewhere in the territory between the literalness of Keyser and the symbolism of Brunner.

4. We may take *theistic evolution* as the solution to our problem of the origin of man.   In our previous discussion of theistic evolution in the chapter on biology we noted how many conservatives either (i) admitted derivation of one species from another and admitted micro-evolution or threshold evolution, or (ii) actually accepted some form of theistic evolution as the *modus operandi* of creation, or (iii) would not object to evolution if it be so defined as not to rule out the Biblical teaching about creation.

Those who admit the possibility of theistic evolution tack man's origin on to their general belief in theistic evolution and believe that at a certain point a pre-human became a human, and that was Adam. The details of the creation of Eve would then be considered as a graphic or metaphorical or dramatic method of indicating the unity of male and female before God. Certainly if a scholar accepts the theory of theistic evolution for man's origin he is no more bound to a literal account of Eve's origin than he is of Adam's.

Before we be tempted to dismiss the theistic evolutionary view of man's origin let us note the arguments of two of its stout defenders. The first is by the Roman Catholic, E. C. Messenger in his *Theology and Evolution* (1949). Messenger had written a work, *Evolution and Theology* (1931), but the plates were destroyed during the bombing of London in World War II. In this first work of his in 1931 he defended a complete theory of the naturalistic evolution of man or, as it was called, "a modified transformist theory of the evolution of the human body." There was a strong reaction to this work in many directions, but whether theologians agreed or concurred they admitted that it was a masterpiece of erudition and destined to become a theological landmark in the history of Catholic theology. His work of 1949 is a series of book reviews of his work of 1931, the purpose being to preserve the thesis of the first book, since its plates were permanently destroyed.

It is apparent from the reviews that the Catholics are faced with many identical problems as evangelicals. But though Catholics and evangelicals are driven into similar quandaries and to similar solutions there is one major difference. Numerous Catholics are theistic evolutionists and receive no censure from the Pope or cardinals or bishops, but the hyper-orthodox treat theistic evolution like a plague. In no other book that we have read have we found such a frank exchange of competent opinion about theistic evolution, fiat creation, and mediate creation. It is a catalogue of mature Catholic reflection on the problem. Another work, not as large but of importance, is that of another Catholic, H. J. T. Johnson (*The Bible and Early Man*, 1948) which surveys the vexing problem of Genesis and anthropology, and decides that theistic evolution is the best solution to the problem of the origin of man.

The argument of Messenger can be summarized as follows: (i) evolution, although not proved with finality, has been verified with sufficient evidence to warrant our belief in it; (ii) there is nothing in the Bible nor in the Church Fathers to militate against evolution, and by a metaphorical exegesis of Genesis and by a careful study of the Fathers, we see that if evolution is not there anticipated, it is at least a permissible Catholic view; (iii) belief in evolution does not negate creation or the supernatural, but evolution is the means

H

whereby creation and the supernatural worked; (iv) if evolution is the general method of creation, it can be applied to man; (v) the creation of man's body, the giving to him a soul, the creation of Eve, are all to be interpreted metaphorically and may not be used to prove fiat creation.   Certainly we are not to imagine, Messenger reasons, that God scooped up a ball of wet clay, formed it into the shape of a man as a baker makes a gingerbread man out of dough, and then breathed into his nostrils as a boy inflates a balloon.   The entire account is metaphorical.   But being metaphorical does not mean the account is *non-historical* but that it is mythological.   The mythological is history under a particular literary form.

Turning now to an evangelical we note a similar argument in James Orr, *God's Image in Man* (1904).   Orr's argument may be stated in the following propositions: (i) evolution is fairly well established by men of science as a theory in biology; (ii) evolution as such is not an enemy of theism; *e.g.* he states:

> No religious interest . . . is imperilled by a theory of evolution, viewed simply as a method of creation . . . The convergence of many lines of evidence has satisfied the great majority of scientific men at the present day that [evolution] is so.[24]

He pens further these significant words:

> I have already made the admission that there is no necessary antagonism between theism and a doctrine of organic evolution as such. That species should have arisen by a method of derivation from some primeval germ (or germs) rather than by unrelated creations, is not only not inconceivable, but may even commend itself as a higher and more worthy conception of the divine working than the older hypothesis.   Assume God—as many devout evolutionists do—to be immanent in the evolutionary process, and His intelligence and purpose to be expressed in it; then evolution, so far from conflicting with theism, may become a new and heightened form of the theistic argument.[25]

(iii) But in that evolution has been used to bolster up materialism and naturalism we must accept a revised evolution or "the new evolution."[26]   (iv) Obviously, if evolution applies to the origin of all forms of life, it applies to man, but with certain considerations.   Evolutionary theory at the time Orr was writing was making much of *jumps* in the theory of evolution.   Man does not gradually emerge from the brute but is a sudden jump or emergence. Man's sudden emergence from pre-human ancestors gives all the leeway the scientist wants with reference to man's origin, and all the theological elements the theologian wants.   This *jump* is that which separates man from the animals and makes him truly God's unique creation.   Orr does not tolerate any weakening of the doctrine of sin and guilt because of man's evolutionary origin:

> Nor can I agree with those theologians who, sometimes with a light heart, make capitulation of the whole position to the evolutionist, and accept the consequences in a weakened doctrine of the origin of sin and guilt.[27]

Orr feels that the evidence amassed at the time of his writing (1904) points towards 12,000 to 15,000 B.C. as the time when man emerged or was created.[28]

5. Another possibility is to affirm that *man is as old as anthropologists say he is*.   This is Miss Fetzer's decision in the essay we have already referred to in *Modern Science and Christian Faith*.   Her position may be stated as follows: (i) By taking the age-day interpretation of Genesis and by realizing that the genealogical tables of Genesis have gaps in them, we free ourselves from any notion that man was made 4004 B.C.[29]   We may feel free to look to science for a decision about the antiquity of man.   (ii) The number of skeletons available for examination of fossil man, the geological stratiagraphy done in connexion with finds of ancient man, and the variations in the size and shapes of the skeleton, prove the claim of the anthropologists for the vast antiquity of man·   (iii) The fact that we cannot make any sort of evolutionary table of ancient fossil man, the fact that no inference of intelligence can be made from brain size, and evidence that fossil man had religious beliefs, are facts which prove that fossil man is genuinely human.   Further, his use of artifacts and fire reveal a measure of rationality.

To get the issue completely before us Miss Fetzer examines how the data proved by the scientists is to be reconciled with Scripture. She rejects the symbolical interpretation of the Genesis account because it does not really help us solve the problem of the origin of man.   On the other hand we may accept the traditional account of the Bible record.   One version of this view states that there were pre-humans till God made man in his own image at about 10,000 B.C.   She rejects this on the grounds that there is evidence of religious life among the Neanderthals at 100,000 B.C.   The other version believes in theistic evolution.   She rejects this on the grounds that (i) it still leaves the problem of man's origin unsolved to the anthropologist, and (ii) we are not sure that evolution is true.

The third possibility is to admit that Adam is as old as the anthropologists say man is.   There are two versions to this.   The first is again theistic evolution which she apparently does not reject as long as evolution is not mechanistically interpreted.   The second is to assert that God made man directly several hundred thousand years ago. She concludes:

> At the present time there is no conclusive scientific evidence which forces the acceptance of either of these alternatives of the early Adam interpretations, but the latter appears simpler and in better harmony with the Biblical account.[30]

All these interpretations are accompanied by serious problems, and materialistic and naturalistic views about man have them as well. If there were pre-humans or pre-Adamites we have no criteria as yet to identify them in any given find unless we arbitrarily assign a date to Biblical man. But such a date must take into consideration the possibility of man's being in America as early as 10,000 B.C.

The chief problem with an origin of man at 500,000 B.C. is the connexion of Gen. 3 with Gen. 4. We might stretch the tables of ancestors a few thousand years, but can we stretch them 200,000 years? In the fourth and fifth chapters of Genesis we have lists of names, ages of people, towns, agriculture, metallurgy, and music. This implies the ability to write, to count, to build, to farm, to smelt, and to compose. Further, this is done by the immediate descendants of Adam. Civilization does not reveal any evidence of its existence till about 8000 B.C. or, to some, 16,000 B.C. We can hardly push it back to 500,000 B.C.[31] It is problematic to interpret Adam as having been created at 200,000 B.C. or earlier, with civilization not coming into existence till say 8000 B.C.

Similarly, the affinities of the Babylonian culture and the Biblical accounts in the early chapters of Genesis cannot be readily harmonized with man created at 500,000 B.C. If this is so, then the entire first ten chapters of Genesis which appear on the surface to be part of a common Semitic tradition, must be classed as pure revelation. Any thought about the origin of man must keep in mind the date of the arrival of the American Indian in America (about 8000 B.C.); the origin of agriculture and civilization (about 8000 B.C.); the advanced culture of Gen. 4; and the common heritage of the Hebrews and Babylonians in the early chapters of Genesis. We are reminded at this time of Torrey's excellent advice about Bible problems:

> *The fact that you cannot solve a difficulty does not prove it cannot be solved, and the fact that you cannot answer an objection does not prove that it cannot be answered* . . . Do not be discouraged because you do not solve every problem in a day. If some difficulty persistently defies your very best efforts at a solution, lay it aside for a while. Very likely when you come back to it, it will have disappeared and you will wonder why you were ever perplexed by it.[32]

We may also take Mivart's advice when he wrote:

> The actual first origin of man must for ever remain a problem insoluble by unaided reason—a matter incapable of direct investigation, and, revelation apart, only to be investigated by conjecture and analogy.   This being so, we must be content to study existing races of men, and thence arrive at the best conclusions we may, with the aid to be derived from history, archaeology, and geology.[33]

We must await more information from science and exegesis before we can propound a pointed theory of the harmony of Genesis and anthropology.   The most vexing part of the problem is the connexion of Gen. 3 with Gen. 4.   The evident recency of the data of Gen. 4 seems to involve us with the recency of man in Gen. 3.   While awaiting a solution to the problem, we can remind ourselves of certain features which we tend to overlook; for anatomy, anthropology, and physiology are not the sole sources of information about man.

B. *Certain features which we tend to overlook.*

1. Both geology and Scripture teach that man is the latest major form to appear on the earth.   If we look at the Genesis record we find man created at the last of the creative drama.   If we grant the anthropologist his 200,000 or 500,000 or 900,000 years, man is still a very recent creature in view of the 3 billion years of geological history and the 500 million years since the appearance of life in the Cambrian rocks.   Fossil man occupies the upper crust of the earth, the Pleistocene.   In this, Scripture and anthropology concur.

2. Anthropology and Scripture agree that man is the highest form of life.   In Biblical language, man is in the likeness and image of God.   Scientifically considered, man has (i) the most generalized body of any organism, (ii) the largest brain in ratio to the weight of the body and diameter of the spinal cord, (iii) the most complex brain; and (iv) is the most intelligent of all life.

3. Anthropology and the Bible both assert that man has much in common with the animals.   The Bible asserts that the animals were made from the earth ("let the earth bring forth"), and that man was made from the dust of the earth.   The strong emphasis in modern science on the continuity of man's body with the animal world is but the realization of what is in the Biblical account already.   Pettigrew writes:

> The special plea here set up for man as a separate and independent creation, originally endowed with prerogatives of a higher order, while it separates him more or less widely from animals, *does not deprive him of his animal characteristics*, he remains one of the animal kingdom, and shares the realm of animality with every living form beneath him.[34]

Mivart asks us to contemplate what we would do, as it were, if we were God and were going to create man.   He says we would be guided by these considerations: (i) to live on his earth man must resemble animals in that he must eat, breathe, etc.; (ii) being an intelligent creature he must have a large nervous system; (iii) as such, no invertebrate nor reptile nor fish nor bird is so built as to be able to support such a huge nervous system; (iv) whales, porpoises, and seals are ruled out as they lack large enough nervous systems, and for the same reason we must (v) rule out the hoofed animals; (vi) this restricts us to the carnivores, and among the carnivores those who have a body most closely suited to what man should possess are the simians.[35]   The many traits that man has in common with animal life, and his marked similarities to the simians, should come then, upon mature reflection, as no great surprise.

4. Geological and anthropological evidence is not the only source of our information about man's origin.   Man's nature investigated through psychology and reflected upon in theology and philosophy, is also evidence as to his divine origin.   It is not possible to account for man's great intelligence, his conscience, his spiritual experiences, his artistic creations, on purely naturalistic premises.   *There is a divine element detectable in human nature now which indicates a divine origin of man in the past.*   Only the Biblical account which asserts the double origin of man (from dust, from God) is true to the total man.   Any present conflict between Genesis and anthropology does not obviate the fact of a present and detectable divine element in human nature, and therefore the necessity of a divine origin of the divine element in that human nature.

5. Perhaps our problem is interpretative.   Maybe our trouble is that we are trying to apply modern methods of historiography to a method of divine revelation which will not yield to such a treatment. It might be that in some clay tablet yet to be unearthed—and Chiera said 90 per cent are still buried!—will come a new clue to the interpretation of these early chapters.   Until we get further light from science or archaeology we must suspend judgment as to any final theory of the harmonization of Genesis and anthropology, realizing that if we are pledged to period geology we perhaps shall have to be pledged to period anthropology.

Before leaving this subject it is profitable to notice how Dawson (*The Meeting-Place of Geology and History*, 1894) struggled with these problems.   He sets the age of the earth at 20 million years and believes that the upper limit for man is 250,000 years and the lower, 7,000.   In answer to the question, Was Adam a Cro-Magnon? he says that it is more probable that Adam was a muscular Cro-Magnon than a Greek Apollos or Adonis.   Dawson identifies the Canstadt fossils with Cain's descendants; the Truchère peoples with the Sethites, and the Cro-Magnon as the mixture of the Sethites and Cainites resulting in the giants of Gen. 6.

The flood which Dawson identifies with a wide-spread but not universal submergence makes the break between so-called primitive man and modern man. In the anthropology texts we read of the Semitic, Turanian, and Aryan peoples which Dawson correlates with Shem, Ham, and Japheth. Dawson admits that man is contemporary with the end of the ice-age, with the sabre-tooth tiger and the giant mammoth, and is therefore as old as they are. His openmindedness, his fearless facing of fact, his loyalty to Scripture are all commendable. He did not know that man actually lived *during* the ice-age, and that by other geological information we are sure he is more than 7000 years old, the date Dawson favoured. His effort was very worth-while in view of the state of science of his time.

V. PARADISE, THE FALL, THE CURSE

A. *Paradise.* Determining the location of the Garden of Eden is not easy as no precise geographical phenomenon can be found which answers to the Genesis description. Good articles on the problem of identification will be found in Bible dictionaries.[36] Frequently the problem of the origin of civilization is confused with the problem of the origin of man and the Garden of Eden. If we take a vast antiquity for the origin of man then the origin of civilization is different from the origin of man. However, if we take Ussher's chronology, or something close to it, then the two problems do greatly overlap. The Scripture mentions the four rivers of the Garden of Eden, which suggest the most probable spot as somewhere near the head of the Persian Gulf, but no specific territory can be named.[37] The parallels between the early chapters of Genesis and the Babylonian tablets strengthen the association of early man with the continent of Asia and the near East.

Archaeologists have suggested China, Egypt, and Mesopotamia as the place where civilization originated, but Mesopotamia and Asia have won. In an essay investigating this very problem Gair analyses the very recent theory that Africa is the home of civilization.[38] He maintains that the Eastern or Caucasian theory has more evidence than the African theory and points to the Iranian, Highland Zone as the most probable origin of civilization. His conclusion is:

> The evidence of science (archaeology, anthropology, philology, geography and geology, and of botany and zoology if space had allowed further discussion) as well as history shows clearly that the Asiatic hypothesis is not without considerable foundation—indeed,

it seems certain that the whole weight of dispassionate inquiry must be held to favour an Iranian origin for civilization, and for the races and peoples today inhabiting Europe.[39]

The second chapter of Genesis states that a certain territory is staked out, as it were, for man, with certain plants and certain animals making it a Paradise.   How large the territory was we do not know, but it was an oasis for man.   His days of probation were spent here.   The animals that Adam named were not the thousands of the world, but those in this staked-off territory.   The calling of these creatures to Adam had, as one purpose, to show that no animal could be the helpmate of man.

B. *The Fall and the Curse.*   Johnson writes that the Fall "forms the most difficult problem in the whole range of Catholic apologetics,"[40] and we could say Protestant apologetics too.   There is no precise historical proof of the Fall of man outside of the Bible. The Christian position has been best stated by Bavinck:

> Science can never reach to the oldest origins and the ultimate destinies of humanity, and historical and critical inquiry will never be able to prove either the veracity or the unveracity of this history. And in the second place, exactly as it now lies before us, this history has already formed for centuries a portion of holy Scripture, an indispensable element in the organism of revelation of salvation, and as such has been accepted in faith by the Hebrew congregation . . . by Christ, by the apostles, and by the whole Christian church.[41]

The evidence for the fall is that (i) it is Biblical, for it is taught in Sacred Scripture.   (ii) It is psychological, for the testimony of each man is to the imperfection of his moral experience, and this testimony is universal.   (iii) It is historical, for, as Butterworth has observed, human history has been written under the terms of the Fall.[42]   The catalogue of human infamy, individual and corporate, is a sad, tragic, sinful, carnal, murderous record, and at times who can doubt its being demonic and Satanic?   What Bavinck says of the Fall and Scripture could be said of the Fall and history:

> The Fall is the silent hypothesis of the whole Biblical doctrine of sin and redemption.[43]

The Fall is the silent hypothesis of human history.

The curse fell upon the man, the woman, and the serpent.   The two matters of the curse which have received the most attention have been the cursing of the ground, and the sentence of death.   The answer to both is the realization that man was in a Paradise and that too frequently commentators have presumed that the same conditions obtained outside of the Garden as inside.   Part of man's judgment was that he be turned out of that park and into the conditions prevalent in the rest of creation. Barrels of ink have been used to describe the effects of sin upon animals and nature. It has been categorically stated that *all* death came from man's sin. When Paul wrote that by sin death entered the world (Romans 5: 12) it was presumed that the word *world* meant creation, not just human-ity.[44] It was argued that before Adam sinned there was no death anywhere in the world and that all creatures were vegetarians.

But this is all imposition on the record. Ideal conditions existed only in the Garden. There was disease and death and bloodshed in Nature long before man sinned. As we have shown in the chapter on geology, we cannot attribute all this death, disease, and blood-shed to the fall of Satan. Certainly the Scriptures do not teach that *death entered the world through Satan!* There is not one clear, unequi-vocal, unambiguous line in the entire Bible which would enable us to point to the vast array of fossil life and state that all the death here involved is by reason of the sin and fall of Satan.

Life can live only on life. All diet must be *protoplasmic*. Are we to believe that the lion and tiger, the ant-eater and the shark, were all vegetarians till Adam fell, and that the sharp claws of the big cats and the magnificent array of teeth in a lion's mouth were for vege-tarian purposes only? One might affirm that such a creation could hardly be called *good,* but that is pre-judging what good means. The cycle of Nature is an amazing thing, and the relationship of life to life sets up a magnificent *balance of Nature*. Unless a very large number of certain forms of life are consumed, *e.g.* insects and fish, the earth would be shortly overpopulated with them. Some fish lay eggs into the millions and if all such eggs hatched the ocean would shortly be all fish. Carnivorous animals and fish keep the balance of Nature.

Outside of the Garden of Eden were death, disease, weeds, thistles, thorns, carnivores, deadly serpents, and intemperate weather. To think otherwise is to run counter to an immense avalanche of fact. Part of the blessedness of man was that he was spared all of these things in his Paradise, and part of the judgment of man was that he had to forsake such a Paradise and enter the world as it was outside of the Garden, where thistles grew and weeds were abundant and where wild animals roamed and where life was pos-sible only by the sweat of man's brow.[45]

VI. The Origin of Races and Languages

The derivation of all races from Noah is only possible if one accepts a universal flood or a flood as universal as man. It is pious fiction to believe that Noah had a black son, a brown son, and a white son.   The derivation of the Negro from Ham is indefensible lingu-istically and anthropologically.   The justification of slavery from Gen. 9: 25–27 is one of the unhappiest examples of improper exegesis in the history of interpretation.   If the flood were local and the judgment of God restricted to the wicked population of the Meso-potamian valley there is no necessity of deriving all races from Noah's sons.   If the evidence is certain that the American Indian was in America around 8000 B.C. to 10,000 B.C., then a universal flood or a universal destruction of man, must be before that time, and due to Genesis and Babylonian parallels there is hardly an evangelical scholar who wishes to put the flood as early as 8000 B.C. to 10,000 B.C.

An examination of the Table of Nations of Gen. 10 discloses that no mention of the Mongoloid or Negroid races is made.[46]   Some anthropologists believe that it is impossible to make any racial distinctions among humans, others make two main divisions, but most accept with modifications and qualifications and exceptions the triadic division of Negroid, Mongoloid, and Caucasoid.   As far as can be determined the early chapters of Genesis centre around that stream of humanity (part of the Caucasoid race) which pro-duced the Semitic family of nations of which the Hebrews were a member.   The sons of Noah were all Caucasian as far as can be determined, and so were all of their descendants.   The Table of Nations gives no hint of any Negroid or Mongoloid peoples.   The Mongoloid and Negroids are not mentioned in the Bible till the times of the prophets.[47]   It is not our intention to try to identify all the peoples of the Table of Nations as that information may be gained from any reliable commentary.   Suffice it to say that the effort to derive the races of the entire world from Noah's sons of the Table of Nations is not necessary from a Biblical standpoint, nor possible from an anthropological one.   Genesis 10 contains a mixture of genealogical, ethnological, and geographical terms.   It is a very important document of great antiquity.   As Pinches reasons, *it is limited to what could be gathered from travellers and merchants*. Places where data could be readily had receive more attention than those where travel would be difficult or occasional.

Dawson has examined this chapter too and records six observa-tions which are very much in accord with the view expressed by Pinches.   (i) The record restricts itself to the sons of Noah and says nothing about other peoples who might have survived the flood. Dawson believes in a local flood and that people outside the flood area would have been untouched by the flood.   Gen. 10 says nothing of these people.   (ii) This document is not a treatise on ethnological theory, but a factual, historical record of the migrations of men from a common centre in Shinar in Mesopotamia.   (iii) As such it refers just to the primary distribution of men from Shinar over certain districts, and does not attempt to teach us anything of subsequent migrations or subsequent history. (iv) It is not an effort to explain the changes that happened after this distribution. Peoples could have moved around, mixed, separated, changed their language, etc. (v) The record says nothing about race or racial characteristics except what may be inferred from heredity. (vi) The language spoken at the Tower of Babel was some primitive Chaldean tongue and therefore cannot be artlessly identified with the Semitic family.[48] These are very valuable comments by Dawson and represent his usual keen understanding of Biblical problems and their scientific implications.

Where did races come from? The person unfamiliar with all the data about race and the problems of determining racial distinctions is hardly in a position to appreciate fully what modern anthropology has discovered about race. Most of us are still in our ancient geographies with their rather neat divisions of red and yellow, black and white. In our racial pride we (i) made a great deal over minor physical differences, (ii) judge races on a very superficial, non-scientific basis, and (iii) fail to see the connexions between culture and our principles of evaluation or judgment. Skin colour is the simplest guide to races for the average person, yet it is unreliable. Theoretically an anthropologist could form a continuum of colour from the darkest African to the blondest Nordic. Indians from India are usually treated as Negroes when in America because of the amateurish knowledge of the average American, yet they are ranked by the anthropologists as Caucasians!

When we note the enormous variations among animals, the variations among humans are rather small. The animal world is capable of far greater variability than the human race. Our very race-conscious eyes tend to make the small variations among human beings to be greater than they actually are.

Race among human beings develops like varieties among animals. Animals were created with a rich store of genes which gives rise to variability among the offspring. Part of the plan of creation was to have *individuality of stock* with *diversity of individuals*. To have meaningful community life there must be the common bond of a common nature, and to have recognition and individuation there must be diversity among individuals. We presume that God stocked the chromosomes of the various species richly. By scientific breeding we can shuffle these genes with their character-istics, and breed traits in or breed them out. Genetics is developing the laws of heredity. In raising livestock or in raising plants or trees, scientists make use of these laws. From a rose with a mixed heritage of colour, a pure yellow or a pure red or a pure white may be bred.   We may breed horses for speed or power, or dogs for racing or hunting or tracking.   Nature has its own controls on breeding.   Isolation among a common stock will eventually lead to a well-defined variety, as will intense *inbreeding*.   Over a period of time peoples who have migrated from a common centre will commence to develop their own individualities.   After a time we have the typical Dutchman or Englishman or Irishman.   The laws of heredity plus principles of separation or selection operating over a period of time will produce the various races of the world.[49]

With reference to the origin of languages, we must make a decision as to a local or universal flood.   If we choose a universal flood we must eventually find all languages stemming from Babel, but if a local flood we need only trace some of the Caucasian languages back to a common point.   It is true that the languages of Europe can be traced back (on paper at least) to the primitive Indo-European.   We know that French, Italian, and Spanish derive from Latin, and that Latin and Greek derive from a common ancestor with Sanskrit.   The convergence of Caucasian languages upon a primitive Indo-European stock may be taken as a suggestive substantiation of the record of the Tower of Babel.

Two things more need to be said about the Tower of Babel.   (i) Such structures called ziggurats have been discovered by archaeologists.   In the clay tablets expressions are found of their reaching to heaven—a figure of speech like our *skyscraper*.   On top of these ziggurats were temples, so that there could have been an anti-God spirit in building these temples for some other deity or deities. (ii) Anthropologists have stated that *the chief barrier among peoples is the language barrier*.   Differences of food, customs, and clothing do not present the barrier that language does when two cultures mix. *No other device known to anthropologists could break the unity of a group like a confusion of tongues*.   We need not speculate how the confusion was done nor how long it took.[50]

VII. The Antediluvians

The proposed longevity of the antediluvians or macrobians presents us with a problem in anthropology.   These men lived up to 900 years, and they did not seem to have children till they were around 100 years old.   Three interpretations have been suggested.

A.   Some have said that the time element needs *reduction*.   Perhaps Moses used the Hebrew word year for some Babylonian word. For example we might take the English pound and equate it with the French franc as both being the unit of money of the two peoples. But to state francs as pounds and pounds as francs requires some method of reduction of pounds to francs.   Babylonian records speak of men living 30,000 years! We would need a reduction factor of about one to ten to reduce 900 down to about 90. But such a reduction ratio has not been found which is satisfactory because it ends up with people having children when they are a year old! Until a feasible system of reduction can be found this method must be rejected.

B. We may assert that these men actually lived 900 years or so, and assert that the flood made a radical difference in world conditions. A change in climate, a change in sunlight and moonlight, an increase in disease, have been suggested as cutting down man's life span.[51] In general, expositors have felt that man coming right from the hand of the Creator was so free from disease that he could live much longer than contemporary man who is the heir of centuries of disease. There is nothing inherently impossible for man to have lived that long, but certainly something very unusual was at work if man did live that long.[52]

C. A third theory goes back to Bunsen's *Bibelwerk* (v. 49)[53] in which Bunsen defends the interpretation that these years are cyclical. They deal with the epochs of the antediluvians, not their chronological ages. Abbé Chevallier explains the eleventh chapter of Genesis the same way in *Annales de Philosophie Chrétienne* (series 6, book 5, p. 28). F. H. Reusch (*Nature and Bible*, 1886) feels that this interpretation is exegetically possible. John Davis in his Bible dictionary and then in the ISBE ("Antediluvian Patriarchs," I, 139–143) defends this theory at length in the twentieth century. He feels that the names represent the *patriarch and his family*.

> The longevity is the period during which the family had prominence and leadership; the age at the son's birth is the date in the family history at which a new family originated and ultimately succeeded to the dominant position.[54]

This theory would relieve us of the problem of time reduction, and the problem of such a long span of life for man. One problem is figuring how Enoch fits into this interpretation for Gen. 5: 21–24 informs us that Enoch walked with God for three hundred years after the birth of Methuselah. Was a whole tribe taken? Or, are we to make a sharp distinction here between Enoch the man, and Enoch the tribe? Certainly Hebrews 11: 5 treats Enoch as a man. Perhaps this objection is not as formidable as it first appears, but it needs some further treatment to fit into Davis' theory which we think is perhaps the most satisfactory of the three offered.

We have now surveyed Genesis and anthropology and found the problems more severe than Genesis and geology. The most uncomfortable problem is the relationship of the antiquity of man, the Fall of man, to the advanced state of culture in Gen. 4.   Although this is a serious problem, it is not a hopeless nor discouraging problem.   Again, we assert that a man may be Christian without the sacrifice of his intelligence.   To the contrary, we feel the Christian interpretation of man is the one which best accounts for the most facts.   If we were to reject all views with serious problems, then no view could be held.   The emergence of *mind, conscience, consciousness* and *will* on naturalistic and materialistic premises constitutes to this writer a far greater problem in anthropology than those problems he faces as a Christian believer in the inspiration of the Genesis record.

NOTES

1. Emil Brunner, *The Christian Doctrine of Creation and Redemption* (1952).   He remarks that it is not Copernicus nor Galileo nor Newton who really disturbs modern man about the Biblical witness, but it is Darwin, and that because of the implications of evolution to Biblical anthropology.   Cf. p. 79.

2. B. B. Warfield, "On the Antiquity and the Unity of the Human Race."   *Biblical and Theological Studies* (1911), p. 261.

3. R. R. Gates, *Human Ancestry* (1948), p. v.   One of the better books of recent publication on these general problems of race is William C. Boyd, *Genetics and the Races of Man* (1950).

4. P. A. Moody, *Introduction to Evolution* (1953), p. 227.

5. F. Weidenreich, *Apes, Giants, and Man* (1946), p. 2.

6. Warfield, *op. cit.,* p. 238.

7. Cf. the charts in Smalley and Fetzer, "A Christian View of Anthropology," *Modern Science and Christian Faith* (revised edition, 1950), p. 169 ff.

8. Fetzer, *op. cit.,* p. 161.   Miss Fetzer's charts and exposition are lucid summaries of anthropological knowledge of man's fossil history.   They are worthy of careful study by any who wish to make a competent judgment about the antiquity of man.   Most books on anthropology or physical anthropology supply pictures or drawings of fossil men so that with a careful eye and a little study their peculiarities may be noted.

9. Strauss, *op. cit.,* p. 266.

10. *Ibid.*

11. *Loc. cit.*

12. Green's famous article will be found in: "Primeval Chronology," BS, 47: 285–303, 1890.   Surprisingly, Byron C. Nelson makes considerable concessions at this point (*Before Abraham: Prehistoric Man in*

Biblical Light, 1948) and accepts Green's strictures on the genealogies. He claims that the Bible can be harmonized with a great antiquity for man although he is sceptical of the way geologists use time in such huge scoops. His two conclusions are that (i) man is very old, and (ii) man is always man. Cf. "No proved or imagined antiquity of man can be too great to be accepted by Christians, since no fundamental doctrine is in any way involved." p. 16. However, there are still those sticking to the comparative recency of man. Cf. G. W. Dunham, "Are the Genealogies Trustworthy, and Chronological?" *Christian Faith and Life,* 38: 400–403, August, 1932. Dunham feels that 4041 years B.C. is "ample to account for all anthropological and archaeological findings," p. 403. Stone hatchets were so misunderstood before modern geology that they were considered weapons used by the angels to drive the devil and his crew from heaven. Cf. White, I, 266.

John Urquhart has tried to fix the age of man from the Biblical genealogies at 10,071 years ago (from 1904) or creation of man at 8167 B.C. He admits that the genealogies are not strict father-son affairs so that a simple bit of addition will not give the age of man. *How Old is Man?* (1902), pp. 113–115.

13. "The Theological and Scientific Theories of the Origin of Man," BS, 48: 510–516, 1891. M. G. Kyle, whose orthodoxy is unimpeachable, said about the same thing when he wrote that "the fact is that the Bible leaves the date of the antiquity of man an open question. We are at liberty, at the same time that we hold strictly to the trustworthiness of the Biblical record, to accept any *established* date, but not mere speculative guesses." "The Antiquity of Man," JTVI, 57: 135 (1925). Italics are his. Kyle gives no date but mentions the "stupendous antiquity of man even since the days of Noah. In the presence of the original antiquity of man before the Flood imagination fails." p. 138.

14. Cf. J. Pohle, *God: The Author of Nature and the Supernatural* (1942), p. 135.

15. A. R. Short, *Modern Discovery and the Bible* (1942), p. 81.

16. R. A. Torrey, *Difficulties in the Bible* (1907), Chapter V, "The Antiquity of Man according to the Bible and according to Science."

17. See the collation of evidence in K. Macgowan, *Early Man in the New World* (1950). It is presumed that it took 20,000 years for man in America to develop 160 language stocks with 1,200 dialect sub-divisions; and that it took 25,000 years to develop all the Indian racial stocks. Although most scholars agree to the figure of about 20,000 years others believe that 10,000 years before Christ is sufficient (cf. p. 24). Smalley takes account of this and realizes that it presents "a serious problem in determining the antiquity of the Flood, Babel and the dispersion" (*Op. cit.,* p. 116).

18. Brunner, *op. cit.,* Chapters I–VII; and P. K. Jewett, "Brunner's Doctrine of the Origin and Unity of the Race," JASA, 4: 7–9, June, 1952

19. Charles E. Raven is a British theologian who has written several books on Christianity and science. He too faces this problem as to when

some pre-human became a man.   He asks: "Where then is the break? What is the novelty that separates man from monkey?"   His answer is: *when man became self-conscious.   Science and Christian Man* (1952), p. 11.

20. This position is argued for at some length by the staunch Christian Reformed scholar, Albertus Pieters, in his *Notes on Genesis* (1943), p. 93 ff., especially with reference to the temptation narrative.   Gen. 3, he reasons, is history, but history clothed in symbolism, or it is "real history symbolically told," p. 95.

21. James Orr, *The Christian View of God and the World* (1897), p. 185. Italics are ours.   For a defence of a crass, literalistic interpretation of man see L. S. Keyser, "The Time Element in Man's Making," *Christian Faith and Life,* 39: 368–730, October, 1933.

22. St. George Mivart, *The Genesis of Species* (1871), p. 300.

23. C. W. Shields, *The Scientific Evidences of Revealed Religion* (1900), p. 124.

24. Orr, *op. cit.,* pp. 87, 88.

25. *Ibid.,* pp. 95, 96.

26. *Ibid.,* p. 110.

27. *Ibid.,* p. 158.

28. *Ibid.,* p. 179.

29. Smalley and Fetzer, *op. cit.,* p. 161 and fn. 161.

30. *Ibid.,* p. 186.

31. Smalley recognizes the seriousness of this problem.   *Op. cit.,* p. 134.   Jack Finegan dates the earliest civilization in Babylonia sometime prior to 5000 B.C.   *Light from the Ancient Past* (1946), p. 14.

32. Torrey, *op. cit.,* pp. 13 and 27.   Italics are his.

33. Mivart, *Lessons from Nature* (1876), pp. 130–131.

34. J. B. Pettigrew, *Design in Nature* (1908), III, 1327.   Italics are mine.

35. *Lessons from Nature,* pp. 170–171.   Cf. a similar judgment in W. B. Dawson, *The Bible Confirmed by Science* (n.d.), p. 130.

36. "Eden," WD, p. 147, contains an excellent summary of the problems and theories about Eden.   Cf. also, G. F. Wright, "Eden," ISBE, II, 899–900.   Wright notes that W. F. Warren believes the original Eden was the North Pole!

37. Both WD and Wright agree that this is the most likely possibility.

38. G. R. Gair, "The Cradle of Mankind," JTVI, 66: 90–105, 1934. W. Howells states that Asia is regarded by anthropologists as the most defensible place for the origin of man.   *Mankind So Far* (1944), pp. 106–107.   Unger observes that it is futile to try to locate the original Eden due to shifting river beds, the changing of the configurations of the country, and the accumulation of enormous deposits of river silt.   M. F. Unger, "Archaeology and Genesis 3–4," BS, 10: 11–17, January, 1953.

39. *Ibid.,* p. 100.

40. *Op. cit.,* p. 18.

41. Herman Bavinck, "The Fall," ISBE, II, 1092.

42. H. Butterfield, *Christianity and History* (1949).

43. Bavinck, *loc. cit.*

44. *Kosmos,* according to the lexicographers, not only means "world" but also "humanity."

45. For general confirmation of these opinions expressed here see B. P. Sutherland, "The Fall and Its Relation to Present Conditions in Nature," JASA, 2: 14–19, December, 1950; and John Pye Smith, *On the Relation Between the Holy Scriptures and some parts of Geological Science* (1840). For example: "Some persons strangely affirm the contrary, and have supposed that, by persevering practice, lions and wolves and all carnivorous creatures might be brought to live on a vegetable diet. Every physiologist must smile at this monstrous absurdity," p. 242. The appeal to millennial conditions is a *non sequitur.* We also have the support of the great Scottish scientist, J. B. Pettigrew, in his monumental *Design in Nature* (3 vols., 1908). After noting that life can only feed on life and that teeth and claws were given to carnivora for a good purpose he states: "Death, from the food point of view, was not therefore the outcome of disobedience and sin." I, 227. Later on he writes: "It must be added that if death became the punishment of disobedience in man it could not be so in the case of animals. As a matter of fact, death has from the first formed part of the great scheme of life." III, 1326.

Dasson's opinion is that the statement in Gen. 1 seemingly restricting the diet of animals to herbs or vegetation is to be explained either as (i) a reference to those animals closely associated with man; or (ii) to the well-known biological fact that all animal life ultimately derives its sustenance from vegetation. J. W. Dawson, *The Origin of the World According to Revelation and Science* (1877), p. 241.

46. Cf. T. G. Pinches, "Table of Nations," ISBE, V, 2898–2901.

47. Cf. T. G. Pinches, "Africa," ISBE, I, 68. See also D. J. Wiseman, *Genesis 10: Some Archaeological Considerations.* JTVI 87: 13–24, 1955.

48. Dawson, *The Meeting-Place of Geology and History,* p. 186 ff. Identical opinions to those of Pinches and Dawson are set forth in A. H. Sayce, *The Higher Criticism and the Monuments* (fifth edition); 1895, p. 119 ff.

49. The conclusion of the great Catholic scholar F. H. Reusch on the origin of race and Scripture is: "The Bible therefore teaches us nothing about the origin of the different races of man, and the only Biblical statement we have to defend in the face of natural science, is the assertion that all men are descended from one pair, all the peoples now existing from the sons of Noah." *Nature and the Bible* (1886), II, 186.

50. An alternate view is that of Smalley (Smalley and Fetzer, *op. cit.,* p. 159) in which he states that the spread of the peoples was the cause of the language change. The usual interpretation is that the difference of language caused the spread. This much can be certainly said for Smalley's veiw: when peoples are separated for any length of time at all their languages change and eventually become mutually unintelligible.

51. Cf. J. L. Butler, "Causes of Antediluvian Longevity," BS, 75: 49–69; and W. R. Vis, "Medical Science and the Bible," *Modern Science and Christian Faith,* pp. 238–249.

52. According to anthropologists an examination of 187 human fossils (Upper Paleolithic, Neo-lithic, Neanderthal) shows a death-age from 20 to 60 years, and only one case beyond 60.   Reported in *L'Anthropologie,* 48: 459, and cited by H. J. T. Johnson, *op. cit.,* p. 144, fn. 20.

53. F. H. Reusch, *op. cit.,* II, 250–251.

54. "Antediluvian Patriarchs," I, 143.   In passing it must be mentioned that longevity is attributed to the Seth line and not the Cain line, *i.e.* not all men lived to such ages but only those who were bearers of the true religion of God and the promises.   Perhaps this is the rationale of the phenomenon.

EPILOGUE

IT has been the intention of the preceding pages to establish two different sets of convictions which we may conveniently describe as (i) denial and (ii) affirmation. We have tried to show in *denial* that certain beliefs attributed to evangelicals are not believed by all evangelicals and are not to be considered part of evangelical faith. Therefore, no man of science may withhold faith by reason of any of the following allegations:

1. It is not true that all evangelicals believe that the world was created 4004 B.C., but to the contrary, evangelicals in large numbers believe that the universe and the earth are as old as the *reliable* evidences of science say they are. Evangelicals may (and many do) believe that the universe is four billion years old.

2. It is not true that all evangelicals believe that man appeared 4004 B.C. Many evangelicals will push the date of man's origin back to the time of the earliest civilization (say, 10,000 B.C.), whereas others are willing to admit that man is hundreds of thousands of years old. A scientist may accept such an antiquity for man in good Christian conscience.

3. It is not true that evangelicals believe that the earth is flat or that the earth is the centre of the solar system. Neither of these is the Biblical position, so evangelicals may believe in a spherical earth and in the Copernican version of the solar system.

4. It is not true that all evangelicals believe that evolution is contrary to the Faith. Most evangelicals are opposed to evolution, to be sure, but we have given evidence to show that men whose orthodoxy is unimpeachable have accepted some form of *theistic* evolution or at least were tolerant toward evolution *theistically* conceived. We indicated that within the strict orthodoxy of the Roman Catholic Church with its huge dogmatic edifice evolution is not condemned.

5. It is not true that evangelicals believe that the last word on specific details of physics, astronomy, chemistry, geology, biology, and psychology is to be found in the Bible. Evangelicals believe that the great metaphysical backdrop and historical setting is given in the Bible for the sciences. But by so asserting this, evangelicalism does not seek to stifle all reason, all research, nor does it seek to dogmatize beyond the facts nor to have theologians dictating to scientists.

Besides these denials we have tried to make the following important *affirmations*.

1. It is impossible to separate Christianity from history and Nature. The hope of some to relegate religion to the world of pure religious experience, and science to the world of physical phenomena, may suit some religious systems but not Christianity. The historical element alone in the Bible is too dominant to permit this treatment, as is the repeated reference to creation. Christianity appears in a universe created by God, and in historical situations under the providence of God. Creation and history are indispensable to a loyal evangelical theology.

Although to some this appears as a weakness in Christianity in reality it is part of the strength of Christianity, for it shows that Christianity is deeply woven in the UNIVERSAL SCHEME OF THINGS.

2. The Bible does not teach final scientific theory, but teaches final theological truth from the culture-perspective of the time and place in which the writers of the Bible wrote. We do not expect modern science in its empirical details in the Bible. In that the Bible had to be meaningful to the people who received its various parts in the course of its writing, the Bible had to be in the culture-terms of the time. *The theological and eternal truths of the Bible are in and through the human and the cultural.* Evangelical Christianity reprimands the religious liberal, who, seeing the cultural accommodation so large, failed to see the divine revelation in and through the cultural.

3. The Biblical statements about Nature are non-postulational or phenomenal; and its statements are free from the grotesque and the mythological. There is no deism, no animism, no pantheism, and no dualism in the Bible. It is free from the absurd views about Nature prevalent among the Greeks and Romans. Scripture is committed to no theory of the solar system nor the structure of matter, etc., and it is at the same time free from the polytheistic, mythological, and grotesque. Therefore, although the revelation in Scripture is in terms of the culture of the people who wrote and received it, divine inspiration spared the writers from adopting the grotesque and mythological, and in turn presented the divine inspired concepts and categories for the understanding of God, man, and God's relationship to Nature and man.

4. We have tried to show that no man of science has a proper reason for not becoming a Christian on the grounds of his science. We have tried to show the inoffensive character of the Biblical statements about Nature; the relevance of so much of Biblical truth to fact; and the credibility of the miraculous. We have not tried to force a man to Christ by these chapters, but if a man is a Christian,

a scientist cannot question on scientific grounds the respectability of that man's faith.

5. Christianity is a religion and not a science. In science the principle of inter-subjectivity or objectivity prevails. What is true for one scientist must be true for all. But this is not true in religion, for if the pure in heart see God, then the impure do not, and what is true for the pure is not true for the impure. God draws near to those who draw near to Him, and He is a rewarder of them who diligently seek Him. He is not known to those who do not draw close to Him or to those who refuse to seek Him. What is true for some is emphatically not true for all.

In the Gospels a very wealthy young man refused to make the motions of faith. He was intrigued by Jesus Christ, but when the issue became sharply one of Christ or his possessions, the tug of his possessions was the stronger, and sorrowfully he left Jesus Christ. He wanted religion without the motions of faith. It is not a rash presumption to believe that many scientists and educated men wish for peace of mind, relief from a guilty conscience, hope for the life to come, and the blessedness of faith in God. But they find themselves caught between their science and their religious hopes, unable to move. Being possessed of great intellectual riches which manage to come first in their sentiments, they leave Jesus Christ.

Just as Jesus refused to pursue the rich young man and make other terms, so today we cannot lessen or cheapen or alter the terms of the gospel for our men of science. There is no other Saviour than Jesus Christ, and there is no other means of having Him than by the motions of repentance and faith. Therefore, if a scientist comes to God he must come in the same way as any other person comes to God. He must make the appropriate spiritual motions. He must repent; he must confess his sin to God; he must believe in Jesus Christ with all his heart.

A CLASSIFIED BIBLIOGRAPHY

I. GENERAL SOURCES (besides those mentioned in our table of abbreviations)[1]

The Hibbert Journal
The Princeton Review
The Princeton Theological Review
Religion and Science
The Expositor
Dictionnaire de Théologie Catholique (15 vols.)
Dictionnaire Apologétique de la Foi Catholique (4 vols. and index)
Dictionnaire de la Bible (10 vols., plus four supplementary vols., plus material for a fifth)
The Catholic Encyclopaedia (15 vols.)
The Jewish Encyclopaedia (12 vols.)

II. BOOKS OF OUTSTANDING MERIT OR OF GREAT HISTORICAL SIGNIFICANCE[2]

Bettex, F., *Modern Science and Christianity*. London: Marshall Brothers, 1903. 349 pp.

Brunner, Emil, *The Christian Doctrine of Creation and Redemption*. Philadelphia: Westminster Press, 1952. 378 pp.

Chambers, Robert, *Vestiges of the Natural History of Creation*. First edition, 1844; twelfth edition, 1884; London: W. and R. Chambers, 1884. 418 pages plus 82 pages on "Proofs, illustrations, authorities."

Dana, James D., "Creation; Or, the Biblical Cosmogony in the Light of Modern Science," BS, 42: 201–224, 1880.

Dawson, J. W., *Facts and Fancies in Modern Science*. Philadelphia: American Baptist Publication Society, 1882. 238 pp.

. . . ., *Nature and the Bible*. New York: Robert Carter, 1875. 254 pp.

. . . ., *The Meeting-Place of Geology and History*. New York: Revell, 1894. 218 pp.

. . . ., *The Origin of the World According to Revelation and Science*. New York: Harper Brothers, 1877. 434 pp.

Dorlodot, Canon, *Darwinism and Catholic Theology*: Vol. I, *The Origin of Species*. New York: Benziger Brothers, 1923. 177 pp.

Everest, Alton, F., editor, *Modern Science and Christian Faith*. Second edition; Wheaton, Ill.: Van Kampen Press, 1950. 301 pp.

Fothergill, Philip G., *Historical Aspects of Organic Evolution*. London: Hollis and Carter, 1952. Bibliography.

Goodwin, C. W., "On the Mosaic Cosmogony," *Essays and Reviews*. Seventh edition; London: Longman, Green, Longman, and Roberts, 1861. Pp. 207–253.

---

[1] Much additional bibliographical information is contained in the exposition of the text and in the footnotes. In many instances books listed under American publishers were also published in Great Britain.

[2] Books with the asterisk also belong to classification IV.

Note: Items of bibliography not included in Index.

Huxley, Thomas, *Essays upon some Controverted Questions*. London: Macmillan and Company, 1892. 625 pp.

............, *Science and Christian Tradition*. New York: Appleton, 1896. 419 pp.

Johnson, H. J. T., *The Bible and Early Man*. New York: The Declan X. McMullen Company, 1948. 159 pp.

Jones, J. Cynddylan, *Primeval Revelation: Studies in Genesis I–VIII*. New York: American Tract Society, 1897.

Kurtz, J. H., *Bible and Astronomy*. Third German edition; Philadelphia, 1857. 527 pp.

Ladd, G. T., "The Doctrine of Sacred Scripture as Related to the Scientific Contents of the Bible," *The Doctrine of Sacred Scripture*, I: 229–285.

Lewis, Tayler, *The Six Days of Creation or the Scriptural Cosmology*. New edition; Edinburgh: T. and T. Clark, 1879. 416 pp.

Messenger, E. C., *Evolution and Theology: The Problem of Man's Origin*. New York: Macmillan and Company, 1932. 302 pp.

............, *Theology and Evolution*. London: Sands and Company, 1951. 332 pp.

Miller, Hugh, *The Testimony of the Rocks, or, Geology and its Bearing on the two Theologies, Natural and Revealed*. Boston: Gould and Lincoln, 1857. 502 pp.

............, *The Foot-Prints of the Creator*. Boston: Gould and Lincoln, 1856. 337 pp.

Mitchel, O. M., *The Astronomy of the Bible*. New York: Blakeman and Mason, 1863. 322 pp.

Mivart, St. George, *Lessons from Nature as Manifested in Mind and Matter*. New York: D. Appleton and Company, 1876. 449 pp.

Moldenke, Harold N., and Alma L., *Plants of the Bible*. Waltham, Mass.: Chronica Botanica Company, 1952. 292 pp. Bibliography.

*Pember, G. H., *Earth's Earliest Ages*. New York: Fleming H. Revell, 1876. 469 pp.

Pratt, John H., *Scripture and Science not at Variance*. Seventh edition; London: Hatchards, Piccadilly, 1872. 321 pp.

*Price, George McCready, *The New Geology*. Mountain View, California: Pacific Press, 1923. 706 pp.

Reusch, F. H., *Nature and the Bible*. Revised edition; 2 vols.; Edinburgh: T. and T. Clark, 1886.

Robinson, H. Wheeler, *Inspiration and Revelation in the Old Testament*. Oxford: Clarendon Press, 1948. 282 pp.

Rust, E. C., *Nature and Man in Biblical Thought*. London: Lutterworth Press, 1953. 303 pp.

Shields, Charles Woodruff, *The Final Philosophy*; New York: Scribner and Armstrong, 1877. 588 pp. (Revised edition in two vols., called *Philosophia Ultima*).

............, *The Scientific Evidences of Revealed Religion*. New York: Charles Scribner's Sons, 1900. 259 pp.

Short, A. Rendle, *Modern Discovery and the Bible*. London: Inter-Varsity Fellowship of Evangelical Unions, 1943. 181 pp.

Smith, John Pye, *On the Relation Between the Holy Scriptures and some parts of Geological Science*. New York: D. Appleton and Company, 1840. 357 pp.

White, Andrew Dickson, *A History of the Warfare of Science with Theology in Christendom*. New York: D. Appleton and Company, 1896. Two vols.

Winchell, Alexander, *Reconciliation of Science and Religion*. New York: Harper and Brothers, 1877. 384 pp.

Wiseman, P. J., *Creation Revealed in Six Days*. London: Marshall, Morgan, and Scott, 1949. 144 pp.

Zahm, J. A., *Evolution and Dogma*. Chicago: D. H. McBride and Company, 1896. 438 pp.

III. BOOKS OF ORDINARY WORTH AND GENERALLY IN A GOOD STYLE AND TRADITION

Bailey, Gilbert S., *The Word and Works of God*. Philadelphia: American Baptist Publication Society, 1882. 239 pp.

Bonney, T. G., *The Present Relations of Science and Religion*. New York: Fleming H. Revell, 1913. 209 pp.

Clark, R. E. D., *Creation*. London: The Tyndale Press, 1946. 72 pp.

............, *Scientific Rationalism and Christian Faith*. Chicago: The Inter-varsity Christian Fellowship, 1945. 99 pp.

Dawson, W. Bell, *The Bible Confirmed by Science*. London: Marshall, Morgan and Scott, n.d. 159 pp.

Dewar, Douglas, *Man: A Special Creation*. London: Thynne and Company, n.d. 119 pp.

Fleming, Ambrose, *Evolution or Creation*. Second edition; London: Marshall, Morgan, and Scott, n.d. 114 pp.

Godet, F., *Studies on the Old Testament*. Ninth edition; London: Hodder and Stoughton, 1874. 343 pp.

Greenwood, W. O., *Biology and Christian Belief*. London: S.C.M. Press, 1938. 190 pp.

Gruber, Franklin L., *The Six Creative Days*. Burlington: Lutheran Literary Board, 1941. 105 pp.

Guyot, Arnold, *Creation or the Biblical Cosmogony in the Light of Modern Science*. New York: Charles Scribner's sons, 1884. 136 pp.

Howard, John Eliot, *Seven Lectures on Scripture and Science*. London: Groombridge and Sons, 1865. 232 pp.

Kinns, Samuel, *The Harmony of the Bible with Science, or, Moses and Geology*. Revised edition; New York: Cassell, 1881 [?] 478 pp.

Larrabee, W. C., *Lectures on the Scientific Evidences of Natural and Revealed Religion*. Cincinnati: Swormstedt and Power, 1851. 395 pp.

Le Comte, Joseph, *Evolution: Its Nature, Its Evidence, and Its Relation to Religious Thought*. Second edition; New York: Appleton, 1901. 375 pp.

Molloy, Gerald, *Geology and Revelation or the Ancient History of the Earth Considered in the Light of Geological Facts and Revealed Religion*. Second edition; London: Burns, Oates, and Company, 1873. 432 pp.

Morris, Herbert W., *Science and the Bible*. Philadelphia: Ziegler and McCurdy, 1871. 566 pp.

Nelson, Byron C., *After Its Kind: The First and Last Word on Evolution*. Minneapolis: Augsburg Publishing House, 1927. 213 pp.

............, *Before Abraham: Prehistoric Man in Biblical Light*. Minneapolis: Augsburg Publishing House, 1948. 116 pp.

Pettigrew, J. B., *Design in Nature*. 3 vols.; London: Longmans, Green, and Company, 1908.

Pieters, Albertus, *Notes on Genesis*. Grand Rapids: Eerdmans, 1947. 179 pp. Bibliography.

Pitcairn, David, *The Ages of the Earth*. London: Samuel Bagsters, 1868. 168 pp.

Pohle, Joseph, *God: The Author of Nature and the Supernatural*. Edited by Preuss; St. Louis: Herder Book Company, 1942. 349 pp.

Porter, J. L., *et al.*, *Science and Revelation*. Belfast: William Mullan, 1875. Pagination commences anew with each essay.

Reimensnyder, J. B., *The Six Days of Creation; The Fall; the Deluge*. Philadelphia: The Lutheran Publication Society, 1886. 361 pp.

Rice, William North, *Christian Faith in an Age of Science*. New York: Armstrong, 1903. 412 pp.

Short, A. Rendle, *Wonderfully Made*. London: Paternoster Press, 1951. 151 pp.

Winchell, Alexander, *Sketches of Creation*. New York: Harper and Brothers, 1870. 445 pp.

IV. WORKS OF LIMITED SCIENTIFIC OR PHILOSOPHIC OR BIBLICAL ORIENTATION

Bartoli, Giorgio, *The Biblical Story of Creation*. Philadelphia: The Sunday School Times, 1926. 155 pp.

Benson, C. H., *The Earth, The Theatre of the Universe*. Chicago: The Bible Institute Colportage Association, 1929. 140 pp.

Chestnut, D. Lee, *The Atom Speaks—and Echoes the Word of God*. Grand Rapids: Eerdmans, 1951. 229 pp.

Christian Faith and Life (a periodical combining the *Essentialist*, and the *Bible Champion*).

De Vries, John, *Beyond the Atom*. Grand Rapids: Eerdmans, 1948. 197 pp.

Higley, A. Allen, *Science and Truth*. New York: Fleming H. Revell, 1940. 280 pp.

Morris, Henry M., *That You Might Believe*. Chicago: Good Books Inc., 1946. 156 pp.

Rimmer, *The Harmony of Science and Scripture*. Third edition; Grand Rapids, Eerdmans, 1936. 283 pp.

.............., *Modern Science and the Genesis Record*. Grand Rapids: Eerdmans: 1937. 370 pp.

Sanden, O. E., *Does Science Support the Scriptures?* Grand Rapids: Zondervan, 1951. 172 pp.

Schwarze, C. Theodore, *The Harmony of Science and the Bible*. Grand Rapids: Zondervan, 1942. 155 pp.

V. GENERAL BACKGROUND BOOKS FOR HISTORICAL OR SCIENTIFIC ORIENTATION

Collier, Katherine Brownell, *Cosmogonies of our Fathers: Some Theories of the Seventeenth and Eighteenth Centuries*. New York: Columbia University Press, 1934. 466 pp. Bibliography.

Collingwood, R. G., *The Idea of Nature*. Oxford: Clarendon Press, 1945. 177 pp.

Dampier-Whetham, William Cecil and Margaret Dampier-Whetham, *Cambridge Readings in the Literature of Science*. Cambridge: Cambridge University Press, 1928. 269 pp.

Frederick, Mary, *Religion and Evolution Since 1859*. Chicago: Loyola University Press, 1934. 186 pp. Bibliography.

Gillispie, Charles Coulston, *Genesis and Geology: A Study in the Relations of Scientific Thought, Natural Theology, and Social Opinion in Great Britain, 1790–1850*. Cambridge: Harvard University Press, 1951. 228 pp. Bibliography.

Grant, Robert M., *Miracle and Natural Law in Graeco-Roman and Early Christian Thought*. Amsterdam: North-Holland Publishing Company, 1952. 270 pp.

Hardwick, John Charlton, *Religion and Science: From Galileo to Bergson*. New York: The Macmillan Company, 1920.

Hart, Henry Chichester, *Scripture Natural History: The Animals Mentioned in the Bible*. London: The Religious Tract Society, 1888. 232 pp.

Hofstadter, R., *Social Darwinism in American Thought: 1860–1915*. Philadelphia: University of Pennsylvania Press, 1945. 176 pp. Bibliography.

Keith, Arthur, *New Discoveries Relating to the Antiquity of Man*. London: Williams and Norgate, 1931. 499 pp.

Leete, F. D., *Christianity in Science*. New York: Abingdon Press, 1928. 387 pp.

Long, Edward LeRoy, *Religious Beliefs of American Scientists*. Philadelphia: The Westminster Press, 1952. 152 pp.

Mathews, Shailer, *et al.*, *Contributions of Science to Religion*. New York: D. Appleton and Company, 1924. 422 pp.

McDougal, William, *Religion and the Science of Life*. Durham, N. C.: Duke University Press, 1934. 263 pp.

Needham, Joseph, editor, *Science, Religion and Reality*. New York: Macmillan Company, 1925. 389 pp.

Oparin, A. I., *The Origin of Life*. New York: The Macmillan Company, 1938. 252 pp.

Osborn, Henry Fairfield, *Evolution and Religion in Education: Polemics of the Fundamentalism Controversy of 1922 to 1926*. New York: Charles Scribner's Sons, 1926. 232 pp. Bibliography.

............, *The Earth Speaks to Bryan*. New York: Charles Scribner's Sons, 1925. 91 pp.

O'Toole, C. J., *The Philosophy of Creation in the Writings of St. Augustine*. Washington, D.C.: Catholic University of America Press, 1944. 119 pp. Bibliography.

Peake, Harold, *The Flood: New Light on an Old Story*. London: Kegan Paul, Trench, Trubner, 1930. 116 pp.

Person, Stow, editor, *Evolutionary Thought in America*. New Haven: Yale University Press, 1950. 452 pp.

Shipley, Maynard, *The War on Modern Science*. New York: Alfred A. Knopf, 1927. 404 pp.

Simpson, James Y., *Landmarks in the Struggle between Science and Religion*. New York: G. H. Doran, 1925 [?] 282 pp.

Smart, W. M., *The Origin of the Earth*. Cambridge: Cambridge University Press, 1951. 235 pp.

Standen, Anthony, *Science is a Sacred Cow*. New York: E. P. Dutton and Company, 1950. 221 pp.

Walsh, C. M., *The Doctrine of Creation*. London: Unwin, 1910. 160 pp.

Warren, William Fairfield, *The Earliest Cosmologies*. New York: Eaton and Mains, 1909. 215 pp.

White, Edward A., *Science and Religion in American Thought*. Stanford: Stanford University Press, 1952. 117 pp.

Wightman, William P., *The Growth of Scientific Ideas*. New Haven: Yale University Press, 1951. 479 pp.

Wood, J. G., *Bible Animals*. Philadelphia: Bradley and Garretson, 1877. 788 pp.

SUBJECT INDEX

NAME INDEX

SCRIPTURE INDEX